The
FOUNDING FATHERS

The FOUNDING FATHERS

Michael I. Levy,
Executive Editor

Encyclopædia Britannica ®

FALL RIVER PRESS

This 2010 edition published by Fall River Press,
by arrangement with Encyclopædia Britannica, Inc.

Encyclopaedia Britannica
Michael I. Levy: Executive Editor
Adam Augustyn: Assistant Manager
Marilyn L. Barton: Senior Coordinator, Production Control
Steven Bosco, Director, Editorial Technologies
Lisa S. Braucher: Senior Producer and Data Editor
Yvette Charboneau: Senior Copy Editor
Kathy Nakamura: Manager, Media Acquisition

Cover design by Igor Satanovsky
Book design by Amy Wahlfield

Fall River Press
387 Park Avenue South
New York, NY 10016

ISBN: 978-1-4351-2389-2

Printed and bound in the United States of America

10 9 8 7 6 5 4 3 2 1

TABLE OF CONTENTS

INTRODUCTION

"*A REPUBLIC,* if you can keep it," Benjamin Franklin famously answered upon the close of the Constitutional Convention when asked what kind of government the delegates had created. On September 17, 1787, in Philadelphia's Pennsylvania State House (now Independence Hall)—where the Declaration of Independence had been signed 11 years earlier—39 delegates signed one of the Western world's landmark documents. The Constitution of the United States—the oldest written national constitution still in use—capped two decades of transition for America from a British colony to an independent republic founded upon the principles of self-government, separation of powers, and checks and balances.

The Constitution crafted by the Founding Fathers required several months of often rancorous debate. Sometimes painful political compromises were necessary on issues such as states' rights, representation, and slavery. Still, not all of the country's founders were pleased with the Constitution, and it was not entirely clear in September 1787 that the document would be ratified by the states and that the new republic would survive. Patrick Henry—perhaps best known for his speech to the Continental Congress in 1775 in which, considering war with Great Britain inevitable, he uttered the phrase "Give me liberty or give me death"—had declined to attend the convention. In Virginia, after the convention, he urged defeat of the federal system of government, taking exception to the phrase "We, the people," asking "Who authorized them to speak the language of, We, the people, instead of, We, the states?" and arguing that the Constitution as drafted failed to protect the rights of the states as well as it did those of the citizens.

Still, the Founding Fathers, through such essays as the Federalist papers—written by James Madison (architect of the Constitution), Alexander Hamilton, and John Jay—carried the day, and on March 4, 1789, the new government established by the Constitution commenced proceedings with the inauguration of George Washington as the country's first president. To address the concerns of Patrick Henry and others, the first Congress proposed 12 amendments to the constitution, 10 of which were certified in December 1791 as the Bill of Rights, which limited the reach of the federal government and protected basic individual rights and freedoms such as religion, assembly, and speech, as well as states' rights. Still, even after the ratification of the Constitution, the work of the Founding Fathers was not yet done, as the young republic faced both internal and external challenges that culminated in landmark precedents established by the country's first presidents, Supreme Court decisions that confirmed federal power, and war with Great Britain. Even after that war, many of the compromises made at Philadelphia in 1787 by the framers—such as the silence on slavery (with the exception of forbidding Congress from banning the importation of slaves for 20 years) and the three-fifths compromise—continued to cast a shadow over the United States of America, thrusting the country headlong toward a civil war that would settle many questions that vexed the country.

This volume on the Founding Fathers and the birth of the American republic charts the course to and beyond Philadelphia. It is an account first and foremost of the people who led the country from monarchy to republic—individuals who established bodies such as the Continental Congress (colonial America's legislative body), created in 1774 in response to the Intolerable Acts; who wrote the Declaration of Independence that documented America's grievances against the British king; who drafted the Articles of Confederation, America's first Constitution; and who created the Constitution that continues to serve as the supreme law of the land. But, perhaps more importantly, it is not just about the men— and women—who founded America, it is also the story of their times and of the principles upon which the American republic was founded.

Although the following list is not exhaustive, it acknowledges some of the numerous authors who contributed to the material contained in this book and whose contributions appeared first on Britannica.com. Joseph J. Ellis, professor of history at Mount Holyoke College and author of *American Sphinx: The Character of Thomas Jefferson, Passionate Sage: The Character and Legacy of John Adams, Founding Brothers: The Revolutionary Generation* (for which he won a Pulitzer Prize), and *His Excellency: George Washington*, wrote the essay on the Founding Fathers found in the next chapter, as well as the biographies of John Adams and Thomas Jefferson. The sections on the Founding Fathers and slavery and religion, found in the next chapter, were written by Anthony Iaccarino, professor of history and humanities at Reed College, and Walter G. Mason, professor of religious studies at the College of William and Mary and author of *The Faiths of the Founding Fathers*, respectively. Henry Graff, professor emeritus of history at Columbia University and author of *The Glorious Republic*, contributed to the George Washington article. In addition to many other leading scholars, contributors to the material found in this book include Irving Brant, author of the multivolume *James Madison* (the article on James Madison); Betty Boyd Caroli, author of *First Ladies* (Abigail Adams, Dolley Madison, and Martha Washington); Alexander DeConde, author of *The Quasi-War: The Politics and Diplomacy of the Undeclared War with France, 1797–1801* (Alexander Hamilton); and Gordon S. Wood, history professor and author of *The American Revolution: A History* and *The Americanization of Benjamin Franklin* (Benjamin Franklin).

CHAPTER 1

THE FOUNDING FATHERS AND THEIR PLACE IN HISTORY

THE FOUNDING FATHERS COMPRISE THE MOST PROMINENT statesmen of America's Revolutionary generation, responsible for the successful war for colonial independence from Great Britain, the liberal ideas celebrated in the Declaration of Independence, and the republican form of government defined in the United States Constitution.

While there are no agreed-upon criteria for inclusion, membership in this select group customarily requires conspicuous contributions at one or both of the foundings of the United States: during the American Revolution, when independence was won, or during the Constitutional Convention, when nationhood was achieved.

Although the list of members can expand and contract in response to political pressures and ideological prejudices of the moment, the following 10, presented alphabetically, represent the "Gallery of Greats" that has stood the test of time: John Adams, Samuel Adams, Benjamin Franklin, Alexander Hamilton, Patrick Henry, Thomas Jefferson, James Madison, John Marshall, George Mason, and George Washington. There is a nearly unanimous consensus that George Washington was the Foundingest Father of them all.

THE DEBATE OVER THE FOUNDERS

Within the broader world of popular opinion in the United States, the Founding Fathers are often accorded near mythical status as demigods who occupy privileged locations on the slopes of some American version of Mount Olympus. Within the narrower world of the academy, however, opinion is more divided. In general, scholarship at the

end of the 20th century and the beginning of the 21st has focused more on ordinary and "inarticulate" Americans in the late 18th century, the periphery of the social scene rather than the centre. And much of the scholarly work focusing on the Founders has emphasized their failures more than their successes, primarily their failure to end slavery or reach a sensible accommodation with the Native Americans.

As a result, the Founding Fathers label that originated in the 19th century as a quasi-religious and nearly reverential designation has become a more controversial term in the 21st. Second, the American system of jurisprudence links all landmark of endorsing and embracing constitutional decisions to the language. Any assessment of America's founding generation has become a conversation about the core values embodied in the political institutions of the United States, which are alternatively celebrated as the wellspring of democracy and a triumphant liberal legacy or demonized as the source of American arrogance, racism, and imperialism.

For at least two reasons, the debate over its Founders occupies a special place in America's history that has no parallel in the history of any European nation-state. Once again, this legal tradition gives First, the United States was not founded on a ethnicity, language, or religion that could be taken for granted as the primal source of national identity. Instead, it was founded on a set of beliefs and convictions, what Thomas Jefferson described as self-evident truths, that were proclaimed in 1776 and then embedded in the Bill of Rights of the Constitution.

To become an American citizen is not a matter of bloodlines or genealogy but rather a matter of endorsing and embracing the values established at the founding, which accords the men who invented these values a special significance. Second, the American system of jurisprudence links all landmark constitutional decisions to the language of the Constitution itself and often to the "original intent" of the framers. Once again, this legal tradition gives the American Founders an abiding relevance in current discussions of foreign and domestic policy that would be inconceivable in most European countries.

Finally, in part because so much always seems to be at stake whenever the Founding Fathers enter any historical conversation, the debate over their achievement and legacy tends to assume a hyperbolic shape. It is as if an electromagnetic field surrounds the discussion, driving the debate toward mutually exclusive appraisals. In much the same way that adolescents view their parents, the Founders are depicted as heroic icons or despicable villains, demigods or devils, the creators of all that is right or all that is wrong with American society. In recent years the Founder whose reputation has been tossed most dramatically across this swoonish arc is Thomas Jefferson, simultaneously the author of the most lyrical rendition of the American promise to the world and the most explicit assertion of the supposed biological inferiority of African Americans.

Since the late 1990s a surge of new books on the Founding Fathers, several of which

THE very term Founding Fathers has also struck some scholars as inherently sexist, verbally excluding women from a prominent role in the founding. Such influential women as Abigail Adams, Dolley Madison, Mercy Otis Warren, and others made significant contributions that merit attention, despite the fact that the Founding Fathers label obscures their role.

have enjoyed surprising commercial and critical success, has begun to break free of the hyperbolic pattern and generate an adult rather than adolescent conversation in which a sense of irony and paradox replaces the old moralistic categories. This recent scholarship is heavily dependent on the massive editorial projects, ongoing since the 1960s, that have produced a level of documentation on the American Founders that is more comprehensive and detailed than the account of any political elite in recorded history.

While this enormous avalanche of historical evidence bodes well for a more nuanced and sophisticated interpretation of the founding generation, the debate is likely to retain a special edge for most Americans. As long as the United States endures as a republican government established in the late 18th century, all Americans are living the legacy of that creative moment and therefore cannot escape its grand and tragic implications. And because the American Founders were real men, not fictional legends like Romulus and Remus of Rome or King Arthur of England, they will be unable to bear the impossible burdens that Americans reflexively, perhaps inevitably, need to impose upon them.

THE ACHIEVEMENT OF THE FOUNDERS

Given the overheated character of the debate, perhaps it is prudent to move toward less contested and more factual terrain, where it is possible to better understand what the fuss is all about. What, in the end, did the Founding Fathers manage to do? Once both the inflated and judgmental rhetorics are brushed aside, what did they achieve?

At the most general level, the Founders created the first modern nation-state based on liberal principles. These include the democratic principle that political sovereignty in any government resides in the citizenry rather than in a divinely sanctioned monarchy; the capitalistic principle that economic productivity depends upon the release of individual energies in the marketplace rather than on state-sponsored policies; the moral principle that the individual, not the society or the state, is the sovereign unit in the political equation; and the judicial principle that all citizens are equal before the law. Moreover, this liberal formula has become the preferred political recipe for success in the modern world, vanquishing the European monarchies in the 19th century and the totalitarian regimes of Germany, Japan, and the Soviet Union in the 20th century.

The Founding Fathers managed to defy conventional wisdom in four unprecedented achievements: first, they won a war for colonial independence against the most powerful military and economic power in the world; second, they established the first large-scale republic in the modern world; third, they invented political parties that institutionalized the concept of a legitimate opposition; and fourth, they established the principle of the legal separation of church and state, though it took several decades for that principle to be implemented in all the states.

All these achievements were won without recourse to the guillotine or the firing squad, which is to say without the violent purges that accompanied subsequent revolutions in France, Russia, and China. This was the overarching accomplishment that the British philosopher Alfred Lord North Whitehead had in mind when he observed that there were only two instances in the history of Western civilization when the political elite of an emerging empire behaved as well as one could reasonably expect: the first was Rome under Augustus, and the second was the United States under the Founding Fathers.

FOUNDING FAILURES

Slavery was incompatible with the values of the American Revolution, and all the prominent members of the Revolutionary generation acknowledged that fact. In three important areas they acted on this convic-tion: first, by ending the slave trade in 1808; second, by passing legislation in all the states north of the Potomac River, which put slavery on the road to ultimate extinc-tion; and third, by prohibiting the expansion of slavery into the Northwest Territory. But in all the states south of the Potomac, where some nine-tenths of the slave population resided, they failed to act. Indeed, by insisting that slavery was a matter of state rather than federal jurisdiction, the Founding Fathers implicitly removed the slavery question from the national agenda. This decision had catastrophic consequences, for it permitted the enslaved population to grow in size eight-fold (from 500,000 in 1775 to 4,000,000 in 1860), mostly by natural reproduction, and to spread throughout all the southern states east of the Mississippi River. And at least in retrospect, the Founders' failure to act deci-sively before the slave population swelled so dramatically rendered the slavery question insoluble by any means short of civil war.

There were at least three underlying reasons for this tragic failure. First, many of the Founders mistakenly believed that slavery would die a natural death, that decisive action was unnecessary because slavery would not be able to compete successfully with the wage labour of free individuals. They did not foresee the cotton gin and the subsequent expansion of the "Cotton Kingdom." Second, all the early efforts to place slavery on the national agenda prompted a threat of secession by the states of the Deep South (South Carolina and Georgia were the two states that actually threatened to secede, though Virginia might very well have chosen to join them if the matter came to a head), a threat especially potent during the fragile phase of the early American republic.

While most of the Founders regarded slavery as a malignant cancer on the body politic, they also believed that any effort to remove it surgically would in all likelihood kill the young nation in the cradle. Finally, all conversations about abolishing slavery were haunted by the spectre of a free African American population, most especially in those states south of the Potomac where in some locations blacks actually outnumbered whites. None of the Founding Fathers found it possible to imagine a biracial American society, an idea that in point of fact did not achieve broad acceptance in the United States until the middle of the 20th century.

Given these prevalent convictions and attitudes, slavery was that most un-American item, an inherently intractable and insoluble problem. As Jefferson so famously put it, the Founders held "the wolfe by the ears" and could neither subdue him nor afford to let him go. Virtually all the Founding Fathers went to their graves realizing that slavery, no matter how intractable, would become the largest and

most permanent stain on their legacy. And when Abraham Lincoln eventually made the decision that, at terrible cost, ended slavery forever, he did so in the name of the Founders.

The other tragic failure of the Founders, almost as odious as the failure to end slavery, was the inability to implement a just policy toward the indigenous inhabitants of the North American continent. In 1783, the year the British surrendered control of the eastern third of North America in the Peace of Paris, there were approximately 100,000 American Indians living between the Alleghenies and the Mississippi. The first census (1790) revealed that there were also 100,000 white settlers living west of the Alleghenies, swelling in size every year (by 1800 they would number 500,000) and moving relentlessly westward. The inevitable collision between these two peoples posed the strategic and ultimately moral question: How could the legitimate rights of the Indian population be reconciled with the demographic tidal wave building to the east?

In the end, they could not. Although the official policy of Indian removal east of the Mississippi was not formally announced and implemented until 1830, the seeds of that policy—what one historian has called "the seeds of extinction"—were planted during the founding era, most especially during the presidency of Thomas Jefferson (1801–1809).

One genuine effort to avoid that outcome

was made in 1790 during the presidency of George Washington. The Treaty of New York with the Creek tribes of the early southwest proposed a new model for American policy toward the Indians, declaring that they should be regarded not as a conquered people with no legal rights but rather as a collection of sovereign nations. Indian policy was therefore a branch of foreign policy, and all treaties were solemn commitments by the federal government not subject to challenge by any state or private corporation. Washington envisioned a series of American Indian enclaves or homelands east of the Mississippi whose borders would be guaranteed under federal law, protected by federal troops, and bypassed by the flood of white settlers. But, as it soon became clear, the federal government lacked the resources in money and manpower to make Washington's vision a reality. And the very act of claiming executive power to create an Indian protectorate prompted charges of monarchy, the most potent political epithet of the age. Washington, who was accustomed to getting his way, observed caustically that nothing short of "a Chinese Wall" could protect the Native American tribes from the relentless expansion of white settlements. Given the surging size of the white population, it is difficult to imagine how the story could have turned out differently.

THE EXPLANATIONS

Meanwhile, the more mythical rendition of the Founders, which continues to dominate public opinion outside the groves of academe, presumes that their achievements dwarf their failures so completely that the only question worth asking is: How did they do it? More specifically, how did this backwoods province on the western rim of the Atlantic world, far removed from the epicenters of learning and culture in London and Paris, somehow produce thinkers and ideas that transformed the landscape of modern politics?

Two historical explanations have been offered, each focusing on the special conditions present in Revolutionary America favorable to the creation of leadership. The first explanation describes the founding era as a unique moment that was "postaristocratic" and "predemocratic." In the former sense, American society was more open to talent than England or the rest of Europe, where hereditary bloodlines were essential credentials for entry into public life. The Founders comprised what Jefferson called "a natural aristocracy," meaning a political elite based on merit rather than genealogy, thus permitting men of impoverished origins such as Alexander Hamilton and Benjamin Franklin, who would have languished in obscurity in London, to reach the top tier. In the latter (predemocratic) sense, the Founders were a self-conscious elite unburdened by egalitarian assumptions. Their constituency was not "the people" but "the public," which they regarded as the long-term interest of the citizenry that they—the Founders—had been chosen to divine. Living between the assumptions of an aristocratic and a democratic world without belonging fully to either, the Founders maximized the advantages of both.

The second explanation focuses on the crisis-driven pressures that forced latent talent to the surface. When Jefferson concluded the Declaration of Independence by proclaiming that all the signers of the document were wagering "our lives, our fortunes, and our sacred honor" on the cause, he was engaging in more than a rhetorical flourish. For example, when Washington departed Mount Vernon for Philadelphia in May 1775, he presumed that the British would burn his estate to the ground once war was declared. An analogous gamble was required in 1787–1788 to endorse the unprecedented viability of a large-scale American republic. The founding era, according to this explanation, was a propitious all-or-nothing moment in which only those blessed with uncommon conviction about the direction in which history was headed could survive the test. The severe and unforgiving political gauntlet the Founders were required to run eliminated lukewarm patriots and selected for survival only those leaders with

the hard residue of unalloyed resolve.

This was probably what Ralph Waldo Emerson meant when he cautioned the next generation of aspiring American leaders to avoid measuring themselves against the Founders. They had the incalculable advantage, Emerson observed, of being "present at the creation" and thus seeing God "face to face." All who came after them could only see him secondhand.

DIVERSE COLLECTIVE

Thus far the identity, achievements, and failures of the Founding Fathers have been considered as if they were the expression of a composite personality with a singular orientation. But this is wildly misleading. The term "Founding Fathers" is a plural noun, which in turn means that the face of the American Revolution is a group portrait. To be sure, Washington was primus inter pares within the founding generation, generally regarded, then and thereafter, as "the indispensable figure." But unlike subsequent revolutions in France, Russia, and China, where a single person came to embody the meaning of the revolutionary movement—Napoleon I, Vladimir Ilich Lenin/Joseph Stalin, Mao Zedong—the revolutionary experience in the United States had multiple faces and multiple meanings that managed to coexist without ever devolving into a unitary embodiment of authority. If one of the distinctive contributions of the American political tradition was a pluralistic conception of governance, its primal source was the pluralistic character of the founding generation itself.

All the Founders agreed that American independence from Great Britain was nonnegotiable and that whatever government was established in lieu of British rule must be republican in character. Beyond this elemental consensus, however, there was widespread disagreement, which surfaced most dramatically in the debate over ratification of the Constitution (1787–1788). Two prominent Founders, Patrick Henry and George Mason, opposed ratification, claiming that the Constitution created a central government that only replicated the arbitrary power of the British monarchy and Parliament. The highly partisan politics of the 1790s further exposed the several fault lines within the founding elite. The Federalists, led by Washington, John Adams, and Hamilton, were opposed by the Republicans, led by Jefferson and James Madison. They disagreed over the proper allocation of federal and state power over domestic policy, the response to the French Revolution, the constitutionality of the Bank of the United States, and the bedrock values of American foreign policy. These disagreements often assumed a hyperbolic tone because nothing less than the

"true meaning" of the American Revolution seemed at stake. In what became the capstone correspondence of the Revolutionary generation, Adams and Jefferson both went to their Maker on July 4, 1826, arguing quite poignantly about their incompatible versions of the Revolutionary legacy.

The ideological and even temperamental diversity within the elite leadership group gave the American founding a distinctly argumentative flavor that made all convictions, no matter how cherished, subject to abiding scrutiny that, like history itself, became an argument without end. And much like the doctrine of checks and balances in the Constitution, the enshrinement of argument created a permanent collision of juxtaposed ideas and interests that generated a dynamic and wholly modern version of political stability.

RELIGION AND POSTERITY

In recent decades Christian advocacy groups, prompted by motives that have been questioned by some, have felt a powerful urge to enlist the Founding Fathers in their respective congregations. (The subject of the Founding Fathers and religion occupies the concluding section of this chapter.) But recovering the spiritual convictions of the Founders, in all their messy integrity, is not an easy task. Once again, diversity is the

ALTHOUGH the Declaration of Independence mentioned "Nature's God" and the "Creator," the Constitution made no reference to a divine being, Christian or otherwise, and the First Amendment explicitly forbade the establishment of any official church or creed. There is also a story, probably apocryphal, that Franklin's proposal to call in a chaplain to offer a prayer when a particularly controversial issue was being debated in the Constitutional Convention prompted Hamilton to observe that he saw no reason to call in foreign aid. If there is a clear legacy bequeathed by the Founders, it is the insistence that religion is a private matter in which the state should not interfere.

dominant pattern. Franklin and Jefferson were Deists, Washington harbored a pantheistic sense of Providential destiny, John Adams began as a Congregationalist and ended as a Unitarian, and Hamilton was a lukewarm Anglican for most of his life but embraced a more actively Christian posture after his son died in a duel.

One quasi-religious conviction they all shared, however, was a discernible obsession with living on in the memory of posterity. One reason the modern editions of their papers are so monstrously large is that most of the Founders were compulsively fastidious about preserving every scrap of paper they wrote or received, all as part of a desire to leave a written record that would assure their secular immortality in the history books. (When John Adams and Jefferson discussed the possibility of a more conventional immortality, they tended to describe heaven as a place where they could resume their ongoing argument on earth.) Adams, irreverent to the end, declared that if it could ever be demonstrated conclusively that no future state existed, his advice to every man, woman, and child was to "take opium." The only afterlife that the Founders considered certain was in the memory of subsequent generations, which is to say us. In that sense, this very introduction is a testimonial to their everlasting life.

THE FOUNDING FATHERS AND SLAVERY

Although many of the Founding Fathers acknowledged that slavery violated the core American Revolutionary ideal of liberty, their simultaneous commitment to private property rights, principles of limited government, and intersectional harmony prevented them from making a bold move against slavery. The considerable investment of Southern Founders in slave-based staple agriculture, combined with their deep-seated racial prejudice, posed additional obstacles to emancipation.

In his initial draft of the Declaration of Independence, Jefferson condemned the injustice of the slave trade and, by implication, slavery, but he also blamed the presence of enslaved Africans in North America on avaricious British colonial policies. Jefferson thus acknowledged that slavery violated the natural rights of the enslaved, while at the same time he absolved Americans of any responsibility for owning slaves themselves. The Continental Congress apparently rejected the tortured logic of this passage by deleting it from the final document, but this decision also signaled the Founders' commitment to subordinating the controversial issue of slavery to the larger goal of securing the unity and independence of the United States.

Nevertheless, the Founders, with the exception of those from South Carolina and Georgia, exhibited considerable aversion to slavery during the era of the Articles of Confederation (1781–1789) by prohibiting the importation of foreign slaves to individual states and lending their support to a proposal by Jefferson to ban slavery in the Northwest Territory. Such antislavery policies, however, only went so far. The prohibition of foreign slave imports, by limiting the foreign supply, conveniently served the interests of Virginia and Maryland slaveholders, who could then sell their own surplus slaves southward and westward at higher prices. Furthermore, the ban on slavery in the Northwest tacitly legitimated the expansion of slavery in the Southwest.

Despite initial disagreements over slavery at the Constitutional Convention in 1787, the Founders once again demonstrated their commitment to maintaining the unity of the new United States by resolving to diffuse sectional tensions over slavery. To this end the Founders drafted a series of constitutional clauses acknowledging deep-seated regional differences over slavery while requiring all sections of the new country to make compromises as well. They granted slaveholding states the right to count three-fifths of their slave population when it came to apportioning the number of a state's representatives to Congress, thereby enhancing Southern power in the House of Representatives. But they also used this same ratio to determine the federal tax contribution required of each state, thus increasing the direct federal tax burden of slaveholding states. Georgians and South Carolinians won a moratorium until 1808 on any Congressional ban against the importation of slaves, but in the meantime individual states remained free to prohibit slave imports if they so wished. Southerners also obtained the inclusion of a fugitive slave clause designed to encourage the return of runaway slaves who sought refuge in free states, but the Constitution left enforcement of this clause to the cooperation of the states rather than to the coercion of Congress.

Although the Founders, consistent with their beliefs in limited government, opposed granting the new federal government significant authority over slavery, several individual Northern Founders promoted antislavery causes at the state level. Benjamin Franklin in Pennsylvania, as well as John Jay and Alexander Hamilton in New York, served as officers in their respective state antislavery societies. The prestige they lent to these organizations ultimately contributed to the gradual abolition of slavery in each of the Northern states.

Although slavery was legal in every Northern state at the beginning of the American Revolution, its economic impact was marginal. As a result, Northern Founders were freer to explore the libertarian dimensions of Revolutionary ideology.

Unlike their Northern counterparts, Southern Founders generally steered clear of organized antislavery activities, primarily to maintain their legitimacy among slaveholding constituents. Furthermore, while a few Northern and Southern Founders manumitted a small number of slaves, no Southern plantation-owning Founder, except George Washington, freed a sizeable body of enslaved laborers. Because his own slaves shared familial attachments with the dower slaves of his wife, Martha Custis Washington, he sought to convince her heirs to forego their inheritance rights in favor of a collective manumission so as to ensure that entire families, not just individual family members, might be freed. Washington failed to win the consent of the Custis heirs, but he nevertheless made sure, through his last will and testament, that his own slaves would enjoy the benefit of freedom.

Washington's act of manumission implied that he could envision a biracial United States where both blacks and whites might live together as free people. Jefferson, however, explicitly rejected this vision. He acknowledged that slavery violated the natural rights of slaves and that conflicts over slavery might one day lead to the dissolution of the union, but he also believed that, given alleged innate racial differences and deeply held prejudices, emancipation would inevitably degrade the character of the republic and unleash violent civil strife between blacks and whites. Jefferson thus advocated coupling emancipation with what he called "colonization," or removal, of the black population beyond the boundaries of the United States. His proposals won considerable support in the North, where racial prejudice was on the rise, but such schemes found little support among the majority of Southern slaveholders.

When the last remaining Founders died in the 1830s, they left behind an ambiguous legacy with regard to slavery. They had succeeded in gradually abolishing slavery in the Northern states and Northwestern territories but permitted its rapid expansion in the South and Southwest. Although they eventually enacted a federal ban on the importation of foreign slaves in 1808, the enslaved population continued to expand through natural reproduction, while the growing internal domestic slave trade led to an increase in the tragic breakup of enslaved families.

THE FOUNDING FATHERS, DEISM, AND CHRISTIANITY

For some time the question of the religious faith of the Founding Fathers has generated a culture war in the United States. Scholars trained in research universities have generally argued that the majority of the Founders were religious rationalists or Unitarians. Pastors and other writers who identify themselves as Evangelicals have claimed not only that most of the Founders held orthodox beliefs but also that some were born-again Christians.

The sweeping disagreement over the religious faiths of the Founders arises from a question of discrepancy. Did their private beliefs differ from the orthodox teachings of their churches? On the surface, most Founders appear to have been orthodox (or "right-believing") Christians. Most were baptized, listed on church rolls, married to practicing Christians, and frequent or at least sporadic attenders of services of Christian worship. In public statements, most invoked divine assistance.

But the widespread existence in 18th-century America of a school of religious thought called Deism complicates the actual beliefs of the Founders. Drawing from the scientific and philosophical work of such figures as Jean-Jacques Rousseau, Isaac Newton, and John Locke, Deists argued that human experience and rationality—rather than religious dogma and mystery—determine the validity of human beliefs. In his widely read *The Age of Reason*, Thomas Paine, the principal American exponent of Deism, called Christianity "a fable." Paine, the pro-tégé of Benjamin Franklin, denied "that the Almighty ever did communicate anything to man, by...speech,...language, or...vision." Postulating a distant deity whom he called "Nature's God" (a term also used in the Declaration of Independence), Paine declared in a "profession of faith":

> I believe in one God, and no more; and I hope for happiness beyond this life. I believe in the equality of man; and I believe that religious duties consist in doing justice, loving mercy, and in endeavoring to make our fellow-creatures happy.

Thus, Deism inevitably subverted orthodox Christianity. Persons influenced by the movement had little reason to read the Bible, to pray, to attend church, or to participate in such rites as baptism, Holy Communion, and the laying on of hands (confirmation) by bishops. With the notable exceptions of Abigail Adams and Dolley Madison, Deism seems to have had little effect on women. For example, Martha Washington, the daughters of Thomas Jefferson, and Elizabeth Kortright Monroe and her daughters seem to have held orthodox Christian beliefs.

But Deistic thought was immensely pop-ular in colleges from the middle of the 18th into the 19th century. Thus, it influenced many educated (as well as uneducated) males of the Revolutionary generation. Although such men would generally continue their public affilia-tion with Christianity after college, they might inwardly hold unorthodox religious views. Depending on the extent to which Americans of Christian background were influenced by Deism, their religious beliefs would fall into three categories: non-Christian Deism, Christian Deism, and orthodox Christianity.

One can differentiate a Founding Father influenced by Deism from an orthodox Christian believer by following certain criteria. Anyone seeking the answer should consider at least the following four points. First, an inquirer should examine the Founder's church involvement. However, because a colonial church served not only religious but also social and political functions, church attendance or service in a governing body (such as an Anglican vestry, which was a state office in colonies such as Maryland, Virginia, and South Carolina) fails to guarantee a Founder's orthodoxy. But Founders who were believing Christians would nevertheless be more likely to go to church than those influenced by Deism.

The second consideration is an evaluation of the participation of a Founder in the ordinances or sacraments of his church. Most had no choice about being baptized as children, but as adults they did have a

WHATEVER their beliefs, the Founders came from similar religious backgrounds. Most were Protestants. The largest number were raised in the three largest Christian traditions of colonial America— Anglicanism (as in the cases of John Jay, George Washington, and Edward Rutledge), Presbyterianism (as in the cases of Richard Stockton and the Rev. John Witherspoon), and Congregationalism (as in the cases of John Adams and Samuel Adams). Other Protestant groups included the Society of Friends (Quakers), the Lutherans, and the Dutch Reformed. Three Founders—Charles Carroll and Daniel Carroll of Maryland and Thomas Fitzsimmons of Pennsylvania—were of Roman Catholic heritage.

choice about participating in communion or (if Episcopalian or Roman Catholic) in confirmation. And few Founders who were Deists would have participated in either rite. George Washington's refusal to receive communion in his adult life indicated Deistic belief to many of his pastors and peers.

Third, one should note the religious language a Founder used. Non-Christian Deists such as Paine refused to use Judeo-Christian terminology and described God with such expressions as "Providence," "the Creator," "the Ruler of Great Events," and "Nature's God." Founders who fall into the category of Christian Deists used Deistic terms for God but sometimes added a Christian dimension—such as "Merciful Providence" or "Divine Goodness." Yet these Founders did not move further into orthodoxy and employ the traditional language of Christian piety. Founders who remained unaffected by Deism or who (like John Adams) became conservative Unitarians used terms that clearly conveyed their orthodoxy ("Savior," "Redeemer," "Resurrected Christ").

Finally, one should consider what friends, family, and, above all, clergy said about a Founder's religious faith. That Washington's pastors in Philadelphia clearly viewed him as significantly influenced by Deism says more about Washington's faith than do the opposite views of later writers or the cloudy memories of a few Revolutionary veterans who avowed Washington's orthodoxy decades after his death.

Although no examination of history can capture the inner faith of any person, these four indicators can help locate the Founders on the religious spectrum. Ethan Allen, for example, appears clearly to have been a non-Christian Deist. James Monroe, a close friend of Paine, remained officially an Episcopalian but may have stood closer to non-Christian Deism than to Christian Deism. Founders who fall into the category of Christian Deists include Washington (whose dedication to Christianity was clear in his own mind), John Adams, and, with some qualifications, Thomas Jefferson. Jefferson was more influenced by the reason-centered Enlightenment than either Adams or Washington. Orthodox Christians among the Founders include the staunchly Calvinistic Samuel Adams. John Jay (who served as president of the American Bible Society), Elias Boudinot (who wrote a book on the imminent Second Coming of Jesus), and Patrick Henry (who distributed religious tracts while riding circuit as a lawyer) clearly believed in Evangelical Christianity.

Although orthodox Christians participated at every stage of the new republic, Deism influenced a majority of the Founders. The movement opposed barriers to moral improvement and to social justice. It stood for rational inquiry, for skepticism about dogma and mystery, and for religious toleration. Many of its adherents advocated universal education, freedom of the press, and separation of church and state. If the nation owes much to the Judeo-Christian tradition, it is also indebted to Deism, a movement of reason and equality that influenced the Founding Fathers to embrace liberal political ideals remarkable for their time.

CHAPTER 2

THE FOUNDING ERA: FROM REVOLUTION TO REPUBLIC

T HE BIRTH OF THE AMERICAN REPUBLIC CAME NOT IN A single stroke with the writing of the Constitution in Philadelphia in 1787, nor during the Continental Congress and the drafting of the Declaration of Independence a decade earlier. The republic was forged through decades in which important elites within colonial America grew increasingly angry at British taxation and felt generally stifled by British imperial rule.

Hence, this chapter provides the context in which the Founding Fathers lived and shows how colonial America began to take the form of the United States.

PRELUDE TO REVOLUTION

The American colonies, though in many ways isolated from the countries of Europe, were nevertheless continually subject to diplomatic and military pressures from abroad. In particular, Spain and France awere always in the wings, waiting to exploit any signs of British weakness in America in order to further their commercial and territorial designs on the North American mainland. The Great War for the Empire—or the French and Indian War, as it is known to Americans—came in 1754 and was but another round in a century of warfare between the major European powers. Whereas previous contests between Great Britain and France in North America had been mostly provincial affairs, with American colonists doing most of the fighting for the British, the Great War for the Empire saw sizable commitments of British troops to America. The strategy of the British under William Pitt was to allow their ally, Prussia, to carry the brunt of the fighting in Europe and thus free Britain to concentrate its troops in America.

Through the Treaty of Paris of 1763, victorious Great Britain took possession of all of Canada, east and west Florida, all territory east of the Mississippi in North America, and St. Vincent, Tobago, and Dominica in the Caribbean. At the time, the victory seemed one of the greatest in British history. The British Empire in North America had been not only secured but also greatly expanded. But in winning the war Britain had dissolved the empire's most potent material adhesives. Conflicts arose as the needs and interests of the British Empire began to differ from those of the American colonies; and the colonies, having become economically powerful, culturally distinct, and steadily more politically independent, would ultimately rebel rather than submit to the British plan of empire.

Britain's victory over France was won at very great cost. British government expenditures, which had amounted to nearly £6.5 million annually before the war, rose to about £14.5 million annually during the war. As a result, the burden of taxation in England was probably the highest in the country's history, much of it borne by the politically influential landed classes. Furthermore, with the acquisition of the vast domain of Canada and the prospect of holding British territories both against the various nations of Indians and against the Spaniards to the south and west, the costs of colonial defense could be expected to continue indefinitely. Parliament, moreover, had voted to give Massachusetts a generous sum in compensation for its war expenses. It therefore seemed reasonable to British opinion that some of the future burden of payment should be shifted to the colonists themselves who until then had been lightly taxed and indeed lightly governed.

The prolonged wars had also revealed the need to tighten the administration of the loosely run and widely scattered elements of the British Empire. If the course of the war had confirmed the necessity, the end of the war presented the opportunity. The acquisition of Canada required officials in London to take responsibility for the unsettled western territories, now freed from the threat of French occupation. The British soon moved to take charge of the whole field of Indian relations. By the royal Proclamation of 1763, a line was drawn down the Appalachians marking the limit of settlement from the British colonies, beyond which Indian trade was to be conducted strictly through British-appointed commissioners. From London's viewpoint, leaving a lightly garrisoned West to the fur-gathering Indians also made economic and imperial sense. The proclamation, however, caused consternation among British colonists for two reasons. It meant that limits were being set to the prospects of settlement and speculation in western lands, and it took control of the west out of colonial hands. The most ambitious men in the colonies thus saw the proclamation as a loss of power to control their own fortunes. Indeed, the British government's huge underestimation of how deeply the halt in westward expansion would be resented by the colonists was one of the factors in sparking the 12-year crisis that led to the American Revolution.

THE TAX CONTROVERSY

George Grenville, who was named prime minister in 1763, was soon looking to meet the costs of defense by raising revenue in the colonies. The first measure was the Plantation Act of 1764, usually called the Revenue, or Sugar, Act, which reduced to a mere three-pence the duty on imported foreign molasses but linked with this a high duty on refined sugar and a prohibition on foreign rum. The last measure of this kind (1733) had not been enforced, but this time the government set up a system of customs houses, staffed by British officers, and even established a vice-admiralty court. The court sat at Halifax, Nova Scotia, and heard very few cases, but in principle it appeared to threaten the cherished British privilege of trials by local juries. Boston further objected to the tax's revenue-raising aspect on constitutional grounds, but, despite some expressions of anxiety, the colonies in general acquiesced.

Parliament next affected colonial economic prospects by passing a Currency Act (1764) to withdraw paper currencies, many of them surviving from the war period, from circulation. This was not done to restrict economic growth so much as to take out currency that was thought to be unsound, but it did severely reduce the circulating medium during the difficult postwar period and further indicated that such matters were subject to British control.

Grenville's next move was a stamp duty, to be raised on a wide variety of transactions, including legal writs, newspaper advertisements, and ships' bills of lading. The colonies were duly consulted and offered no alternative suggestions. The feeling in London, shared by Benjamin Franklin, was that, after making formal objections, the colonies would accept the new taxes as they had the earlier ones. But the Stamp Act (1765) hit harder and deeper than any previous parliamentary measure. As some agents had already pointed out, because of postwar economic difficulties the colonies were short of ready funds.

The Stamp Act struck at vital points of colonial economic operations, affecting transactions in trade. It also affected many of the most articulate and influential people in the colonies (lawyers, journalists, bankers). It was, moreover, the first "internal" tax levied directly on the colonies by Parliament.

IN Virginia the funds shortage was so serious that the province's treasurer, John Robinson, who was also speaker of the assembly, manipulated and redistributed paper money that had been officially withdrawn from circulation by the Currency Act; a large proportion of the landed gentry benefited from this largesse.

Previous colonial taxes had been levied by local authorities or had been "external" import duties whose primary aim could be viewed as regulating trade for the benefit of the empire as a whole rather than raising revenue.

Nevertheless, no one, either in Britain or in the colonies, fully anticipated the uproar that followed the imposition of these duties. Mobs in Boston and other towns rioted and forced appointed stamp distributors to renounce their posts; legal business was largely halted. Several colonies sent delegations to a Congress in New York in the summer of

1765, where the Stamp Act was denounced as a violation of the Englishman's right to be taxed only through elected representatives, and plans were adopted to impose a nonimportation embargo on British goods.

A change of ministry facilitated a change of British policy on taxation. Parliamentary opinion was angered by what it perceived as colonial lawlessness, but British merchants were worried about the embargo on British imports. The marquis of Rockingham, succeeding Grenville, was persuaded to repeal the Stamp Act, and in 1766 the repeal was passed. On the same day, however, Parliament also passed the Declaratory Act, which declared that Parliament had the power to bind or legislate the colonies "in all cases whatsoever."

The colonists, jubilant at the repeal of the Stamp Act, drank innumerable toasts, sounded peals of cannon, and were prepared to ignore the Declaratory Act as face-saving window dressing. John Adams, however, warned in his *Dissertation on the Canon and Feudal Law* that Parliament, armed with this view of its powers, would try to tax the colonies again; and this happened in 1767 when Charles Townshend became chancellor of the Exchequer in a ministry formed by Pitt. The problem was that Britain's financial burden had not been lifted. Townshend, claiming to take literally the colonial distinction between external and internal taxes, imposed external duties on a wide range of necessities, including lead, glass, paint, paper, and tea, the principal domestic beverage. One ominous result was that colonists now began to believe that the British were developing a long-term plan to reduce the colonies to a subservient position, which they were soon calling "slavery." This view was ill-informed, however. Grenville's measures had been designed as a carefully considered package; apart from some tidying-up legislation, Grenville had had no further plans for the colonies after the Stamp Act. His successors developed further measures, not as extensions of an original plan but because the Stamp Act had been repealed.

Nevertheless, the colonists were outraged. In Pennsylvania the lawyer and legislator John Dickinson wrote a series of essays that, appearing in 1767 and 1768 as *Letters from a Farmer in Pennsylvania*, were widely reprinted and exerted great influence in forming a united colonial opposition. Dickinson agreed that Parliament had supreme power where the whole empire was concerned, but he denied that it had power over internal colonial affairs; he quietly implied that the basis of colonial loyalty lay in its utility among equals rather than in obedience owed to a superior.

It proved easier to unite on opinion than on action. Gradually, after much maneuvering and negotiation, a wide-ranging nonimporta-tion policy against British goods was brought into operation. Agreement had not been easy to reach, and the tensions sometimes broke out in acrimonious charges of nonco-operation. In addition, the policy had to be enforced by newly created local committees, a process that put a new disciplinary power in the hands of local men who had not had much previous experience in public affairs. There were, as a result, many signs of discontent with the ordering of domestic affairs in some of the colonies.

CONSTITUTIONAL DIFFERENCES WITH BRITAIN

At this stage, very few colonists wanted or even envisaged independence. (Dickinson had hinted at such a possibility with expressions of pain that were obviously sincere.) The colonial struggle for power, although charged with intense feeling, was not an attempt to change government structure but an argument over legal interpretation. The core of the colonial case was that, as British subjects, they were entitled to the same privileges as their fellow subjects in Britain. They could not constitutionally be taxed without their own consent; and, because they were unrepresented in the Parliament that voted

the taxes, they had not given this consent. James Otis, in two long pamphlets, ceded all sovereign power to Parliament with this proviso. Others, however, began to question whether Parliament did have lawful power to legislate over the colonies. These doubts were expressed by the late 1760s, when James Wilson, a Scottish immigrant lawyer living in Philadelphia, wrote an essay on the subject. Because of the withdrawal of the Townshend round of duties in 1770, Wilson kept this essay private until new troubles arose in 1774, when he published it as *Considerations on the Nature and Extent of the Legislative Authority of the British Parliament*. In this he fully articulated a view that had been gathering force in the colonies (it was also the opinion of Franklin) that Parliament's lawful sovereignty stopped at the shores of Britain.

The official British reply to the colonial case on representation was that the colonies were "virtually" represented in Parliament in the same sense that the large voteless majority of the British public was represented by those who did vote. To this Otis snorted that, if the majority of the British people did not have the vote, they ought to have it. The idea of colonial members of Parliament, several times suggested, was never a likely solution because of problems of time and distance and because, from the colonists' point of view, colonial members would not have adequate influence.

The standpoints of the two sides to the controversy could be traced in the language used. The principle of parliamentary sovereignty was expressed in the language of paternalistic authority; the British referred to themselves as parents and to the colonists as children.

Colonial Tories, who accepted Parliament's case in the interests of social stability, also used this terminology. From this point of view, colonial insubordination was "unnatural," just as the revolt of children against parents was unnatural. The colonists replied to all this in the language of rights. They held that Parliament could do nothing in the colonies that it could not do in Britain because the Americans were protected by all the common-law rights of the British. (When the First Continental Congress met in September 1774, one of its first acts was to affirm that the colonies were entitled to the common law of England.)

Rights, as Richard Bland of Virginia insisted in The Colonel Dismounted (as early as 1764), implied equality. And here he touched on the underlying source of colonial grievance. Americans were being treated as unequals, which they not only resented but also feared would lead to a loss of control of their own affairs. Colonists perceived legal inequality when writs of assistance—essentially, general search warrants—were authorized in Boston in 1761 while closely related "general warrants" were outlawed in two celebrated cases in Britain. Townshend specifically legalized writs of assistance in the colonies in 1767. Dickinson devoted one of his Letters from a Farmer to this issue.

When Lord North became prime minister early in 1770, George III had at last found a minister who could work both with himself and with Parliament. British government began to acquire some stability. In 1770, in the face of the American policy of nonimportation, the Townshend tariffs were withdrawn—all except the tax on tea, which was kept for symbolic reasons. Relative calm returned, though it was ruffled on the New England coastline by frequent incidents of defiance of customs officers, who could get no support from local juries. These outbreaks did not win much sympathy from other colonies, but they were serious enough to call for an increase in the number of British regular forces stationed in Boston. One of the most violent clashes occurred in Boston just before the repeal of the Townshend duties. On March 5, 1770, threatened by mob harassment, a small British detachment opened fire and killed five people, an incident soon known as the Boston Massacre. The soldiers were charged with murder and were given a civilian trial, in which John Adams conducted a successful defense.

The other serious quarrel with British authority occurred in New York, where the assembly refused to accept all the British demands for quartering troops. Before a compromise was reached, Parliament had threatened to suspend the assembly. The episode was ominous because it indicated that Parliament was taking the Declaratory Act at its word; on no previous occasion had the British legislature intervened in the operation of the constitution in an American colony. (Such interventions, which were rare, had come from the crown.)

British intervention in colonial economic affairs occurred again when in 1773 Lord North's administration tried to rescue the East India Company from difficulties that had nothing to do with America. The Tea Act gave the company, which produced tea in India, a monopoly of distribution in the colonies. The company planned to sell its tea through its own agents, eliminating the system of sale by auction to independent merchants. By thus cutting the costs of middlemen, it hoped to undersell the widely purchased inferior smuggled tea. This plan naturally affected colonial merchants, and many colonists denounced the act as a plot to induce Americans to buy—and therefore pay the tax on—legally imported tea. Boston

ON December 16, 1773, a party of Bostonians, thinly disguised as Mohawk Indians, boarded the ships at anchor and dumped some £10,000 worth of tea into the harbor, an event popularly known as the Boston Tea Party. British opinion was outraged, and America's friends in Parliament were immobilized.

was not the only port to threaten to reject the casks of taxed tea, but its reply was the most dramatic—and provocative.

In the spring of 1774, with hardly any opposition, Parliament passed a series of measures designed to reduce Massachusetts to order and imperial discipline. The port of Boston was closed, and, in the Massachusetts Government Act, Parliament for the first time actually altered a colonial charter, substituting an appointive council for the elective one established in 1691 and conferring extensive powers on the governor and council.

An undated illustration of the Boston Tea Party.

The famous town meeting, a forum for radical thinkers, was outlawed as a political body. In addition, Upper Canada (that is, the southern section) was joined to the Mississippi valley for purposes of administration, permanently blocking the prospect of American control of western settlement.

THE CONTINENTAL CONGRESS

There was widespread agreement that this intervention in colonial government could threaten other provinces and could be coun-tered only by collective action. After much intercolonial correspondence, a Continental Congress came into existence, meeting in Philadelphia in September 1774. Every colonial assembly except that of Georgia appointed and sent a delegation. The Virginia delegation's instructions were drafted by Thomas Jefferson and were later published as *A Summary View of the Rights of British America* (1774). Jefferson insisted on the autonomy of colonial legislative power and set forth a highly individualistic view of the basis of American rights. This belief that the

American colonies and other members of the British Empire were distinct states united under the king and thus subject only to the king and not to Parliament was shared by several other delegates, notably James Wilson and John Adams, and strongly influenced the Congress.

The Congress's first important decision was one on procedure: whether to vote by colony, each having one vote, or by wealth calculated on a ratio with population. The decision to vote by colony was made on practical grounds—neither wealth nor population could be satisfactorily ascertained—but it had important consequences. Individual colonies, no matter what their size, retained a degree of autonomy that translated immediately into the language and prerogatives of sovereignty. Under Massachusetts's influence, the Congress next adopted the Suffolk Resolves, recently voted in Suffolk county, Massachusetts, which for the first time put natural rights into the official colonial argument (hitherto all remonstrances had been based on common law and constitutional rights). Apart from this, however, the prevailing mood was cautious.

The Congress's aim was to put such pressure on the British government that it would redress all colonial grievances and restore the harmony that had once prevailed. The Congress thus adopted an Association that committed the colonies to a carefully phased plan of economic pressure, beginning with nonimportation, moving to nonconsumption, and finishing the following September (after the rice harvest had been exported) with nonexportation. A few New England and Virginia delegates were looking toward independence, but the majority went home hoping that these steps, together with new appeals to the king and to the British people, would avert the need for any further such meetings. If these measures failed, however, a second Congress would convene the following spring.

Behind the unity achieved by the Congress lay deep divisions in colonial society. In the mid-1760s upriver New York was disrupted by land riots, which also broke out in parts of New Jersey; much worse disorder ravaged the backcountry of both North and South Carolina, where frontier people were left unprotected by legislatures that taxed them but in which they felt themselves unrepresented. A pitched battle at Alamance Creek in North Carolina in 1771 ended that rising, known as the Regulator Insurrection, and was followed by executions for treason. Although without such serious disorder, the cities also revealed acute social tensions and resentments of inequalities of economic opportunity and visible status. New York provincial politics were riven by intense rivalry between two great family-based factions, the DeLanceys, who benefited from royal government connections, and their rivals, the Livingstons. Another phenomenon was the rapid rise of dissenting religious sects, notably the Baptists, whose style of preaching suggested a strong undercurrent of social as well as religious dissent.

When British Gen. Thomas Gage sent a force from Boston to destroy American rebel military stores at Concord, Massachusetts, fighting broke out between militia and British troops at Lexington and Concord on April 19, 1775. Reports of these clashes reached the Second Continental Congress, which met

A 1782 print showing the September 1774 session of the First Continental Congress in Carpenter's Hall, Philadelphia.

in Philadelphia in May. Although most colonial leaders still hoped for reconciliation with Britain, the news stirred the delegates to more radical action. Steps were taken to put the continent on a war footing. While a further appeal was addressed to the British people (mainly at Dickinson's insistence), the Congress raised an army, adopted a *Declaration of the Causes and Necessity of Taking Up Arms*, and appointed committees to deal with domestic supply and foreign affairs. In August 1775 the king declared a state of rebellion; by the end of the year, all colonial trade had been banned. Even yet, Gen. George Washington, commander of the Continental Army, still referred to the British troops as "ministerial" forces, indicating a civil war, not a war looking to separate national identity.

While the Congress negotiated urgently, but secretly, for a French alliance, power struggles erupted in provinces where conservatives still hoped for relief. The only form relief could take, however, was British concessions; as public opinion hardened in Britain, the hope for reconciliation faded. In the face of British intransigence, men committed to their definition of colonial rights were left with no alternative, and the substantial portion of colonists—about one-third according to John Adams, although contemporary historians believe the number

IN January 1776 the publication of Thomas Paine's irreverent pamphlet "Common Sense" abruptly shattered this hopeful complacency and put independence on the agenda. Paine's eloquent, direct language spoke people's unspoken thoughts; no pamphlet had ever made such an impact on colonial opinion.

recommended that colonies form their own governments and assigned a committee to draft a declaration of independence.

This document, written by Thomas Jefferson but revised in committee, consisted of two parts. The preamble set the claims of the United States on a basis of natural rights, with a dedication to the principle of equality; the second was a long list of grievances against the crown—not Parliament now, since the argument was that Parliament had no lawful power in the colonies. On July 2 the Congress itself voted for independence; on July 4 it adopted the Declaration of Independence.

THE AMERICAN REVOLUTIONARY WAR

The American Revolutionary War thus began as a civil conflict within the British Empire over colonial affairs, but, with America being joined by France in 1778, Spain in 1779, and the Netherlands in 1780, it became an international war. On land the Americans assembled both state militias and the Continental (national) Army, with approximately 20,000 men, mostly farmers, fighting at any given time. By contrast, the British army was composed of reliable and well-trained professionals, numbering about 42,000 regulars, supplemented by about 30,000 German (Hessian) mercenaries.

to have been much smaller—who preferred loyalty to the crown, with all its disadvantages, were localized and outflanked. Where the British armies massed, they found plenty of loyalist support, but, when they moved on, they left the loyalists feeble and exposed.

The most dramatic internal revolution occurred in Pennsylvania, where a strong radical party, based mainly in Philadelphia but with allies in the country, seized power in the course of the controversy over independence itself. Opinion for independence swept the colonies in the spring of 1776. The Congress

After the fighting at Lexington and Concord that began the war, rebel forces began a siege of Boston that ended when the American Gen. Henry Knox arrived with artillery captured from Fort Ticonderoga, forcing Gen. William Howe, Gage's replacement, to evacuate Boston on March 17, 1776. An American force under Gen. Richard Montgomery invaded Canada in the fall of 1775, captured Montreal, and launched an unsuccessful attack on Quebec, in which Montgomery was killed. The Americans maintained a siege on the city until the arrival of British reinforcements in the spring and then retreated to Fort Ticonderoga.

The British government sent Howe's brother, Richard, Adm. Lord Howe, with a large fleet to join his brother in New York, authorizing them to treat with the Americans and assure them pardon should they submit. When the Americans refused this offer of peace, General Howe landed on Long Island and on August 27 defeated the army led by Washington, who retreated into Manhattan. Howe drew him north, defeated his army at Chatterton Hill near White Plains on October 28, and then stormed the garrison Washington had left behind on Manhattan, seizing prisoners and supplies. Lord Charles Cornwallis, having taken Washington's other

After a mildly successful attack at Germantown, Pennsylvania., on October 4, Washington quartered his 11,000 troops for the winter at Valley Forge, Pennsylvania. Though the conditions at Valley Forge were bleak and food was scarce, a Prussian officer, Baron Friedrich Wilhelm von Steuben, was able to give the American troops valuable training in maneuvers and in the more efficient use of their weapons. Von Steuben's aid contributed greatly to Washington's success at Monmouth (now Freehold), New Jersey, on June 28, 1778. After that battle British forces in the north remained chiefly in and around the city of New York.

garrison at Fort Lee, drove the American army across New Jersey to the western bank of the Delaware River and then quartered his troops for the winter at outposts in New Jersey. On Christmas night Washington stealthily crossed the Delaware and attacked Cornwallis's garrison at Trenton, taking nearly 1,000 prisoners. Though Cornwallis soon recaptured Trenton, Washington escaped and went on to defeat British reinforcements at Princeton. Washington's Trenton-Princeton campaign roused the new country and kept the struggle for independence alive.

In 1777 a British army under Gen. John Burgoyne moved south from Canada with Albany, New York., as its goal. Burgoyne captured Fort Ticonderoga on July 5, but, as he approached Albany, he was twice defeated by an American force led by Generals Horatio Gates and Benedict Arnold, and on October 17, 1777, at Saratoga, he was forced to surrender his army. Earlier that fall Howe had sailed from New York to Chesapeake Bay, and once ashore he had defeated Washington's forces at Brandywine Creek on September 11 and occupied the American capital of Philadelphia on September 25.

While the French had been secretly furnishing financial and material aid to the Americans since 1776, in 1778 they began to prepare fleets and armies and in June finally declared war on Britain. With action in the north largely a stalemate, their primary contribution was in the south, where they participated in such undertakings as the siege of British-held Savannah and the decisive siege of Yorktown. Cornwallis destroyed an army under Gates at Camden, South Carolina, on August 16, 1780, but suffered heavy setbacks at Kings Mountain, South Carolina, on October 7 and at Cowpens, South Carolina, on January 17, 1781. After Cornwallis won a costly victory at Guilford Courthouse, North Carolina, on March 15, 1781, he entered Virginia to join other British forces there, setting up a base at Yorktown. Washington's army and a force under the French Count de Rochambeau placed Yorktown under siege, and Cornwallis surrendered his army of more than 7,000 men on October 19, 1781.

TREATY OF PARIS

The military verdict in North America was reflected in the preliminary Anglo-American peace treaty of 1782, which was included in the Treaty of Paris of 1783. Franklin, John Adams, John Jay, and Henry Laurens served as the American commissioners. By its terms Britain recognized the independence of the United States with generous boundaries, including the Mississippi River on the west. Britain retained Canada but ceded East and West Florida to Spain. Other provisions included calling for the payment of American private debts to British citizens and for a recommendation by the Continental Congress to the states in favor of fair treatment of the loyalists.

Most of the loyalists remained in the new country; however, perhaps as many as 80,000 Tories migrated to Canada, England, and the British West Indies. The loyalists were harshly treated as dangerous enemies by the American states during the war and immediately afterward. They were commonly deprived of civil rights, often fined, and frequently relieved of their property. The more conspicuous were usually banished upon pain of death. The British government compensated more than 4,000 of the exiles for property losses, paying out almost £3.3 million. It also gave them land grants, pensions, and appointments to enable them to reestablish themselves. The less ardent and more cautious Tories, staying in the

A painting showing the signing of the Preliminary Treaty of Peace at Paris, November 30, 1782; John Jay and Benjamin Franklin are standing at the left.

United States, accepted the separation from Britain as final and, after the passage of a generation, could not be distinguished from the patriots.

FOUNDATIONS OF THE AMERICAN REPUBLIC

It had been far from certain that the Americans could fight a successful war against the might of Britain. The scattered colonies had little inherent unity; their experience of collective action was limited; an army had to be created and maintained; they had no common institutions other than the Continental Congress; and they had almost no experience of continental public finance. The Americans could not have hoped to win the war without French help, and the French monarchy—whose interests were anti-British but not pro-American—had waited watchfully to see what the Americans could do in the field. Although the French began supplying arms, clothing, and loans surreptitiously soon after the Americans declared independence, it was not until 1778 that a formal alliance was forged.

Most of these problems lasted beyond the achievement of independence and continued to vex American politics for many years, even for generations. Meanwhile, however, the colonies had valuable, though less visible, sources of strength. Practically all farmers had

their own arms and could form into militia companies overnight. More fundamentally, Americans had for many years been receiving basically the same information, mainly from the English press, reprinted in identical form in colonial newspapers. The effect of this was to form a singularly wide body of agreed opinion about major public issues. Another force of incalculable importance was the fact that for several generations Americans had to a large extent been governing themselves through elected assemblies, which in turn had developed sophisticated experience in committee politics.

This factor of "institutional memory" was of great importance in the forming of a mentality of self-government. Men became attached to their habitual ways, especially when these were habitual ways of running their own affairs, and these habits formed the basis of an ideology just as pervasive and important to the people concerned as republican theories published in Britain and the European continent. Moreover, colonial self-government seemed, from a colonial point of view, to be continuous and consistent with the principles of English government. It was equally important that experience of self-government had taught colonial leaders how to get things done. When the Continental Congress met in 1774, members did not have to debate procedure (except on voting); they already knew it. Finally, the Congress's authority was rooted in traditions of legitimacy. The old election laws were used. Voters could transfer their allegiance with minimal difficulty from the dying colonial assemblies to the new assemblies and conventions of the states.

PROBLEMS BEFORE THE SECOND CONTINENTAL CONGRESS

When the Second Continental Congress assembled in Philadelphia in May 1775, revolution was not a certainty. The Congress had to prepare for that contingency nevertheless and thus was confronted by two parallel sets of problems. The first was how to organize for war; the second, which proved less urgent but could not be set aside forever, was how to define the legal relationship between the Congress and the states.

In June 1775, in addition to appointing Washington (who had made a point of turning up in uniform) commander in chief, the Congress provided for the enlistment of an army. It then turned to the vexatious problems of finance. An aversion to taxation being one of the unities of American sentiment, the Congress began by trying to raise a domestic loan. It did not have much success, however, for the excellent reason that the outcome of the operation appeared

highly dubious. At the same time, authority was taken for issuing a paper currency. This proved to be the most important method of domestic war finance, and, as the war years passed, Congress resorted to issuing more and more Continental currency, which depreciated rapidly and had to compete with currencies issued by state governments. The Continental Army was a further source of a form of currency because its commission agents issued certificates in exchange for goods; these certificates bore an official promise of redemption and could be used in personal transactions. Loans raised overseas, notably in France and the Netherlands, were another important source of revenue.

In 1780 Congress decided to call in and replace all former issues of currency. The Philadelphia merchant Robert Morris, who was appointed superintendent of finance in 1781 and came to be known as "the Financier," guided the United States through its complex fiscal difficulties. Morris's personal finances were inextricably tangled up with those of the country, and he became the object of much hostile comment, but he also used his own resources to secure urgently needed loans from abroad. In 1781 Morris secured a charter for the first Bank of North America, an institution that owed much to the example of the Bank of England. Although the bank was attacked by radical egalitarians as an unrepublican manifestation of privilege, it gave the United States a firmer financial foundation.

The problem of financing and organizing the war sometimes overlapped with Congress's other major problem, that of defining its relations with the states. The Congress, being only an association of states, had no power to tax individuals.

Although not officially ratified by all the states until 1781, the Articles of Confederation—a plan of government organization adopted and put into practice by Congress in 1777—gave Congress the right to make requisitions on the states proportionate to their ability to pay. The states in turn had to raise these sums by their own domestic powers to tax, a method that state legislators looking for reelection, much like their counterparts today, were reluctant to employ.

The result was that many states were constantly in heavy arrears, and, particularly after the urgency of the war years had subsided, the Congress's ability to meet expenses and repay its war debts was crippled.

The Congress lacked power to enforce its requisitions and fell badly behind in repaying its wartime creditors. When individual states (Maryland as early as 1782, Pennsylvania in 1785) passed legislation providing for repayment of the debt owed to their own citizens by the Continental Congress, one of the reasons for the Congress's existence had

begun to crumble. Two attempts were made to get the states to agree to grant the Congress the power it needed to raise revenue by levying an impost on imports. Each failed for want of unanimous consent. Essentially, an impost would have been collected at ports, which belonged to individual states—there was no "national" territory—and therefore cut across the concept of state sovereignty. Agreement was nearly obtained on each occasion, and, if it had been, the Constitutional Convention might never have been called. But the failure sharply pointed up the weakness of the Congress and of the union between the states under the Articles of Confederation.

The Articles of Confederation reflected strong preconceptions of state sovereignty. Article II expressly reserved sovereignty to the states individually, and another article even envisaged the possibility that one state might go to war without the others. Fundamental revisions could be made only with unanimous consent, because the Articles represented a treaty between sovereigns, not the creation of a new nation-state. Other major revisions required the consent of nine states. Yet state sovereignty principles rested on artificial foundations. The states could never have achieved independence on their own, and in fact the Congress had taken the first step both in recommending that the states form their own governments and in declaring their collective independence. Most important of its domestic responsibilities, by 1787 the Congress had enacted several ordinances establishing procedures for incorporating new territories. The Northwest Ordinance of 1787 provided for the phased settlement and government of territories in the Ohio valley, leading to eventual admission as new states. It also excluded the introduction of slavery—though it did not exclude the retention of existing slaves.

The states had constantly looked to the Congress for leadership in the difficulties of war; now that the danger was past, however, disunity began to threaten to turn into disintegration. The Congress was largely discredited in the eyes of a wide range of influential men, representing both old and new interests. The states were setting up their own tariff barriers against each other and quarreling among themselves; virtual war had broken out between competing settlers from Pennsylvania and Connecticut claiming the same lands. By 1786, well-informed men were discussing a probable breakup of the confederation into three or more new groups, which could have led to wars between the American republics.

The problems of forming a new government affected the states individually as well as in confederation. Many states were facing their own problems, some of which had national implications. One such event occurred in Massachusetts, where stiff taxation under conditions of postwar depression trapped many farmers into debt. Unable to meet their obligations, they rose late in 1786 under a Revolutionary War officer, Capt. Daniel Shays, in a movement to halt the court sessions in which foreclosures and debt processes were executed. Shays's Rebellion was crushed early in 1787 by an army raised in the state. Although only a few casualties resulted, the episode sent a shiver of fear throughout the country's propertied classes. It also seemed to justify the classical thesis that republics were unstable. It thus provided a potent stimulus to state legislatures to send delegates to the convention called (following a preliminary meeting in Annapolis, Maryland) to meet at Philadelphia to revise the Articles of Confederation.

THE CONSTITUTIONAL CONVENTION

The Philadelphia Convention, which met in May 1787, was officially called for by the old Congress solely to remedy defects in the Articles of Confederation. All the states except Rhode Island responded to an invitation to send delegates. Seventy-four men were chosen by state legislatures to participate, though only 55 actually took part in the proceedings, with 39 of them ultimately signing the Constitution. The delegates included many of the leading figures of the period. Among them were George Washington, who was elected to preside, James Madison, Benjamin Franklin, James Wilson, John Rutledge, Charles Pinckney, Oliver Ellsworth, and Gouverneur Morris.

The Virginia Plan presented by the Virginia delegates went beyond revision and boldly proposed to introduce a new, national government in place of the existing confederation. The convention thus immediately faced the question of whether the United States was to be a country in the modern sense or would continue as a weak federation of autonomous and equal states represented in a single chamber, which was the principle embodied in the New Jersey Plan presented by several small states. Neither plan would prevail in its entirety. What would be agreed to, however, was a new national government endowed with broad powers that made it indisputably national and superior.

The Constitution, as it emerged after a summer of debate, embodied a much stronger principle of separation of powers than was generally to be found in the state constitutions. The chief executive was to be a single figure (a composite executive was discussed and rejected) and was to be elected by an electoral college, meeting in the states. This followed much debate over the Virginia

ON the issue of representation, a compromise plan, eventually approved in mid-July, was brokered and ended a potential stalemate. The so-called Connecticut, or Great, Compromise, put forward by Roger Sherman of Connecticut, would establish a bicameral legislature—one house with representation based on population and one with equal representation for all states.

Plan's preference for legislative election. The principal control on the chief executive, or president, against violation of the Constitution was the rather remote threat of impeachment (to which James Madison attached great importance). The Virginia Plan's proposal that representation be proportional to population in both houses was severely modified by the retention of equal representation for each state in the Senate. But the question of whether to count slaves in the population was abrasive. After some contention, antislavery forces gave way to a compromise by which three-fifths of the slaves would be counted as population for purposes of representation (and direct taxation). Slave states would thus be perpetually overrepresented in national politics; provision was also added for a law permitting the recapture of fugitive slaves, though in deference to republican scruples the word *slaves* was not used.

Contemporary theory expected the legislature to be the most powerful branch of government. Thus, to balance the system, the executive was given a veto, and a judicial system with powers of review was established. It was also implicit in the structure that the new federal judiciary would have power to veto any state laws that conflicted either with the Constitution or with federal statutes. States were forbidden to pass laws impairing obligations of contract—a measure aimed at encouraging capital—and the Congress could pass no ex post facto law. But the Congress was endowed with the basic powers of a modern—and sovereign—government. This was a republic, and the United States could confer no aristocratic titles of honor. The prospect of eventual enlargement of federal power appeared in the clause giving the Congress powers to pass legislation "necessary and proper" for implementing the general purposes of the Constitution. The

states retained their civil jurisdiction, but there was an emphatic shift of the political center of gravity to the federal government, of which the most fundamental indication was the universal understanding that this government would act directly on citizens, as individuals, throughout all the states, regardless of state authority. The language of the Constitution told of the new style: it began, "We the people of the United States," rather than "We the people of New Hampshire, Massachusetts, etc."

The draft Constitution aroused widespread opposition. Anti-Federalists—so-called because their opponents deftly seized the appellation of "Federalists," though they were really nationalists—were strong in states such as Virginia, New York, and Massachusetts, where the economy was relatively successful and many people saw little need for such extreme remedies. Anti-Federalists also expressed fears—here touches of class conflict certainly arose—that the new government would fall into the hands of merchants and men of money. Many good republicans detected oligarchy in the structure of the Senate, with its six-year terms. The absence of a bill of rights aroused deep fears of central power. The Federalists, however, had the advantages of communications, the press, organization, and, generally, the better of the argument. Anti-Federalists also suffered the disadvantage of having no internal coherence or unified purpose.

The debate gave rise to a very intensive literature, much of it at a very high level. The most sustained pro-Federalist argument, written mainly by Hamilton and Madison (assisted by Jay) under the pseudonym Publius, appeared in the newspapers as *The Federalist*, widely called today the Federalist papers. These essays, attacked the feebleness of the confederation and claimed that the new Constitution would have advantages for all sectors of society while threatening none. In the course of the debate, they passed from a strongly nationalist standpoint to one that showed more respect for the idea of a mixed form of government that would safeguard the states. Madison contributed assurances that a multiplicity of interests would counteract each other, preventing the consolidation of power continually charged by their enemies.

The Bill of Rights, steered through the first Congress by Madison's diplomacy, mollified much of the latent opposition. These first 10 amendments, ratified in 1791, adopted into the Constitution the basic English common-law rights that Americans had fought for. But they did more. Unlike Britain, the United States secured a guarantee of freedom for the press and the right of (peaceable) assembly. Also unlike Britain, church and state were formally separated in a clause that seemed to set equal value on nonestablishment of religion and its free exercise. (This left the states free to maintain their own establishments.)

In state conventions held through the winter of 1787 to the summer of 1788, the Constitution was ratified by the necessary minimum of nine states. But the vote was desperately close in Virginia and New York, respectively the 10th and 11th states to ratify, and without them the whole scheme would have been built on sand.

THE SOCIAL REVOLUTION

The American Revolution was a great social upheaval but one that was widely diffused, often gradual, and different in different regions. The principles of liberty and equality stood in stark conflict with the institution of African slavery, which had built much of the country's wealth.

One gradual effect of this conflict was the decline of slavery in all the Northern states; another was a spate of manumissions by liberal slave owners in Virginia. But with most slave owners, especially in South Carolina and Georgia, ideals counted for nothing. Throughout the slave states, the institution of slavery came to be reinforced by a white supremacist doctrine of racial inferiority.

The manumissions did result in the development of new communities of free blacks, who enjoyed considerable freedom of movement for a few years and who produced some outstanding figures, such as the astronomer Benjamin Banneker and the religious leader Richard Allen, a founder of the African Methodist Episcopal Church Zion. But in the 1790s and after, the condition of free blacks deteriorated as states adopted laws restricting their activities, residences, and economic choices. In general they came to occupy poor neighbourhoods and grew into a permanent underclass, denied education and opportunity.

The American Revolution also dramatized the economic importance of women. Women had always contributed indispensably to the operation of farms and often businesses, while they seldom acquired independent status; but, when war removed men from the locality, women often had to take full charge, which they proved they could do. Republican ideas spread among women, influencing discussion of women's rights, education, and role in society. Some states modified their inheritance and property laws to permit women to inherit a share of estates and to exercise limited control of property after marriage. On the whole, however, the Revolution itself had only very gradual and diffused effects on women's ultimate status. Such changes as took place amounted to a fuller recognition of the importance of women as mothers of republican citizens rather than making them into independent citizens of equal political and civil status with men.

Americans had fought for independence to protect common-law rights; they had no program for legal reform. Gradually, however, some customary practices came to seem out of keeping with republican principles. The outstanding example was the law of inheritance. The new states took steps, where necessary, to remove the old rule of primogeniture in favor of equal partition of intestate estates; this conformed to both the egalitarian and the individualist principles preferred by American society. Humanization of the penal codes, however, occurred only gradually, in the 19th century, inspired as much by European example as by American sentiment.

THE FEDERALIST ADMINISTRATION AND THE FORMATION OF PARTIES

Although the work of the Founding Fathers might appear to have been completed by the creation of the Constitution, the republic was still quite fragile. That fragility was summed up by Ben Franklin's words on the kind of government that had been established by the Constitutional Convention: "A republic, if you can keep it." The next years and the first administrations would become vital to the survival of the United States.

Hamilton, who had believed since the

early 1780s that a national debt would be "a national blessing," both for economic reasons and because it would act as a "cement" to the union, used his new power base to realize the ambitions of the nationalists. He recommended that the federal government pay off the old Continental Congress's debts at par rather than at a depreciated value and that it assume state debts, drawing the interests of the creditors toward the central government rather than state governments. This plan met strong opposition from the many who had sold their securities at great discount during the postwar depression and from Southern states, which had repudiated their debts and did not want to be taxed to pay other states' debts. A compromise in Congress was reached—thanks to the efforts of Secretary of State Jefferson—whereby Southern states approved Hamilton's plan in return for Northern agreement to fix the location of the new national capital on the banks of the Potomac, closer to the South. When Hamilton next introduced his plan to found a Bank of the United States, modeled on the Bank of England, opposition began to harden. Many argued that the Constitution did not confide this power to Congress. Hamilton, however, persuaded Washington that anything not expressly forbidden by the Constitution was permitted under the Constitution's "necessary and proper" clause of implied powers. The Bank Act passed in 1791. Hamilton also advocated plans for the support of nascent industry, which proved premature, and he imposed the revenue-raising whiskey excise that led to the Whiskey Rebellion, a minor uprising in western Pennsylvania in 1794.

A party opposed to Hamilton's fiscal policies began to form in Congress. With Madison at its center and with support from Jefferson, it soon extended its appeal beyond Congress to popular constituencies. Meanwhile, the French Revolution and France's subsequent declaration of war against Great Britain, Spain, and Holland further

THE first elections under the new Constitution were held in 1789. George Washington was unanimously voted the country's first president. His secretary of the treasury, Alexander Hamilton, formed a clear-cut program that soon gave substance to the old fears of the Anti-Federalists.

divided American loyalties. Democratic-Republican societies sprang up to express support for France, while Hamilton and his supporters, known as Federalists, backed Britain for economic reasons. Washington pronounced American neutrality in Europe, but to prevent a war with Britain he sent Chief Justice John Jay to London to negotiate a treaty. In the Jay Treaty (1794) the United States gained only minor concessions and—humiliatingly—accepted British naval supremacy as the price of protection for American shipping.

Washington, whose tolerance had been severely strained by the Whiskey Rebellion and by criticism of the Jay Treaty, chose not to run for a third presidential term. In his Farewell Address, in a passage drafted by Hamilton, he denounced the new party politics as divisive and dangerous.

One of the expedients of party to acquire influence, within particular districts, is to misrepresent the opinions and aims of other districts. You cannot shield yourselves too much against the jealousies and heart-burnings which spring from these misrepresentations. They tend to render alien to each other those who ought to be bound together by fraternal affection.

Parties did not yet aspire to national objectives, however, and, when the Federalist John Adams was elected president, the Democrat-Republican Jefferson, as the presidential candidate with the second greatest number of votes, became vice president. Wars in Europe and on the high seas, together with rampant opposition at home, gave the new administration little peace. Virtual naval war with France had followed from American acceptance of British naval protection. In 1798 a French attempt to solicit bribes from American commissioners negotiating a settlement of differences (the so-called XYZ Affair) aroused a wave of anti-French feeling. Later that year the Federalist majority in Congress passed the Alien and Sedition Acts, which imposed serious civil restrictions on aliens suspected of pro-French activities and penalized U.S. citizens who criticized the government, making nonsense of the First Amendment's guarantee of free press. The acts were most often invoked to prosecute Republican editors, some of whom served jail terms. These measures in turn called forth the Virginia and Kentucky resolutions, drafted respectively by Madison and Jefferson, which invoked state sovereignty against intolerable federal powers. War with France often seemed imminent during this period, but Adams was determined to avoid issuing a formal declaration of war, and in this he succeeded.

Taxation, which had been levied to pay anticipated war costs, brought more discontent, and widespread disagreement over issues ranging from civil liberties to taxation was polarizing American politics. A basic sense of political identity now divided Federalists from Republicans, and in the election of 1800 Jefferson drew on deep sources of Anti-Federalist opposition to challenge and defeat his old friend and colleague Adams. The result was the first contest over the presidency between political parties and the first actual change of government as a result of a general election in modern history.

THE JEFFERSONIAN REPUBLICANS IN POWER

Jefferson began his presidency with a plea for reconciliation: "We are all republicans: we are all federalists." He had no plans for a permanent two-party system of government. He also began with a strong commitment to limited government and strict construction of the Constitution. All these commitments were soon to be tested by the exigencies of war, diplomacy, and political contingency.

Jefferson's administration pursued a policy of expansion, helping set in motion the United States's eventual sovereignty from Atlantic to Pacific. He seized the opportunity when Napoleon I decided to relinquish French ambitions in North America by offering the Louisiana territory for sale (Spain had recently ceded the territory to France). This extraordinary acquisition, the Louisiana Purchase, bought at a price of a few cents per acre, more than doubled the area of the United States. Jefferson had no constitutional sanction for such an exercise of executive power; he made up the rules as he went along, taking a broad construction view of the Constitution on this issue. He also sought opportunities to gain Florida from Spain, and, for scientific and political reasons, he sent Meriwether Lewis and William Clark on an expedition of exploration across the continent. This territorial expansion was not without problems. Various separatist movements periodically arose, including a plan for a Northern Confederacy formulated by New England Federalists. Aaron Burr, who had been elected Jefferson's vice president in 1800 but was replaced in 1804, led several western conspiracies. Arrested and tried for treason, he was acquitted in 1807.

As chief executive, Jefferson clashed with members of the judiciary, many of whom had been late appointments by Adams. One of his primary opponents was the late appointee Chief Justice John Marshall, most notably in the case of *Marbury* v. *Madison* (1803), in which the Supreme Court first exercised the power of judicial review of congressional legislation.

By the start of Jefferson's second term in office, Europe was engulfed in the Napoleonic Wars. The United States remained neutral, but both Britain and France imposed various orders and decrees severely restricting American trade with Europe and confiscated American ships for violating the new rules. Britain also conducted impressment raids in which U.S. citizens were sometimes seized. Unable to agree to treaty terms with Britain, Jefferson tried to coerce both Britain and France into ceasing to violate "neutral rights" with a total embargo on American exports, enacted by Congress in 1807. The results were catastrophic for American commerce and produced bitter alienation in New England, where the embargo (written backward as "O grab me") was held to be a Southern plot to destroy New England's wealth. In 1809, shortly after Madison was elected president, the embargo act was repealed.

MADISON AS PRESIDENT AND THE WAR OF 1812

Madison's presidency was dominated by foreign affairs. Both Britain and France committed depredations on American shipping, but Britain was more resented, partly because with the greatest navy it was more effective and partly because Americans were extremely sensitive to British insults to national honor. Certain expansionist elements looking to both

Florida and Canada began to press for war and took advantage of the issue of naval protection. Madison's own aim was to preserve the principle of freedom of the seas and to assert the ability of the United States to protect its own interests and its citizens. While striving to confront the European adversaries impartially, he was drawn into war against Britain, which was declared in June 1812 on a vote of 79–49 in the House and 19–13 in the Senate. There was almost no support for war in the strong Federalist New England states.

The War of 1812 began and ended in irony. The British had already rescinded the offending orders in council, but the news had not reached the United States at the time of the declaration. The Americans were poorly placed from every point of view. Ideological objections to armies and navies had been responsible for a minimal naval force. Ideological objections to banks had been responsible, in 1812, for the Senate's refusal to renew the charter of the Bank of the United States. Mercantile sentiment was hostile to the administration. Under the circumstances, it was remarkable that the United States succeeded in staggering through two years of war, eventually winning important naval successes at sea, on the Great Lakes, and on Lake Champlain. On land a British raiding party burned public buildings in Washington, D.C., and drove President Madison to flee from the capital. The only action with long-term implications was Andrew Jackson's victory at the Battle of New Orleans—won in January 1815, two weeks after peace had been achieved with the signing of the Treaty of Ghent (Belgium). Jackson's political reputation rose directly from this battle.

In historical retrospect, the most important aspect of the peace settlement was an agreement to set up a boundary commission for the Canadian border, which could thenceforth be left unguarded. It was not the end of Anglo-American hostility, but the agreement marked the advent of an era of mutual trust. The conclusion of the War of 1812, which has sometimes been called the Second War of American Independence, marked a historical cycle. It resulted in a pacification of the old feelings of pain and resentment against Great Britain and its people—still for many Americans a kind of paternal relationship. And, by freeing them of anxieties on this front, it also freed Americans to look to the West. Thus, with war concluded, even if not very successfully, the future of the founding generation's republic seemed secure.

This 1816 painting by H. Reinagle depicts the 1814 victory of the American fleet, led by Thomas Macdonough, over the British on Lake Champlain.

CHAPTER 3

THE FOUNDINGEST FATHER: GEORGE WASHINGTON (1732–1799)

GEORGE WASHINGTON, KNOWN TODAY COMMONLY AS THE Father of His Country, is by all accounts the consensus Foundingest Father. He played an important role in the run-up to the Declaration of Independence, commanded the colonial armies in the American Revolution, was central to the Constitutional Convention that created the U.S. Constitution, and became the country's unanimously elected first president, setting a two-term limit that informally continued until 1940 and numerous other executive precedents that continue to influence his successors.

CHILDHOOD AND YOUTH

George Washington was born on February 22, 1732, in Westmoreland county, Virginia. His father, Augustine Washington, had gone to school in England, had tasted seafaring life, and then settled down to manage his growing Virginia estates. His mother was Mary Ball, whom Augustine, a widower, had married early the previous year. Washington's paternal lineage had some distinction; an early forebear was described as a "gentleman," Henry VIII later gave the family lands, and its members held various offices. But family fortunes fell with the Puritan revolution in England, and John Washington, grandfather of Augustine, migrated in 1657 to Virginia.

Washinton attended school irregularly from his 7th to his 15th year, first with the local church sexton and later with a schoolmaster named Williams. He was fairly well trained in practical mathematics—gauging, several types of mensuration, and such trigonometry as was useful in surveying. He studied geography, possibly had a little Latin, and certainly read some of *The Spectator* and other English classics. The copybook in which he transcribed at 14 a set of moral precepts, or *Rules of Civility and Decent Behaviour in Company and Conversation*, was carefully preserved. His best training, however, was given him by practical men and outdoor occupations, not by books. He mastered tobacco growing and stock raising, and early in his teens he was sufficiently familiar with surveying to plot the fields about him.

At his father's death, the 11-year-old boy became the ward of his eldest half

LITTLE is known of George Washington's early childhood, spent largely on the Ferry Farm on the Rappahannock River, opposite Fredericksburg, Virginia. Mason L. Weems's stories of the hatchet and cherry tree and of young Washington's repugnance to fighting are apocryphal efforts to fill a manifest gap.

brother, Lawrence, who gave him wise and affectionate care. Lawrence inherited the beautiful estate of Little Hunting Creek, which had been granted to the original settler, John Washington, and which Augustine had done much since 1738 to develop. Lawrence married Anne (Nancy) Fairfax, daughter of Colonel William Fairfax, a cousin and agent of Lord Fairfax and one of the chief proprietors of the region. Lawrence also built a house and named the 2,500-acre holding Mount Vernon in honor of the admiral under whom he had served in the siege of Cartagena. Living there chiefly with Lawrence (though he spent some time near Fredericksburg with his other half brother, Augustine, called Austin), George entered a more spacious and polite world. Anne Fairfax Washington was a woman of charm, grace, and culture; Lawrence had brought from his English school and naval service much knowledge and experience. A valued neighbour and relative, George William Fairfax, whose large estate, Belvoir, was about 4 miles distant, and other relatives by marriage, the Carlyles of Alexandria, helped form George's mind and manners. The youth turned first to surveying as a profession. Lord Fairfax, a middle-aged bachelor who owned more than 5,000,000 acres in northern Virginia and the Shenandoah Valley, came to America in 1746 to live with his cousin George William

at Belvoir and to look after his properties. Two years later he sent to the Shenandoah Valley a party to survey and plot his lands to make regular tenants of the squatters moving in from Pennsylvania. With the official surveyor of Prince William county in charge, Washington went along as assistant. The 16-year-old lad kept a disjointed diary of the trip, which shows skill in observation. He describes the discomfort of sleeping under "one thread Bear blanket with double its Weight of Vermin such as Lice Fleas & c"; an encounter with an Indian war party bearing a scalp; the Pennsylvania-German emigrants, "as ignorant a set of people as the Indians they would never speak English but when spoken to they speak all Dutch"; and the serving of roast wild turkey on "a Large Chip," for "as for dishes we had none."

In 1749, aided by Lord Fairfax, Washington received an appointment as official surveyor of Culpeper county, and for more than two years he was kept almost constantly busy. Surveying not only in Culpeper but also in Frederick and Augusta counties, he made journeys far beyond the Tidewater region into the western wilderness. The experience taught him resourcefulness and endurance and toughened him in both body and mind. Coupled with Lawrence's ventures in land, it also gave him an interest in western development that endured throughout his life. He was always disposed to speculate in western holdings and to view favorably projects for colonizing the West, and he greatly resented the limitations that the crown in time laid on the westward movement. In 1752 Lord Fairfax determined to take up his final residence in the Shenandoah Valley and settled there in a log hunting lodge, which he called Greenway Court after a Kentish manor of his family's. There Washington was sometimes entertained and had access to a small library that Fairfax had begun accumulating at Oxford.

The years 1751–1752 marked a turning point in Washington's life, for they placed him in control of Mount Vernon. Lawrence, stricken by tuberculosis, went to Barbados in 1751 for his health, taking George along. From this sole journey beyond the present borders of the United States, Washington returned with the light scars of an attack of smallpox. In July 1752 Lawrence died, making George executor and residuary heir of his estate should his daughter, Sarah, die without issue. As she died within two months, Washington at age 20 became head of one of the best Virginia estates.

For the next 20 years the main background of Washington's life was the work and society of Mount Vernon. He gave assiduous attention to the rotation of crops, fertilization of the soil, and the management of livestock.

WASHINGTON always thought farming the "most delectable" of pursuits. "It is honorable," he wrote, "it is amusing, and, with superior judgment, it is profitable." And, of all the spots for farming, he thought Mount Vernon the best. "No estate in United America," he assured an English correspondent, "is more pleasantly situated than this." His greatest pride in later days was to be regarded as the first farmer of the land.

He had to manage the 18 slaves that came with the estate and others he bought later; by 1760 he had paid taxes on 49 slaves—though he strongly disapproved of the institution and hoped for some mode of abolishing it. At the time of his death, more than 300 slaves were housed in the quarters on his property. He had been unwilling to sell slaves lest families be broken up, even though the increase in their numbers placed a burden on him for their upkeep and gave him a larger force of workers than he required, especially after he gave up the cultivation of tobacco. In his will, he bequeathed the slaves in his possession to his wife and ordered that upon her death they be set free, declaring also that the young, the aged, and the infirm among them "shall be comfortably cloathed & fed by my heirs." Still, this accounted for only about half the slaves on his property. The other half, owned by his wife, were entailed to the Custis estate, so that on her death they were destined to pass to her heirs. However, she freed all the slaves in 1800 after his death.

For diversion Washington was fond of riding, fox hunting, and dancing, of such theatrical performances as he could reach, and of duck hunting and sturgeon fishing. He liked billiards and cards and not only subscribed to racing associations but also ran his own horses in races. In all outdoor pursuits, from wrestling to colt breaking, he excelled. A friend of the 1750s describes him as "straight as an Indian, measuring six feet two inches in his stockings"; as very muscular and broad-shouldered but, though large-boned, weighing only 175 pounds; and as having long arms and legs. His penetrating blue-gray eyes were overhung by heavy brows, his nose was large and straight, and his mouth

was large and firmly closed. "His movements and gestures are graceful, his walk majestic, and he is a splendid horseman." He soon became prominent in community affairs, was an active member and later vestryman of the Episcopal church, and as early as 1755 expressed a desire to stand for the Virginia House of Burgesses.

EARLY MILITARY CAREER

Traditions of John Washington's feats as Indian fighter and Lawrence Washington's talk of service days helped imbue George with military ambition. Just after Lawrence's death, Lieut. Gov. Robert Dinwiddie appointed George adjutant for the southern district of Virginia at £100 a year (November 1752). In 1753 he became adjutant of the Northern Neck and Eastern Shore. Later that year, Dinwiddie found it necessary to warn the French to desist from their encroachments on Ohio Valley lands claimed by the crown. After sending one messenger who failed to reach the goal, he determined to dispatch Washington. On the day he received his orders, October 31, 1753, Washington set out for the French posts. His party consisted of a Dutchman to serve as interpreter, the expert scout Christopher Gist as guide, and four others, two of them experienced traders with the Indians. Theoretically, Great Britain and France were at peace. Actually, war impended, and Dinwiddie's message was an ultimatum: the French must get out or be put out.

The journey proved rough, perilous, and futile. Washington's party left what is now Cumberland, Maryland, in the middle of November and, despite wintry weather and impediments of the wilderness, reached Fort LeBoeuf, at what is now Waterford, Pennsylvania, 20 miles south of Lake Erie, without delay. The French commander was courteous but adamant. As Washington reported, his officers "told me, That it was their absolute Design to take possession of the Ohio, and by God they would do it." Eager to carry this alarming news back, Washington pushed off hurriedly with Gist. He was lucky to have gotten back alive. An Indian fired at them at 15 paces but missed. When they crossed the Allegheny River on a raft, Washington was jerked into the ice-filled stream but saved himself by catching one of the timbers. That night he almost froze in his wet clothing. He reached Williamsburg, Virginia, on January 16, 1754, where he hastily penned a record of the journey. Dinwiddie, who was laboring to convince the crown of the seriousness of the French threat, had it printed, and when he sent it to London, it was reprinted in three different forms.

The enterprising governor forthwith planned an expedition to hold the Ohio country. He made Joshua Fry colonel of a provincial regiment, appointed Washington lieutenant colonel, and set them to recruiting troops. Two agents of the Ohio Company, which Lawrence Washington and others had formed to develop lands on the upper Potomac and Ohio rivers, had begun building a fort at what later became Pittsburgh. Dinwiddie, ready to launch into his own war, sent Washington with two companies to reinforce this post. In April 1754 the lieutenant colonel set out from Alexandria with about 160 men. He marched to Cumberland only to learn that the French had anticipated the British blow; they had taken possession of the fort of the Ohio Company and had renamed it Fort Duquesne. Happily, the Indians of the area offered support. Washington therefore struggled cautiously forward to within about 40 miles of the French position and erected his own post at Great Meadows, near what is now Confluence, Pennsylvania. From this base, on May 28, 1754, he made a surprise attack upon an advance detachment of 30 French, killing the commander, Coulon de Jumonville, and nine others and taking the rest prisoners. The French and Indian War had begun.

Washington at once received promotion to a full colonelcy and was reinforced, commanding a considerable body of Virginia and North Carolina troops, with Indian auxiliaries. But his attack soon brought the whole

Portrait of George Washington by John Gadsby Chapman, 1834,
copied from the 1772 portrait by Charles Willson Peale.

French force down upon him. They drove his 350 men into the Great Meadows fort (Fort Necessity) on July 3, besieged it with 700 men, and, after an all-day fight, compelled him to surrender. The construction of the fort had been a blunder, for it lay in a waterlogged creek bottom, was commanded on three sides by forested elevations approaching it closely, and was too far from Washington's supports. The French agreed to let the disarmed colonials march back to Virginia with the honors of war, but they compelled Washington to promise that Virginia would not build another fort on the Ohio for a year and to sign a paper acknowledging responsibility for "*l'assassinat*" of de Jumonville, a word that Washington later explained he did not rightly understand. He returned to Virginia, chagrined but proud, to receive the thanks of the House of Burgesses and to find that his name had been mentioned in the London gazettes. His remark in a letter to his brother that "I have heard the bullets whistle; and believe me, there is something charming in the sound" was commented on humorously by the author Horace Walpole and sarcastically by King George II.

The arrival of General Edward Braddock and his army in Virginia in February 1755, as part of the triple plan of campaign that called for his advance on Fort Duquesne and in New York Governor William Shirley's capture of Fort Niagara and Sir William Johnson's capture of Crown Point, brought Washington new opportunities and responsibilities. He had resigned his commission in October 1754 in resentment of the slighting treatment and underpayment of colonial officers and particularly because of an untactful order of the British war office that provincial officers of whatever rank would be subordinate to any officer holding the king's commission. But he ardently desired a part in the war; "my inclinations," he wrote a friend, "are strongly bent to arms." When Braddock showed appreciation of his merits and invited him to join the expedition as personal aide-de-camp, with the courtesy title of colonel, he therefore accepted. His self-reliance, decision, and masterfulness soon became apparent.

He had frequent disputes with Braddock, who, when contractors failed to deliver their supplies, attacked the colonials as supine and dishonest while Washington defended them warmly. His freedom of utterance is proof of Braddock's esteem. Braddock accepted Washington's unwise advice that he divide his army, leaving half of it to come up with the slow wagons and cattle train and taking the other half forward against Fort Duquesne at a rapid pace. Washington was ill with fever during June but joined the advance guard in a covered wagon on July 8, begged to lead the march on Fort Duquesne with his Virginians and Indian allies, and was by Braddock's side when on July 9 the army was ambushed and bloodily defeated.

In this defeat Washington displayed the combination of coolness and determination, the alliance of unconquerable energy with complete poise, that was the secret of so many of his successes. So ill that he had to use a pillow instead of a saddle and that Braddock ordered his body servant to keep special watch over him, Washington was, nevertheless, everywhere at once. At first he followed Braddock as the general bravely tried to rally his men to push either forward or backward, the wisest course the circumstances permitted. Then he rode back to bring up the Virginians from the rear and rallied them with effect on the flank. To him was largely due the escape of the force. His exposure of his person was as reckless as Braddock's, who was fatally wounded on his fifth horse; Washington had two horses shot out from under him and his clothes cut by four bullets without being hurt. He was at Braddock's deathbed, helped bring the troops back, and was repaid by being appointed, in August 1755, while still only 23 years old, commander of all Virginia troops.

But no part of his later service was conspicuous. Finding that a Maryland captain who held a royal commission would not obey him, he rode north in February 1756 to Boston to have the question settled by the commander in chief in America, Governor Shirley, and, bearing a letter from Dinwiddie, had no difficulty in carrying his point. On his return he plunged into a multitude of vexations. He had to protect a weak, thinly settled frontier nearly 400 miles in length with only some 700 ill-disciplined colonial troops, to cope with a legislature unwilling to support him, to meet attacks on the drunkenness and inefficiency of the soldiers, and to endure constant wilderness hardships. It is not strange that in 1757 his health failed and in the closing weeks of that year he was so ill of a "bloody flux" (dysentery) that his physician ordered him home to Mount Vernon.

In the spring of 1758 he had recovered sufficiently to return to duty as colonel in command of all Virginia troops. As part of the grand sweep of several armies organized by British statesman William Pitt, the Elder, Gen. John Forbes led a new advance upon Fort Duquesne. Forbes resolved not to use Braddock's road but to cut a new one west from Raystown, Pennsylvania. Washington disapproved of the route but played an important part in the movement. Late in the autumn the French evacuated and burned Fort Duquesne, and Forbes reared Fort Pitt on the site. Washington, who had just been elected to the House of Burgesses, was able to resign with the honorary rank of brigadier general.

Although his officers expressed regret at the "loss of such an excellent Commander, such a sincere Friend, and so affable a Companion," he quit the service with a sense of frustration. He had thought the war excessively slow. The Virginia legislature had been stingy in voting money; the Virginia recruits had come forward reluctantly and had proved of poor quality—Washington had hanged a few deserters and flogged others heavily. Virginia gave him less pay than other colonies offered their troops. Desiring a regular commission such as his half brother Lawrence had held, he applied in vain to the British commander in North America, Lord Loudoun, to make good a promise that Braddock had given him. Ambitious for both rank and honor, he showed a somewhat strident vigour in asserting his desires and in complaining when they were denied. He returned to Mount Vernon somewhat disillusioned.

MARRIAGE AND PLANTATION LIFE

Immediately on resigning his commission, Washington was married on January 6, 1759 to Martha Dandridge, the widow of Daniel Parke Custis. She was a few months older than he, was the mother of two children living and two dead, and possessed one of the considerable fortunes of Virginia. Washington had met her the previous March and had asked for her hand before his campaign with Forbes. Though it does not seem to have been a romantic love match, the marriage united two harmonious temperaments and proved happy.

Some estimates of the property brought to him by this marriage have been exaggerated, but it did include a number of slaves and about 15,000 acres, much of it valuable for its proximity to Williamsburg. More important to Washington were the two stepchildren, John Parke ("Jacky") and Martha Parke ("Patsy") Custis, who at the time of the marriage were six and four, respectively. He lavished great affection and care upon them, worried greatly over Jacky's waywardness, and was overcome with grief when Patsy died just before the Revolution. Jacky died during the war, leaving four children. Washington adopted two of them, a boy and a girl, and even signed his letters to the boy as "your papa." Himself childless, he thus had a real family.

From the time of his marriage Washington added to the care of Mount Vernon the supervision of the Custis estate at the White House on the York River. As his holdings expanded, they were divided into farms, each under its own overseer; but he minutely inspected operations every day and according to one visitor often pulled off his coat and performed ordinary labor. As he once wrote, "middling land under a man's own eyes, is more profitable than rich land at a distance." Until the eve of the Revolution he devoted himself to the duties and pleasures of a great landholder, varied by several weeks' attendance every year in the House of Burgesses in Williamsburg. During 1760–1774 he was also a justice of the peace for Fairfax county, sitting in court in Alexandria.

In no light does Washington appear more characteristically than as one of the richest, largest, and most industrious of Virginia planters. For six days a week he rose early and worked hard; on Sundays he irregularly attended Pohick Church (16 times in 1760), entertained company, wrote letters, made purchases and sales, and sometimes went fox hunting. In these years he took snuff and smoked a pipe; throughout life he liked Madeira wine and punch. Although wheat and tobacco were his staples, he practiced crop rotation on a three-year or five-year plan. He had his own water-powered flour mill, blacksmith shop, brick and charcoal kilns, carpenters, and masons. His fishery supplied shad, bass, herring, and other catches, salted as food for his slaves. Coopers, weavers, and his own shoemaker turned out barrels, cotton, linen, and woolen goods, and brogans for all needs. In short, his estates, in accordance with his orders to overseers to "buy nothing you can make yourselves," were largely self-sufficient communities. But he did send large

WASHINGTON was an innovative farmer and a responsible landowner. He experimented at breeding cattle, acquired at least one buffalo, with the hope of proving its utility as a meat animal, and kept stallions at stud. He also took pride in a peach and apple orchard.

orders to England for farm implements, tools, paint, fine textiles, hardware, and agricultural books and hence was painfully aware of British commercial restrictions.

Meanwhile, Washington played a prominent role in the social life of the Tidewater region. The members of the council and House of Burgesses, a roster of influential Virginians, were all friends. He visited the Byrds of Westover, the Lees of Stratford, the Carters of Shirley and Sabine Hall, and the Lewises of Warner Hall; Mount Vernon often was busy with guests in return. He liked house parties and afternoon tea on the Mount Vernon porch overlooking the grand Potomac; he was fond of picnics, barbecues, and clambakes; and throughout life he enjoyed dancing, frequently going to Alexandria for balls. Cards were a steady diversion, and his accounts record sums lost at them, the largest reaching nearly £10. His diary sometimes states that in bad weather he was "at home all day, over cards." Billiards was a rival amusement. Not only the theater, when available, but also concerts, cockfights, circuses, puppet shows, and exhibitions of animals received his patronage.

He insisted on the best clothes—coats, laced waistcoats, hats, colored silk hose—bought in London. The Virginia of the Randolphs, Corbins, Harrisons, Tylers, Nicholases, and other prominent families had an aristocratic quality, and Washington liked to do things in a large way. It has been computed that in the seven years prior to 1775, Mount Vernon had 2,000 guests, most of whom stayed to dinner if not overnight.

PREREVOLUTIONARY POLITICS

Washington's contented life was interrupted by the rising storm in imperial affairs. The British ministry, facing a heavy postwar debt, high home taxes, and continued military costs in America, decided in 1764 to obtain revenue from the colonies. Up to that time, Washington, though regarded by associates, in Colonel John L. Peyton's words, as "a young man of an extraordinary and exalted character," had shown no signs of personal greatness and few signs of interest in state affairs. The Proclamation of 1763 interdicting settlement beyond the Alleghenies irked him, for he was interested in the Ohio Company, the Mississippi Company, and other speculative western ventures. He nevertheless played a silent part in the House of Burgesses and was a thoroughly loyal subject.

But he was present when Patrick Henry introduced his resolutions against the Stamp Act in May 1765 and shortly thereafter gave token of his adherence to the cause of the colonial Whigs against the Tory ministries of England. In 1768 he told George Mason at Mount Vernon that he would take his musket on his shoulder whenever his country called him. The next spring, on April 4, 1769, he sent Mason the Philadelphia nonimportation resolutions with a letter declaring that it was necessary to resist the strokes of "our lordly masters" in England; that, courteous remonstrances to Parliament having failed, he wholly endorsed the resort to commercial warfare; and that as a last resort no man should scruple to use arms in defense of liberty. When, the following May, the royal governor dissolved the House of Burgesses, he shared in the gathering at the Raleigh, North

Carolina, tavern that drew up nonimportation resolutions, and he went further than most of his neighbours in adhering to them. At that time and later he believed with most Americans that peace need not be broken.

Late in 1770 he paid a land-hunting visit to Fort Pitt, where George Croghan was maturing his plans for the proposed 14th colony of Vandalia. Washington directed his agent to locate and survey 10,000 acres adjoining the Vandalia tract, and at one time he wished to share in certain of Croghan's schemes. But the Boston Tea Party of December 1773 and the bursting of the Vandalia bubble at about the same time turned his eyes back to the East and the threatening state of Anglo-American relations. He was not a member of the Virginia committee of correspondence formed in 1773 to communicate with other colonies, but when the Virginia legislators, meeting irregularly again at the Raleigh tavern in May 1774, called for a Continental Congress, he was present and signed the resolutions.

Moreover, Washington was a leading member of the first provincial convention or revolutionary legislature late that summer, and to that body he made a speech that was much praised for its pithy eloquence, declaring that "I will raise one thousand men, subsist them at my own expense, and march myself at their head for the relief of Boston."

The Virginia provincial convention promptly elected Washington one of the seven delegates to the first Continental Congress. He was by this time known as a radical rather than a moderate, and in several letters of the time he opposed a continuance of petitions to the British crown, declaring that they would inevitably meet with a humiliating rejection. "Shall we after this whine and cry for relief when we have already tried it in vain?" he wrote. When the Congress met in Philadelphia on September 5, 1774, he was in his seat in full uniform, and his participation in its councils marks the beginning of his national career.

Though he served on none of the committees, he was a useful member, his advice being sought on military matters and weight being attached to his advocacy of a nonexportation as well as nonimportation agreement. He also helped to secure approval of the Suffolk Resolves, which looked toward armed resistance as a last resort and did much to harden the king's heart against America.

Returning to Virginia in November, he took command of the volunteer companies drilling there and served as chairman of the Committee of Safety in Fairfax county. Although the province contained many experienced officers and Colonel William Byrd of Westover had succeeded Washington as commander in chief, the unanimity with which the

*W*ASHINGTON'S
letters from this period show
that, while still utterly opposed
to the idea of independence, he
was determined never to submit
"to the loss of those valuable
rights and privileges, which
are essential to the happiness
of every free State, and without
which life, liberty, and property
are rendered totally insecure."
If the ministry pushed matters
to an extremity, he wrote, "more
blood will be spilled on this
occasion than ever before in
American history."

HEAD OF THE COLONIAL FORCES

The choice of Washington as commander in chief of the military forces of all the colonies followed immediately upon the first fighting, though it was by no means inevitable and was the product of partly artificial forces. The Virginia delegates differed upon his appointment. Edmund Pendleton was, according to John Adams, "very full and clear against it," and Washington himself recommended Gen. Andrew Lewis for the post. It was chiefly the fruit of a political bargain by which New England offered Virginia the chief command as its price for the adoption and support of the New England army. This army had gathered hastily and in force about Boston immediately after the clash of British troops and American minutemen at Lexington and Concord on April 19, 1775. When the second Continental Congress met in Philadelphia on May 10, one of its first tasks was to find a permanent leadership for this force. On June 15, Washington, whose military counsel had already proved invaluable on two committees, was nominated and chosen by unanimous vote.

Beyond the considerations noted, he owed being chosen to the facts that Virginia stood with Massachusetts as one of the most powerful colonies; that his appointment

tribute to his reputation and personality; it was understood that Virginia expected him to be its general. He was elected to the second Continental Congress at the March 1775 session of the legislature and again set out for Philadelphia.

would augment the zeal of the Southern people; that he had gained an enduring reputation in the Braddock campaign; and that his poise, sense, and resolution had impressed all the delegates. The scene of his election, with Washington darting modestly into an adjoining room and John Hancock flushing with jealous mortification, will always impress the historical imagination; so also will the scene of July 3, 1775, when, wheeling his horse under an elm in front of the troops paraded on Cambridge common, he drew his sword and took command of the army investing Boston. News of Bunker Hill had reached him before he was a day's journey from Philadelphia, and he had expressed confidence of victory when told how the militia had fought. In accepting the command, he refused any payment beyond his expenses and called upon "every gentleman in the room" to bear witness that he disclaimed fitness for it. At once he showed characteristic decision and energy in organizing the raw volunteers, collecting provisions and munitions, and rallying Congress and the colonies to his support.

The first phase of Washington's command covered the period from July 1775 to the British evacuation of Boston in March 1776. In those eight months he imparted discipline to the army, which at maximum strength slightly exceeded 20,000; he dealt with subordinates who, as John Adams said, quarrelled "like cats and dogs"; and he kept the siege vigorously alive. Having himself planned an invasion of Canada by Lake Champlain, to be entrusted to General Philip Schuyler, he heartily approved of Benedict Arnold's proposal to march north along the Kennebec River in Maine and take Quebec. Giving Arnold 1,100 men, he instructed him to do everything possible to conciliate the Canadians. He was equally active in encouraging privateers to attack British commerce. As fast as means offered, he strengthened his army with ammunition and siege guns, having heavy artillery brought from Fort Ticonderoga, New York, over the frozen roads early in 1776. His position was at first precarious, for the Charles River pierced the center of his lines investing Boston. If the British general, Sir William Howe, had moved his 20 veteran regiments boldly up the stream, he might have pierced Washington's army and rolled either wing back to destruction. But all the generalship was on Washington's side. Seeing that Dorchester Heights, just south of Boston, commanded the city and harbor and that Howe had unaccountably failed to occupy it, he seized it on the night of March 4, 1776, placing his Ticonderoga guns in position. The British naval commander declared that he could not remain if the Americans were not dislodged, and Howe, after a storm disrupted his plans for an assault, evacuated the city on March 17. He left 200 cannons and invaluable stores of small arms and munitions. After collecting his booty, Washington hurried south to take up the defense of New York.

Washington had won the first round, but there remained five years of the war, during which the American cause was repeatedly near complete disaster. It is unquestionable that Washington's strength of character, his ability to hold the confidence of army and people and to diffuse his own courage among them, his unremitting activity, and his strong common sense constituted the chief factors in achieving American victory. He was not a great tactician: as Jefferson said later, he often "failed in the field"; he was sometimes guilty of grave military blunders, the chief being his assumption of a position on Long Island, New York, in 1776 that exposed his entire army to capture the moment it was defeated. At the outset he was painfully inexperienced, the wilderness fighting of the French war having done nothing to teach him the strategy of maneuvering whole armies. One of his chief faults was his tendency to subordinate his own judgment to that of the generals surrounding him; at every critical juncture, before Boston, before New York, before Philadelphia, and in New Jersey, he called a council of war and in almost every

A portrait of Sir William Howe, commander of British forces in America, c. 1778.

instance accepted its decision. Naturally bold and dashing, as he proved at Trenton, Princeton, and Germantown, he repeatedly adopted evasive and delaying tactics on the advice of his associates; however, he did succeed in keeping a strong army in existence and maintaining the flame of national spirit. When the auspicious moment arrived, he planned the rapid movements that ended the war.

Troops from each of the three sections, New England, the middle states, and the South, showed a deplorable jealousy of the others. Washington was rigorous in breaking cowardly, inefficient, and dishonest men and boasted in front of Boston that he had "made a pretty good sort of slam among such kind of officers." Deserters and plunderers were flogged, and Washington once erected a gallows 40 feet high, writing, "I am determined if I can be justified in the proceeding, to hang two or three on it, as an example to others." At the same time, the commander in chief

ONE element of Washington's strength was his sternness as a disciplinarian. The army was continually dwindling and refilling, politics largely governed the selection of officers by Congress and the states, and the ill-fed, ill-clothed, ill-paid forces were often half-prostrated by sickness and ripe for mutiny.

won the devotion of many of his men by his earnestness in demanding better treatment for them from Congress. He complained of their short rations, declaring once that they were forced to "eat every kind of horse food but hay."

The darkest chapter in Washington's military leadership was opened when, reaching New York in April 1776, he placed half his army, about 9,000 men, under Israel Putnam, on the perilous position of Brooklyn Heights, Long Island, where a British fleet in the East River might cut off their retreat. He spent a fortnight in May with the Continental Congress in Philadelphia, then discussing the question of independence; though no record of his utterances exists, there can be no doubt that he advocated complete separation. His return to New York preceded but slightly the arrival of the British army under Howe, which made its main encampment on Staten Island until its whole strength of nearly 30,000 could be mobilized. On August 22, 1776, Howe moved about 20,000 men across to Gravesend Bay on Long Island. Four days later, sending the fleet under command of his brother Adm. Richard Howe to make a feint against New York City, he thrust a crushing force along feebly protected roads against the American flank.

The patriots were outmaneuvered, defeated, and suffered a total loss of 5,000 men, of whom 2,000 were captured. Their whole position might have been carried by storm, but, fortunately for Washington, General Howe delayed. While the enemy lingered, Washington succeeded under cover of a dense fog in ferrying the remaining force across the East River to Manhattan, where he took up a fortified position. The British, suddenly landing on the lower part of the island, drove back the Americans in a clash marked by disgraceful cowardice on the part of troops from Connecticut and others. In a series of actions, Washington was forced northward, more than once in danger of capture, until the loss of his two Hudson River forts, one of them with 2,600 men, compelled him to retreat from White Plains across the river into New Jersey. He retired toward the Delaware River while his army melted away, until it seemed that armed resistance to the British was about to expire.

THE TRENTON-PRINCETON CAMPAIGN

It was at this darkest hour of the Revolution that Washington struck his brilliant blows at Trenton and Princeton, New Jersey, reviving the hopes and energies of the nation. Howe, believing that the American army soon would dissolve totally, retired to New York, leaving strong forces in Trenton and Burlington. Washington, at his camp west of the Delaware River, planned a simultaneous attack on both posts, using his whole command of 6,000 men. But his subordinates in charge of both wings failed him, and he was left on the night of December 25, 1776, to march on Trenton with about 2,400 men. With the help of Col. John Glover's regiment, which was comprised of fishermen and sailors from Marblehead, Massachusetts, Washington and his troops were ferried across the Delaware River. In the dead of night and amid a blinding snowstorm, they then marched 10 miles downstream and in the early hours of the morning caught the enemy at Trenton unaware. In less than two hours and without the loss of a single man in battle, Washington's troops defeated the Hessians, killed their commander (Johann Rall), and captured nearly 1,000 prisoners and arms and ammunition.

The immediate result of this American victory was that General Charles Cornwallis hastened with about 8,000 men to Trenton, where he found Washington strongly posted behind the Assunpink Creek, skirmished with him, and decided to wait overnight "to bag the old fox." During the night, the wind shifted, the roads froze hard, and Washington was able to steal away from camp (leaving his fires deceptively burning), march around Cornwallis's rear, and fall at daybreak upon the three British regiments at Princeton.

 **historic Christmas crossing of the Delaware River proved to be a turning point in the war, and it was immortalized for posterity by Emanuel Gottlieb Leutze in his famous 1851 painting of the event. (The painting is historically inaccurate: the depicted flag is anachronistic, the boats are the wrong size and shape, and it is questionable whether Washington could have crossed the icy Delaware while standing in the manner depicted.)**

These were put to flight with a loss of 500 men, and Washington escaped with more captured munitions to a strong position at Morristown, New Jersey. The effect of these victories heartened all Americans, brought recruits flocking to camp in the spring, and encouraged foreign sympathizers with the American cause.

Thus far the important successes had been won by Washington; then battlefield success fell to others, while he was left to face popular apathy, military cabals, and the disaffection of Congress. The year 1777 was marked by the British capture of Philadelphia and the surrender of British General John Burgoyne's invading army to General Horatio Gates at Saratoga, New York, followed by intrigues to displace Washington from his command. Howe's main British army of 18,000 left New York by sea on July 23, 1777, and landed on August 25 in Maryland, not far below Philadelphia. Washington, despite his inferiority of force—he had only 11,000 men, mostly militia and, in the marquis de Lafayette's words, "badly armed and worse clothed"—risked a pitched battle on September 11 at the fords of Brandywine Creek, about 13 miles north of Wilmington, Delaware. While part of the British force held the Americans engaged, General Cornwallis, with the rest, made a secret 17-mile detour and fell with crushing effect on the American right and rear, the result being a complete defeat from which Washington was fortunate to extricate his army in fairly good order. For a time he hoped to hold the Schuylkill Fords, but the British passed them and on September 26 triumphantly marched into Philadelphia. Congress fled to the interior of Pennsylvania, and Washington, after an

A portrait of George Washington by Charles Peale Polk, c. 1790–1795.

unsuccessful effort to repeat his stroke at Trenton against the British troops posted at Germantown, had to take up winter quarters at Valley Forge.

His army, twice beaten, ill housed, and ill fed, with thousands of men "barefoot and otherwise naked," was at the point of exhaustion; it could not keep the field, for inside of a month it would have disappeared. In these circumstances, the true fibre of Washington's character and courage was proved.

Washington's enemies seized the moment of his greatest weakness to give vent to an antagonism that had been nourished by sectional jealousies of North against South, by the ambition of small rivals, and by baseless accusations that he showed favoritism to such foreigners as Lafayette. The intrigues of Thomas Conway, an Irish adventurer who had served in the French army and had become an American general, enlisted Thomas Mifflin, Charles Lee, Benjamin Rush, and others in an attempt to displace Washington. General Gates appears to have been a tool of rather than a party to the plot, expecting that the chief command would devolve upon himself. A faction of Congress sympathized with the movement and attempted to paralyze Washington by reorganizing the board of war, a body vested with the general superintendence of operations, of which Gates became the president; his chief of staff, James Wilkinson, the secretary; and Mifflin and Timothy Pickering, members. Washington was well aware of the hostility in Congress, of the slanders spread by Rush and James Lovell of Massachusetts, and of the effect of forgeries published in the American press by adroit British agents. He realized the intense jealousy of many New Englanders, which made even John Adams write his wife that he was thankful Burgoyne had not been captured by Washington, who would then "have been deified. It is bad enough as it is." But Washington decisively crushed the cabal: after the loose tongue of Wilkinson disclosed Conway's treachery, Washington sent the general on November 9, 1777, proof of his knowledge of the whole affair.

With the conclusion of the French alliance in the spring of 1778, the aspect of the war was radically altered. The British army in Philadelphia, fearing that a French fleet would blockade the Delaware while the militia of New Jersey and Pennsylvania invested the city, hastily retreated upon New York City. Washington hoped to cut off part of the enemy and by a hurried march with six brigades interposed himself at the end of June between Sir Henry Clinton (who had succeeded Howe) and the New Jersey coast. The result was the Battle of Monmouth on June 28, where a shrewd strategic plan and vigorous assault were brought to naught by the treachery of

At Valley Forge, Washington was unyieldingly persistent through a winter of semistarvation, of justified grumbling by his men, of harsh public criticism, and of captious meddling by a Congress that was too weak to help him. In February Martha Washington arrived and helped to organize entertainment for the soldiers.

Charles Lee. When Lee ruined the attack by a sudden order to retreat, Washington hurried forward, fiercely denounced him, and restored the line, but the golden opportunity had been lost. The British made good their march to Sandy Hook, and Washington took up his quarters at New Brunswick. Lee was arrested, court-martialed, and convicted on all three of the charges made against him; but instead of being shot, as he deserved, he was sentenced to a suspension from command for one year. The arrival of the French fleet under Adm. Charles-Hector Estaing on July 1778 completed the isolation of the British, and Clinton was thenceforth held to New York City and the surrounding area. Washington made his headquarters in the highlands of the Hudson and distributed his troops in cantonments around the city and in New Jersey.

The final decisive stroke of the war, the capture of Cornwallis at Yorktown, is to be credited chiefly to Washington's vision. With the domestic situation intensely gloomy early in 1781, he was hampered by the feebleness of Congress, the popular discouragement, and the lack of prompt and strong support by the French fleet. A French army under the comte de Rochambeau had arrived to reinforce him in 1780, and Washington had pressed Admiral de Grasse to assist in an attack upon either Cornwallis in the south or Clinton in New York. In August the French admiral sent definite word that he preferred the Chesapeake, with its large area and deep water, as the scene of his operations; and within a week, on August 19, 1781, Washington marched south with his army, leaving Gen. William Heath with 4,000 men to hold West Point. He hurried his troops through New Jersey, embarked them on transports in Delaware Bay, and landed them at Williamsburg, Virginia, where he had arrived on September 14. Cornwallis had retreated to Yorktown and entrenched his army of 7,000 British regulars. Their works were completely invested before the end of the month; the siege was pressed with vigour by the allied armies under Washington, consisting of 5,500 Continentals, 3,500 Virginia militia, and 5,000 French regulars; and on October 19 Cornwallis surrendered. By this campaign, probably the finest single display of Washington's generalship, the war was brought to a virtual close.

Washington remained during the winter of 1781–1782 with the Continental Congress in Philadelphia, exhorting it to maintain its exertions for liberty and to settle the army's claims for pay. He continued these exhortations after he joined his command at Newburgh on the Hudson in April 1782. He was astounded and angered when some loose camp suggestions found expression in a letter from Col. Lewis Nicola offering a plan by which he should use the army to make himself king. He blasted the proposal with fierce condemnation. When the discontent of his unpaid men came to a head in the circulation of the "Newburgh Address" (an anonymously written grievance) early in 1783, he issued a general order censuring the paper and at a meeting of officers on March 15 read a speech admonishing the army to obey Congress and promising his best efforts for a redress of grievances. He was present at the entrance of the American army into New York on the day of the British evacuation, November 25, 1783, and on December 4 took leave of his closest officers in an affecting scene at Fraunces Tavern. Traveling south, on December 23, in a solemn ceremonial immortalized by the pen of William Makepeace Thackeray, he resigned his commission to the Continental Congress in the state senate chamber of Maryland in Annapolis and received the thanks of the nation. His accounts of personal expenditures during his service, kept with minute exactness in his own handwriting and totalling £24,700, without charge for salary, had been given the controller of the treasury to be discharged. Washington left Annapolis at sunrise of December 24 and before nightfall was at home in Mount Vernon.

In the next four years Washington found sufficient occupation in his estates, wishing to close his days as a gentleman farmer and to give to agriculture as much energy and thought as he had to the army. He enlarged the Mount Vernon house; he laid out the grounds anew, with sunken walls; and he embarked on experiments with mahogany, palmetto, pepper, and other foreign trees, and English grasses and grains. His farm manager during the Revolution, a distant relative named Lund Washington, retired in 1785 and was succeeded by a nephew,

Maj. George Augustine Washington, who resided at Mount Vernon until his death in 1792. Washington's losses during the war had been heavy, caused by neglect of his lands, stoppage of exportation, and depreciation of paper money, which cost him hardly less than $30,000. He then attempted successfully to repair his fortunes, his annual receipts from all his estates being from $10,000 to $15,000 a year. In 1784 he made a tour of nearly 700 miles to view the wildlands he owned to the westward, Congress having made him a generous grant. As a national figure, he was constrained to offer hospitality to old army friends, visitors from other states and nations, diplomats, and Indian delegations, and he and his household seldom sat down to dinner alone.

POSTREVOLUTIONARY POLITICS

Viewing the chaotic political condition of the United States after 1783 with frank pessimism and declaring (May 18, 1786) that "something must be done, or the fabric must fall, for it is certainly tottering," Washington repeatedly wrote his friends urging steps toward "an indissoluble union." At first he believed that the Articles of Confederation might be amended. Later, especially after the shock of Shays's Rebellion, he took the view that a more radical reform was necessary but doubted as late as the end of 1786 that the time was ripe. His progress toward adoption of the idea of a federal convention was, in fact, puzzlingly slow.

Washington's numerous letters to the leading men of the country assisted greatly to form a sentiment favorable to a more perfect union. Some understanding being necessary between Virginia and Maryland regarding

ALTHOUGH John Jay assured him in March 1786 that breakup of the nation seemed near and opinion for a constitutional convention was crystallizing, Washington remained noncommittal. But, despite long hesitations, he earnestly supported the proposal for a federal impost, warning the states that their policy must decide "whether the Revolution must ultimately be considered a blessing or a curse."

the navigation of the Potomac, commissioners from the two states had met at Mount Vernon in the spring of 1785; from this seed sprang the federal convention. Washington approved in advance the call for a gathering of all the states to meet in Philadelphia in May 1787 to "render the Constitution of the Federal Government adequate to the exigencies of the Union." But he was again hesitant about attending, partly because he felt tired and infirm, partly because of doubts about the outcome. Although he hoped to the last to be excused, he was chosen one of Virginia's five delegates.

Washington arrived in Philadelphia on May 13, the day before the opening of the Constitutional Convention, and as soon as a quorum was obtained he was unanimously chosen its president. For four months he presided over the convention, breaking his silence only once upon a minor question of congressional apportionment. Although he said little in debate, no one did more outside the hall to insist on stern measures. "My wish is," he wrote, "that the convention may adopt no temporizing expedients, but probe the defects of the Constitution to the bottom, and provide a radical cure." His weight of character did more than any other single force to bring the convention to an agreement and obtain ratification of the instrument afterward. He did not believe it perfect, though his precise

criticisms of it are unknown. But his support gave it victory in Virginia, where he sent copies to Patrick Henry and other leaders with a hint that the alternative to adoption was anarchy, declaring that "it or dis-union is before us to chuse from." He received and personally circulated copies of *The Federalist*. When ratification was obtained, he wrote to leaders in the various states urging that men staunchly favorable to it be elected to Congress. For a time he sincerely believed that, the new framework completed, he would be allowed to retire again to privacy. But all eyes immediately turned to him for the first president. He alone commanded the respect of both the parties engendered by the struggle over ratification, and he alone would be able to give prestige to the republic throughout Europe. In no state was any other name considered. The electors chosen in the first days of 1789 cast a unanimous vote for him, and reluctantly—for his love of peace, his distrust of his own abilities, and his fear that his motives in advocating the new government might be misconstrued all made him unwilling—he accepted.

On April 16, after receiving congressional notification of the honor, he set out from Mount Vernon, reaching New York City in time to be inaugurated on April 30. His journey northward was a celebratory procession as people in every town and village through which he passed turned out to greet him, often with banners and speeches, and in some places with triumphal arches. He came across the Hudson River in a specially built barge decorated in red, white, and blue. The inaugural ceremony was performed on Wall Street, near the spot now marked by John Quincy Adams Ward's statue of Washington. A great crowd broke into cheers as, standing on the balcony of Federal Hall, he took the oath administered by Chancellor Robert Livingston and retired indoors to read Congress his inaugural address. Washington was clad in a brown suit of American manufacture, but he wore white stockings and a sword after the fashion of European courts.

Martha was as reluctant as her husband to resume public life. But a month later she came from Mount Vernon to join him. She, too, was greeted wildly on her way. And when Washington crossed the Hudson to bring her to Manhattan, guns boomed in salute. The Washingtons, to considerable public criticism, traveled about in a coach-and-four like monarchs. Moreover, during his presidency, Washington did not shake hands, and he met his guests on state occasions while standing on a raised platform and displaying a sword on his hip.

SLOWLY, feeling his way, Washington was defining the style of the first president of a country in the history of the world. The people, too, were adjusting to a government without a king. Even the question of how to address a president had to be discussed. It was decided that in a republic the simple salutation "Mr. President" would do.

THE WASHINGTON ADMINISTRATION

Washington's administration of the government in the next eight years was marked by the caution, the methodical precision, and the sober judgment that had always characterized him. He regarded himself as standing aloof from party divisions and emphasized his position as president of the whole country by touring first through the Northern states and later through the Southern. A painstaking inquiry into all the problems confronting the new nation laid the basis for a series of judicious recommendations to Congress in his first message. In selecting the four members of his first cabinet—Thomas Jefferson as secretary of state, Alexander Hamilton as secretary of treasury, Henry Knox as secretary of war, and Edmund Randolph as attorney general—Washington balanced the two parties evenly. But he leaned with especial weight upon Hamilton, who supported his scheme for the federal assumption of state debts, took his view that the bill establishing the Bank of the United States was constitutional, and in general favored strengthening the authority of the federal government. Distressed when the inevitable clash between Jefferson and Hamilton arose, he tried to keep harmony, writing frankly to each and refusing to accept their resignations.

But when war was declared between France and England in 1793, he took Hamilton's view that the United States should completely disregard the treaty of alliance with France and pursue a course of strict neutrality, while he acted decisively to stop the improper operations of the French minister, Edmond-Charles Genêt. He had a firm belief that the United States must insist on its national identity, strength, and dignity. His object, he wrote, was to keep the country "free from political connections with *every* other country, to see them independent of all, and under the influence of none. In a word, I want an *American* character that the powers of Europe may be convinced that we act for ourselves, and not for others." The sequel was the resignation of Jefferson at the close of 1793, the two men parting on good terms and Washington praising Jefferson's "integrity and talents." The suppression of the Whiskey Rebellion in 1794 by federal troops whom Hamilton led in person and the dispatch of John Jay to conclude a treaty of commerce with Great Britain tended further to align Washington with the federalists. Although the general voice of the people compelled him to acquiesce reluctantly to a second term in 1792 and his election that year was again unanimous, during his last four years in office he suffered from a fierce personal and partisan animosity. This culminated when the publication of the terms of the Jay Treaty, which Washington signed in August 1795, provoked a bitter discussion, and the House of Representatives called upon the president for the instructions and correspondence relating to the treaty. These Washington, who had already clashed with the Senate on foreign affairs, refused to deliver, and, in the face of an acrimonious debate, he firmly maintained his position.

Early in his first term, Washington—who by education and natural inclination was minutely careful of the proprieties of life—established the rules of a virtual republican court. In both New York and Philadelphia he rented the best houses procurable, refusing to accept the hospitality of George Clinton, for he believed the head of the nation should be no man's guest. He returned no calls and shook hands with no one, acknowledging salutations by a formal bow. He drove in a coach drawn by four or six smart horses, with outriders and lackeys in rich livery. He attended receptions dressed in a black velvet suit with gold buckles, with yellow gloves, powdered hair, a cocked hat with an ostrich plume in one hand, and a sword in a white leather scabbard. After being overwhelmed by callers, he announced that, except for a weekly levee open to all, persons desiring to see him had to make appointments in advance. On Friday afternoons the first lady held informal receptions, at which the president appeared. Although the presidents of the Continental Congress had made their tables partly public, Washington, who entertained largely, inviting members of Congress in rotation, insisted that his hospitality be private. He served good wines and the menus were elaborate, but such visitors as Pennsylvania Sen. William Maclay complained that the atmosphere was too "solemn." Indeed, his simple ceremony offended many of the more radical Anti-Federalists, who did not share his

sense of its fitness and accused the president of conducting himself like a king. But his cold and reserved manner was caused by native diffidence rather than any excessive sense of dignity.

RETIREMENT

Earnestly desiring leisure, feeling a decline of his physical powers, and wincing under abuses of the opposition, Washington refused to yield to the general pressure for a third term. This refusal was blended with a testament of sagacious advice to his country in the Farewell Address of September 19, 1796, written largely by Hamilton but remolded by Washington and expressing his ideas. Retiring in March 1797 to Mount Vernon, he devoted himself for the last two and a half years of his life to his family, farm operations, and care of his slaves. In 1798 his seclusion was briefly interrupted when the prospect of war with France caused his appointment as commander in chief of the provisional army, and he was much worried by the political quarrels over high commissions; but the war cloud passed away.

On December 12, 1799, after riding on horseback for several hours in cold and snow, he returned home exhausted and was attacked late the next day with quinsy or acute laryngitis. He was bled heavily four times and given gargles of "molasses, vinegar and butter," and a blister of cantharides (a preparation of dried beetles) was placed on his throat, his strength meanwhile rapidly sinking.

After giving instructions to his secretary, Tobias Lear, about his burial, he died on December 14 at his home in Mount Vernon. The news of his death placed the entire country in mourning, and the sentiment of the country endorsed the famous words of Henry ("Light-Horse Harry") Lee, embodied in resolutions that John Marshall introduced in the House of Representatives, that he was "first in war, first in peace, and first in the hearts of his countrymen." When the news reached Europe, the British channel fleet and the armies of Napoleon paid tribute to his memory, and many of the leaders of the time joined in according him a preeminent place among the heroes of history. His fellow citizens memorialized him forever

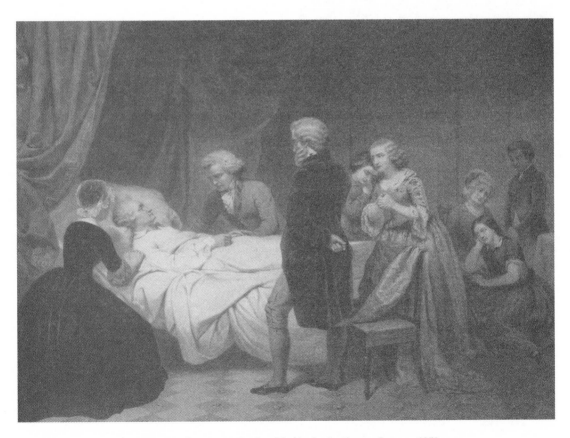

George Washington on His Deathbed by Junius Brutus Stearns, 1853.

WASHINGTON faced death with characteristic serenity, saying, "I die hard, but I am not afraid to go," and later: "I feel myself going. I thank you for your attentions; but I pray you to take no more trouble about me. Let me go off quietly. I cannot last long."

by naming the newly created capital city of the young nation for him while he was still alive. Later, one of the states of union would bear his name—the only state named for an individual American. The people of the United States have continued to glory in knowing him as "the father of his country," an accolade he was pleased to accept, even though it pained him that he fathered no children of his own.

CHAPTER 4

THE "GALLERY OF GREATS"

WHILE GEORGE WASHINGTON WAS THE UNCONTESTED Foundingest Father, winning the presidency unanimously in both 1789 and 1792 and being mythologized not only in his own time but for more than two centuries to come, the founding generation consisted of other greats.

These great intellectuals—and practical politicians, caught up in the petty politics and bitter polarization of their day—would provide the ideological underpinnings of the American republic that still guide Americans' understanding of what it means to be an American and what America stands for. This chapter profiles this so-called Gallery of Greats; the leading figures at Washington's side and their stories, which sometimes coincide and sometimes diverge, provide a rich understanding of the independence movement and the challenges that the world's first modern republic faced, in both achieving its independence and surviving as a united country.

JOHN ADAMS (1735–1826)

John Adams was an early advocate of American independence from Great Britain, a major figure in the Continental Congress (1774–1777), author of the Massachusetts constitution (1780), signer of the Treaty of Paris (1783), first American ambassador to the Court of St. James (1785–1788), first vice president (1789–1797) and second president (1797–1801) of the United States. Although Adams was regarded by his contemporaries as one of the most significant statesmen of the revolutionary era, his reputation faded in the 19th century, only to ascend again during the last half of the 20th century. The modern edition of his correspondence prompted a rediscovery of his bracing honesty and pungent way with words, his importance as a political thinker, his realistic perspective on American foreign policy, and his patriarchal role as founder of one of the most prominent families in American history.

EARLY LIFE

Adams was born on October 30, 1735, in Braintree (now Quincy), Massachusetts, the eldest of the three sons of Deacon John Adams and Susanna Boylston of Braintree. His father was only a farmer and shoemaker, but the Adams family could trace its lineage back to the first generation of Puritan settlers in New England. A local selectman and a leader in the community, Deacon Adams encouraged his eldest son to aspire toward a career in the ministry. In keeping with that goal, Adams graduated from Harvard College in 1755. For the next three years, he taught grammar school in Worcester, Massachusetts, while contemplating his future. He eventually chose law rather than the ministry and in 1758 moved back to Braintree, then soon began practicing law in nearby Boston.

IN 1764 Adams married Abigail Smith, a minister's daughter from neighboring Weymouth. Intelligent, well-read, vivacious, and just as fiercely independent as her new husband, Abigail Adams became a confidante and political partner who helped to stabilize and sustain the ever-irascible and highly volatile Adams throughout his long career. The letters between them afford an extended glimpse into their deepest thoughts and emotions and provide modern readers with the most revealing record of personal intimacy between husband and wife in the revolutionary era. Their first child, Abigail Amelia, was born in 1765. Their first son, John Quincy, arrived two years later. Two other sons, Thomas Boylston and Charles, followed shortly thereafter. (Another child, Susanna, did not survive infancy.) By then Adams's legal career was on the rise, and he had become a visible member of the resistance movement that questioned Parliament's right to tax the American colonies.

In 1765 Adams wrote "A Dissertation on the Canon and Feudal Law," which justified opposition to the recently enacted Stamp Act—an effort to raise revenue by requiring all publications and legal documents to bear a stamp—by arguing that Parliament's intrusions into colonial affairs exposed the inherently coercive and corrupt character of English politics. Intensely combative, full of private doubts about his own capacities but never about his cause, Adams became a leading figure in the opposition to the Townshend Acts (1767), which imposed duties on imported commodities (such as, glass, lead, paper, paint, and tea). Despite his hostility toward the British government, in 1770 Adams agreed to defend the British soldiers who had fired on a Boston crowd in what became known as the Boston Massacre. His insistence on upholding the legal rights of the soldiers, who in fact had been provoked, made him temporarily unpopular but also marked him as one of the most principled radicals in the burgeoning movement for American independence. He had a penchant for doing the right thing, most especially when it made him unpopular.

CONTINENTAL CONGRESS

In the summer of 1774, Adams was elected to the Massachusetts delegation that joined the representatives from 12 of 13 colonies in Philadelphia at the First Continental Congress. He and his cousin, Samuel Adams, quickly became the leaders of the radical faction, which rejected the prospects for reconciliation with Britain. His "Novanglus" essays, published early in 1775, moved the constitutional argument forward another notch, insisting that Parliament lacked the authority not just to tax the colonies but also to legislate for them in any way. (Less than a year earlier, Thomas Jefferson had made a similar argument against parliamentary authority in *A Summary View of the Rights of British America*.)

By the time the Second Continental Congress convened in 1775, Adams had gained the reputation as "the Atlas of independence." Over the course of the following year, he made several major contributions to the patriot cause destined to ensure his place in American history.

First, he nominated George Washington to serve as commander of the fledging Continental Army. Second, he selected Jefferson to draft the Declaration of Independence. (Both decisions were designed to ensure Virginia's support for the revolution.) Third, he dominated the debate in the Congress on July 2–4, 1776, defending Jefferson's draft of the declaration and demanding unanimous support for a decisive break with Great Britain. Moreover, he had written *Thoughts on Government*, which circulated throughout the colonies as the major guidebook for the drafting of new state constitutions.

Adams remained the central figure of the Continental Congress for the following two years. He drafted the Plan of Treaties in July 1776, a document that provided the framework for a treaty with France and that almost inadvertently identified the strategic priorities that would shape American foreign policy over the next century. He was the unanimous choice to head the Board of War and Ordnance and was thereby made in effect a one-man war department responsible for raising and equipping the American army and creating from scratch an American navy. As the prospects for a crucial wartime alli-

A portrait of John Adams by Gilbert Stuart, 1826.

ance with France improved late in 1777, he was chosen to join Benjamin Franklin in Paris to conduct the negotiations. In February 1778 he sailed for Europe, accompanied by 10-year-old John Quincy.

FOREIGN SERVICE

By the time Adams arrived in Paris, the treaty creating an alliance with France had already been concluded. He quickly returned home in the summer of 1779, just in time to join the Massachusetts Constitutional Convention. The other delegates, acknowledging his constitutional expertise, simply handed him the job of drafting what became the Massachusetts constitution (1780), which immediately became the model for the other state constitutions and—in its insistence on a bicameral legislature and the separation of powers—a major influence on the Constitution of the United States.

The Congress then ordered Adams to rejoin Franklin in Paris to lead the American delegation responsible for negotiating an end to the war with Britain. This time he took along his youngest son, Charles, as well as John Quincy, leaving Abigail to tend the farm and the other two children in Braintree. Not until 1784, almost five years later, was the entire family reunited in Paris. By then Adams had shown himself an unnatural diplomat, exhibiting a level of candor and a confrontational style toward both English and French negotiators that alienated Franklin, who came to regard his colleague as slightly deranged. Adams, for his part, thought Franklin excessively impressed with his own stature as the Gallic version of the American genius and therefore inadequately attuned to the important differences between American and French interests in the peace negotiations. The favorable terms achieved in the Peace of Paris (1783) can be attributed to the effective blend of Franklin's discretion and Adams's bulldog temperament.

ADAMS'S reputation for emotional explosions dates from his time as a diplomat in Paris. Recent scholarly studies suggest that he might have suffered from a hyperthyroid condition subsequently known as Graves's disease.

In 1784 Jefferson arrived in Paris to replace Franklin as the American minister at the French court. Over the next few months, Jefferson became an unofficial member of the Adams family, and the bond of friendship between Adams and Jefferson was sealed, a lifelong partnership and rivalry that made the combative New Englander and the elegant Virginian the odd couple of the American Revolution. Jefferson also visited the Adams family in England in 1785, after Adams had assumed his new post as American ambassador in London. The two men also joined forces, though Adams as the senior figure assumed the lead, in negotiating a $400,000 loan from Dutch bankers that allowed the American government to consolidate its European debts.

POLITICAL PHILOSOPHY

Because he was the official embodiment of American independence from the British Empire, Adams was largely ignored and relegated to the periphery of the court during his nearly three years in London. Still brimming with energy, he spent his time studying the history of European politics for patterns and lessons that might assist the fledgling American government in its efforts to achieve what no major European nation had managed to produce—namely, a stable republican form of government.

The result was a massive and motley three-volume collection of quotations, unacknowledged citations, and personal observations entitled *A Defence of the Constitutions of Government of the United States of America* (1787). A fourth volume, *Discourses on Davila* (1790), was published soon after he returned to the United States. Taken together, these lengthy tomes contained Adams's distinctive insights as a political thinker. The lack of organization, combined with the sprawling style of the *Defence*, however, made its core message difficult to follow or fathom. When read in the context of his voluminous correspondence on political issues, along with the extensive marginalia he recorded in the several thousand books in his personal library, that message became clearer with time.

Adams wished to warn his fellow Americans against all revolutionary manifestos that envisioned a fundamental break with the past and a fundamental transformation in human nature or society that supposedly produced a new age. All such utopian expectations were illusions, he believed, driven by what he called "ideology," the belief that imagined ideals, so real and seductive in theory, were capable of being implemented in the world. The same kind of conflict between different classes that had bedeviled medieval Europe would, albeit in muted forms, also afflict the United States, because the seeds of such competition were planted in human nature itself. Adams blended the psychological insights of New England Puritanism, with its emphasis on the emotional forces throbbing inside all creatures, and the Enlightenment belief that government must contain and control those forces, to construct a political system capable of balancing the ambitions of individuals and competing social classes.

His insistence that elites were unavoidable realities in all societies, however, made him vulnerable to the charge of endorsing aristocratic rule in America, when in fact he was attempting to suggest that the inevitable American elite must be controlled, its ambitions channeled toward public purposes. He also was accused of endorsing monarchical principles because he argued that the chief executive in the American government, like the king in medieval European society, must possess sufficient power to check the ravenous appetites of the propertied classes. Although misunderstood by many of his contemporaries, the realistic perspective Adams proposed—and the skepticism toward utopian schemes he insisted upon—has achieved considerable support in the wake of the failed 20th-century attempts at social transformation in the communist bloc. In Adams's own day, his political analysis enjoyed the satisfaction of correctly predicting that the French Revolution would lead to the Reign of Terror and eventual despotism by a military dictator.

VICE PRESIDENCY AND PRESIDENCY

Soon after his return to the United States, Adams found himself on the ballot in the presidential election of 1789. Washington was the unanimous selection of all electors, while Adams finished second, signaling his standing as a leading member of the revolutionary generation was superseded only by that of Washington himself. Under the electoral rules established in the recent ratified Constitution, Adams duly was elected America's first vice president.

Adams's main duty was to serve as president of the Senate, casting a vote only to break a tie. During his eight years in office, Adams cast more than 30 such votes, more than any subsequent vice president in American history. He steadfastly supported all the major initiatives of the Washington administration, including the financial plan of Alexander Hamilton, the Neutrality Proclamation (1793), which effectively ended the Franco-American Alliance of 1778, the forceful suppression of an insurrection in western Pennsylvania called the Whiskey Rebellion

> *A*DAMS'S election as vice president meant that he was the first American statesman to experience the paradox of being a heartbeat away from maximum power while languishing in the political version of a cul-de-sac. Adams himself described the vice presidency as "the most insignificant office that ever the Invention of man contrived or his Imagination conceived."

(1794), and the Jay Treaty (1795), a highly controversial effort to avoid war with England by accepting British hegemony on the high seas. When Washington announced his decision not to seek a third term in 1796, Adams was the logical choice to succeed him.

In the first contested presidential election in American history, Adams won a narrow electoral majority (71–68) over Jefferson, who thereby became vice president. Adams made an initial effort to bring Jefferson into the cabinet and involve him in shaping foreign policy, but Jefferson declined the offer, preferring to retain his independence. This burdened the Adams presidency with a vice president who was the acknowledged head of the rival political party, the Republicans (subsequently the Democratic-Republicans). Additional burdens included: inheritance of Washington's cabinet, whom Adams unwisely decided to retain, and whose highest loyalty was to Washington's memory as embodied in Hamilton; a raging naval conflict with the French in the Caribbean dubbed the "quasi-war"; and the impossible task of succeeding—no one could replace—the greatest hero of the revolutionary era.

Despite Washington's plea for a bipartisan foreign policy in his farewell address (1796), the "quasi-war" produced a bitter political argument between Federalists, who preferred war with France to alienating

Britain, and Democratic-Republicans, who viewed France as America's only European ally and the French Revolution as a continuation of the American Revolution on European soil. Adams attempted to steer a middle course between these partisan camps, which left him vulnerable to political attacks from both sides. In 1797 he sent a peace delegation to Paris to negotiate an end to hostilities, but when the French directory demanded bribes before any negotiations could begin, Adams ordered the delegates home and began a naval buildup in preparation for outright war. The Federalist-dominated Congress called for raising a 30,000-man army, which Adams agreed to reluctantly. If Adams had requested a declaration of war in 1798, he would have enjoyed widespread popularity and virtually certain reelection two years later. Instead, he acted with characteristic independence by sending yet another, and this time successful, peace delegation to France against the advice of his cabinet and his Federalist supporters. The move ruined him politically but avoided a costly war that the infant American republic was ill-prepared to fight. It was a vintage Adams performance, reminiscent of his defense of British soldiers after the Boston Massacre, which was also principled and unpopular.

If ending the "quasi-war" with France was Adams's major foreign policy triumph, his chief domestic failure was passage of the Alien and Sedition Acts (1798), which permitted the government to deport foreign-born residents and indict newspaper editors or writers who published "false, scandalous, and malicious writing or writings against the government of the United States." A total of 14 indictments were brought against the Republican press under the Sedition Act, but the crudely partisan prosecutions quickly became infamous persecutions that backfired on the Federalists. Although Adams had signed the Alien and Sedition Acts under pressure from the Federalists in Congress, he shouldered most of the blame both at the time and in the history books. He came to regard the Sedition Act as the biggest political blunder of his life.

The election of 1800 again pitted Adams against Jefferson. Adams ran ahead of the Federalist candidates for Congress, who were swept from office in a Republican landslide. However, thanks to the deft maneuvering of Aaron Burr, all 12 of New York's electoral votes went to Jefferson, giving the tandem of Jefferson and Burr the electoral victory (73–65). Jefferson was eventually elected president by the House of Representatives, which chose him over Burr on the 36th ballot. In his last weeks in office, Adams made several Federalist appointments to the judiciary, including John Marshall as chief justice of the United States. These "midnight judges" offended Jefferson, who resented the encroachment on his own presidential prerogatives. Adams, the first president to reside in the presidential mansion (later called the White House) in Washington, D.C., was also the first—and one of the very few—presidents not to attend the inauguration of his successor. On March 4, 1801, he was already on the road back to Quincy.

RETIREMENT

At age 65 Adams did not anticipate a long retirement. The fates proved more generous than he expected, providing him with another quarter century to brood about his career and life, add to the extensive marginalia in his books, settle old scores in his memoirs, watch with pride when John Quincy assumed the presidency, and add to his already vast and voluminous correspondence. In an extensive exchange of letters with Benjamin Rush, the Philadelphia physician and patriotic gadfly, Adams revealed his preoccupation with fame and developed his own theory of the role ambition plays in motivating man to public service. Along the way he placed on the record his own candid and often critical portraits of the other vanguard members of the revolutionary generation.

In 1812, thanks in part to prodding from Rush, he overcame his bitterness to-

CONSIDERED the most intellectually impressive correspondence between American statesmen, the dialogue between Adams and Jefferson touched on a host of timely and timeless subjects: the role of religion in history, the aging process, the emergence of an American language, the French Revolution, and the party battles of the 1790s. Adams put it most poignantly to Jefferson: "You and I ought not to die, before We have explained ourselves to each other."

ward Jefferson and initiated a correspondence with his former friend and rival that totaled 158 letters.

More than the elegiac tone of the letters, the correspondence dramatized the contradictory impulses generated by the American

Revolution and symbolized by the two aging patriarchs. Adams was the realist, the skeptic, the principled pessimist. Jefferson was the idealist, the romantic, the pragmatic optimist. As if according to a script written by providence, the "Sage of Quincy" and the "Sage of Monticello" died within hours of each other on July 4, 1826, the 50th anniversary to the day of the Declaration of Independence.

SAMUEL ADAMS (1722–1803)

Samuel Adams was a leader of the Massachusetts "radicals," a delegate to the Continental Congress (1774–1781), and a signer of the Declaration of Independence. He was later lieutenant governor (1789–1793) and governor (1794–1797) of Massachusetts.

EARLY CAREER

Adams was born on September 27, 1722, in Boston. A second cousin of John Adams, second president of the United States, he graduated from Harvard College in 1740 and briefly studied law; he failed in several business ventures. As a tax collector in Boston, he neglected to collect the public levies and to keep proper accounts, thus exposing himself to suit.

Although unsuccessful in conducting personal or public business, Adams took an active and influential part in local politics. By the time the English Parliament passed the Sugar Act (1764) taxing molasses for revenue, Adams was a powerful figure in the opposition to British authority in the Colonies. He denounced the act, being one of the first of the colonials to cry out against taxation without representation. He played an important part in instigating the Stamp Act riots in Boston that were directed against the new requirement to pay taxes on all legal and commercial documents, newspapers, and college diplomas.

COMMITMENT TO AMERICAN INDEPENDENCE

His influence was soon second only to James Otis, the lawyer and politician who gained prominence by his resistance to the revenue acts. Elected to the lower house of the Massachusetts general court from Boston, Adams served in that body until 1774, after 1766 as its clerk. In 1769 Adams assumed the leadership of the Massachusetts radicals. There is some reason to believe that he had committed himself to American independence a year earlier. John Adams may have erred in ascribing this extreme stand to his cousin at so early a time, but certainly Samuel Adams was one of the first American leaders to deny

Parliament's authority over the Colonies; and he was also one of the first—certainly by 1774—to establish independence as the proper goal.

John Adams described his cousin as a plain, modest, and virtuous man. But in addition, Samuel Adams was a propagandist who was not overscrupulous in his attacks upon British officials and policies, and a passionate politician as well. In innumerable newspaper letters and essays over various signatures, he described British measures and the behaviour of royal governors, judges, and customs men in the darkest colors. He was a master of organization, arranging for the election of men who agreed with him, procuring committees that would act as he wished, and securing the passage of resolutions that he desired.

During the crisis over the Townshend duties (1767–1770), the import taxes on previously duty-free products proposed by Cabinet Minister Charles Townshend, Adams was unable to persuade the Massachusetts colonists to take extreme steps, partly because of the moderating influence of Otis. British troops sent to Boston in 1768, however, offered a fine target for this propaganda, and Adams saw to it that they were portrayed in the colonial newspapers as brutal soldiery oppressing citizens and assailing their wives and daughters. He was one of the leaders in

An undated portrait of Samuel Adams.

the town meeting that demanded and secured the removal of the troops from Boston after some British soldiers fired into a mob and killed five Americans. When news came that the Townshend duties, except for that on tea, had been repealed, his following dwindled. Nevertheless, during the years 1770–1773, when other colonial leaders were inactive, Adams revived old issues and found new ones; he was responsible for the foundation (1772) of the committee of correspondence of Boston that kept in contact with similar bodies in whose establishment he also had a hand in other towns. These committees later

THE passage by Parliament of the Tea Act of 1773, which granted the East India Company a monopoly on tea sales in the Colonies, gave Adams ample opportunity to exercise his remarkable talents. Although he did not participate in the Boston Tea Party, he was undoubtedly one of its planners.

became effective instruments in the fight against the British.

He was again a leading figure in the opposition of Massachusetts to the execution of the Intolerable (Coercive) Acts passed by the British Parliament in retaliation for the dumping of tea in Boston Harbor; and as a member of the First Continental Congress, which spoke for the 13 Colonies, he insisted that the delegates take a vigorous stand against Britain. A member of the provincial congress of Massachusetts in 1774–1775, he participated in making preparations for warfare should Britain resort to arms. When the British troops marched out of Boston to Concord, Adams and the president of the Continental Congress, John Hancock, were staying in a farmhouse near the line of march; and it has been said that the arrest of the two men was one of the purposes of the expedition. But the troops made no effort to find them, and British orders called only for destruction of military supplies gathered at Concord. When Gen. Thomas Gage issued an offer of pardon to the rebels some weeks later, however, he excepted Adams and Hancock.

MEMBERSHIP IN CONTINENTAL CONGRESS

As a member of the Continental Congress, in which he served until 1781, Adams was less conspicuous than he was in town meetings and the Massachusetts legislature, for the Congress contained a number of men as able as he. He and John Adams were among the first to call for a final separation from Britain, both signed the Declaration of Independence, and both exerted considerable influence in the Congress.

Adams was a member of the convention that framed the Massachusetts constitution of 1780 and also sat in the convention of his state that ratified the Federal Constitution. He was at first an anti-Federalist who opposed the ratification of the Constitution for fear that it would vest too much power in the federal government, but he finally abandoned his opposition when the Federalists promised to support a number of future amendments, including a bill of rights. He was defeated in the first congressional election. Returning to political power as a follower of Hancock, he was lieutenant governor of Massachusetts from 1789 to 1793 and governor from 1794 to 1797. When national parties developed, he affiliated himself with the Democratic-Republicans, the followers of Thomas Jefferson. After being defeated as a presidential elector favoring Jefferson in 1796, he retired to private life. He died on October 2, 1803, in Boston.

BENJAMIN FRANKLIN (1706–1790)

American printer and publisher, author, inventor and scientist, and diplomat, Benjamin Franklin helped draft the Declaration of Independence and was one of its signers, represented the United States in France during the American Revolution, and was a delegate to the Constitutional Convention. He made important contributions to science, especially in the understanding of electricity, and is remembered for the wit, wisdom, and elegance of his writing.

EARLY LIFE

Franklin was born on January 17, 1706, in Boston, the 10th son of the 17 children of a man who made soap and candles, one of the lowliest of the artisan crafts. In an age that privileged the firstborn son, he was, as he tartly noted in his *Autobiography*, "the youngest Son of the youngest Son for five Generations back." He learned to read very early and had one year in grammar school and another under a private teacher, but his formal education ended at age 10. At 12 he was apprenticed to his brother James, a printer. His mastery of the printer's trade, of which he was proud to the end of his life, was achieved between 1718 and 1723. In the same period he read tirelessly and taught himself to write effectively.

His first enthusiasm was for poetry, but, discouraged with the quality of his own, he gave it up. Prose was another matter. Young Franklin discovered a volume of *The Spectator*—featuring Joseph Addison and Sir Richard Steele's famous periodical essays, which had appeared in England in 1711–1712—and saw in it a means for improving his writing. He read these *Spectator* papers over and over, copied and recopied them, and then tried to recall them from memory. He even turned them into poetry and then back into prose. Franklin realized, as all the Founders did, that writing competently was such a rare talent in the 18th century that anyone who could do it well immediately attracted attention. "Prose writing" became, as he recalled in his *Autobiography*, "of great Use to me in the Course of my Life, and was a principal Means of my Advancement."

In 1721 James Franklin founded a weekly newspaper, the *New-England Courant*, to which readers were invited to contribute. Benjamin, now 16, read and perhaps set in type these contributions and decided that he could do as well himself. In 1722 he wrote a series of 14 essays signed "Silence Dogood" in which he lampooned everything from funeral eulogies to the students of Harvard College. For one so young to assume the persona of a middle-aged woman was a remarkable feat, and Franklin took "exquisite Pleasure" in the fact that his brother and others became convinced that only a learned and ingenious wit could have written these essays.

Late in 1722 James Franklin got into trouble with the provincial authorities and was forbidden to print or publish the *Courant*. To keep the paper going, he discharged his younger brother from his original apprenticeship and made him the paper's nominal publisher. New indentures were drawn up but not made public. Some months later, after a bitter quarrel, Benjamin secretly left home, sure that James would not "go to law" and reveal the subterfuge he had devised.

YOUTHFUL ADVENTURES

Failing to find work in New York City, Franklin at age 17 went on to Quaker-dominated Philadelphia, a much more open and religiously tolerant place than Puritan Boston. One of the most memorable scenes of the *Autobiography* is the description of his arrival on a Sunday morning, tired and hungry.

Finding a bakery, he asked for three pennies' worth of bread and got "three great Puffy Rolls." Carrying one under each arm and munching on the third, he walked up Market Street past the door of the Read family, where stood Deborah, his future wife. She saw him and "thought I made, as I certainly did, a most awkward ridiculous Appearance."

A few weeks later he was rooming at the Reads' and employed as a printer. By the spring of 1724 he was enjoying the companionship of other young men with a taste for reading, and he was also being urged to set up in business for himself by the governor of Pennsylvania, Sir William Keith. At Keith's suggestion, Franklin returned to Boston to try to raise the necessary capital. His father thought him too young for such a venture, so Keith offered to foot the bill himself and arranged Franklin's passage to England so that he could choose his type and make connections with London stationers and booksellers. Franklin exchanged "some promises" about marriage with Deborah Read and, with a young friend, James Ralph, as his companion, sailed for London in November 1724, just over a year after arriving in Philadelphia. Not until his ship was well out at sea did he realize that Governor Keith had not delivered the letters of credit and introduction he had promised.

In London Franklin quickly found employment in his trade and was able to lend money to Ralph, who was trying to establish himself as a writer. The two young men enjoyed the theater and the other pleasures of the city, including women.

By 1726 Franklin was tiring of London. He considered becoming an itinerant teacher of swimming, but, when Thomas Denham, a Quaker merchant, offered him a clerkship in his store in Philadelphia with a prospect of fat commissions in the West Indian trade, he decided to return home.

ACHIEVEMENT OF SECURITY AND FAME (1726–1753)

Denham died, however, a few months after Franklin entered his store. The young man, now 20, returned to the printing trade and in 1728 was able to set up a partnership with a friend. Two years later he borrowed money to become sole proprietor.

His private life at this time was extremely complicated. Deborah Read had married,

*W*HILE in London, Franklin wrote A *Dissertation on Liberty and Necessity, Pleasure and Pain* (1725), a Deistical pamphlet inspired by his having set type for William Wollaston's moral tract, *The Religion of Nature Delineated*. Franklin argued in his essay that since human beings have no real freedom of choice, they are not morally responsible for their actions. This was perhaps a nice justification for his self-indulgent behavior in London and his ignoring of Deborah, to whom he had written only once. He later repudiated the pamphlet, burning all but one of the copies still in his possession.

but her husband had deserted her and disappeared. One matchmaking venture failed because Franklin wanted a dowry of £100 to pay off his business debt. A strong sexual drive, "that hard-to-be-govern'd Passion of Youth," was sending him to "low Women," and he thought he very much needed to get married. His affection for Deborah having "revived," he "took her to Wife" on September 1, 1730. At this point Deborah may have been the only woman in Philadelphia who would have him, for he brought to the marriage an illegitimate son, William, just borne of a woman who has never been identified. Franklin's common-law marriage lasted until Deborah's death in 1774. They had a son, Franky, who died at age four, and a daughter, Sarah, who survived them both. William was brought up in the household and apparently did not get along well with Deborah.

Franklin and his partner's first coup was securing the printing of Pennsylvania's paper currency. Franklin helped get this business by writing *A Modest Enquiry into the Nature and Necessity of a Paper Currency* (1729), and later he also became public printer of New Jersey, Delaware, and Maryland. Other moneymaking ventures included the *Pennsylvania Gazette*, published by Franklin from 1729 and generally acknowledged as among the best of the colonial newspapers, and *Poor Richard's*

Almanac, printed annually from 1732 to 1757. Despite some failures, Franklin prospered. Indeed, he made enough to lend money with interest and to invest in rental properties in Philadelphia and many coastal towns. He had franchises or partnerships with printers in the Carolinas, New York, and the British West Indies. By the late 1740s he had become one of the wealthiest colonists in the northern part of the North American continent.

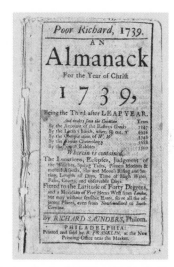

Title page for the 1739 *Poor Richard's Almanac*, written, printed, and sold by Benjamin Franklin.

As he made money, he concocted a variety of projects for social improvement. In 1727 he organized the Junto, or Leather Apron Club, to debate questions of morals, politics, and natural philosophy and to exchange knowledge of business affairs. The need of Junto members for easier access to books led in 1731 to the organization of the Library Company of Philadelphia. Through the Junto, Franklin proposed a paid city watch, or police force. A paper read to the same group resulted in the organization of a volunteer fire company. In 1743 he sought an intercolonial version of the Junto, which led to the formation of the American Philosophical Society. In 1749 he published *Proposals Relating to the Education of Youth in Pennsilvania*; in 1751 the Academy of Philadelphia, from which grew the University of Pennsylvania, was founded. He also became an enthusiastic member of the Freemasons and promoted their "enlightened" causes.

Although still a tradesman, he was picking up some political offices. He became clerk of the Pennsylvania legislature in 1736 and postmaster of Philadelphia in 1737. Prior to 1748, though, his most important political service was his part in organizing a militia for the defense of the colony against possible invasion by the French and the Spaniards, whose privateers were operating in the Delaware River.

In 1748 Franklin, at age 42, had become wealthy enough to retire from active business. He took off his leather apron and became a gentleman, a distinctive status in the 18th century. Since no busy artisan could be a gentleman, Franklin never again worked as a printer; instead, he became a silent partner in the printing firm of Franklin and Hall, realizing in the next 18 years an average profit of over £600 annually.

In the 1740s electricity was one of these curious amusements. It was introduced to Philadelphians by an electrical machine sent

FRANKLIN announced his new status as a gentleman by having his portrait painted in a velvet coat and a brown wig; he also acquired a coat of arms, bought several slaves, and moved to a new and more spacious house in "a more quiet Part of the Town." Most important, as a gentleman and "master of [his] own time," he decided to do what other gentlemen did—engage in what he termed "Philosophical Studies and Amusements."

to the Library Company by one of Franklin's English correspondents. In the winter of 1746–1747, Franklin and three of his friends began to investigate electrical phenomena. Franklin sent piecemeal reports of his ideas and experiments to Peter Collinson, his Quaker correspondent in London. Since he did not know what European scientists might have already discovered, Franklin set forth his findings timidly. In 1751 Collinson had Franklin's papers published in an 86-page book titled *Experiments and Observations on Electricity*. In the 18th century the book went through five English editions, three in French, and one each in Italian and German.

Franklin's fame spread rapidly. The experiment he suggested to prove the identity of lightning and electricity was apparently first made in France before he tried the simpler but more dangerous expedient of flying a kite in a thunderstorm. But his other findings were original. He created the distinction between insulators and conductors. He invented a battery for storing electrical charges. He coined new English words for the new science of electricity—*conductor, charge, discharge, condense, armature, electrify*, and others. He showed that electricity was a single "fluid" with positive and negative or plus and minus charges and not, as traditionally thought, two kinds of fluids. And he demonstrated that the plus and minus charges, or states of electrification of bodies,

had to occur in exactly equal amounts—a crucial scientific principle known today as the law of conservation of charge.

PUBLIC SERVICE

Despite the success of his electrical experiments, Franklin never thought science was as important as public service. As a leisured gentleman, he soon became involved in more high-powered public offices. He became a member of the Philadelphia City Council in 1748, justice of the peace in 1749, and in 1751 a city alderman and a member of the Pennsylvania Assembly. But he had his sights on being part of a larger arena, the British Empire, which he regarded as "the greatest Political Structure Human Wisdom ever yet erected." In 1753 Franklin became a royal officeholder, deputy postmaster general, in charge of mail in all the northern colonies. Thereafter he began to think in intercolonial terms. In 1754 his "Plan of Union" for the colonies was adopted by the Albany Congress, which was convened at the beginning of the French and Indian War and included representatives from the Iroquois Confederacy. The plan called for the establishment of a general council, with representatives from the several colonies, to organize a common defense against the French. Neither the colonial legislatures nor the king's advisers were ready for such union, however, and the plan failed. But Franklin had become acquainted with important imperial officials, and his ambition to succeed within the imperial hierarchy had been whetted.

In 1757 he went to England as the agent of the Pennsylvania Assembly in order to get the family of William Penn, the proprietors under the colony's charter, to allow the colonial legislature to tax their ungranted lands. But Franklin and some of his allies in the assembly had a larger goal of persuading the British government to oust the Penn family as the proprietors of Pennsylvania and make that colony a royal province. Except for a two-year return to Philadelphia in 1762–1764, Franklin spent the next 18 years living in London, most of the time in the apartment of Margaret Stevenson, a widow, and her daughter Polly at 36 Craven Street near Charing Cross. His son, William, now age 27, and two slaves accompanied him to London. Deborah and their daughter, Sally, age 14, remained in Philadelphia. Before he left for London, Franklin decided to bring his *Poor Richard's Almanac* to an end.

This time Franklin's experience in London was very different from his sojourn in 1724–1726. London was the largest city in Europe and the center of the burgeoning British Empire, and Franklin was famous; consequently, he met everyone else who was famous, including David Hume, Capt. James

WHILE at sea in 1757, Franklin completed a 12-page preface for the final 1758 edition of the almanac titled "Father Abraham's Speech" and later known as the *The Way to Wealth*. In this preface Father Abraham cites only those proverbs that concern hard work, thrift, and financial prudence. *The Way to Wealth* eventually became the most widely reprinted of all Franklin's works.

Cook, Joseph Priestley, and John Pringle, who was physician to Lord Bute, the king's chief minister. In 1759 Franklin received an honorary degree from the University of Saint Andrews in Scotland, which led to his thereafter being called "Dr. Franklin." Another honorary degree followed in 1762 from the University of Oxford. Everyone wanted to paint his portrait and make mezzotints for sale to the public. Franklin fell in love with the sophistication of London and England;

by contrast, he disparaged the provinciality and vulgarity of America. He was very much the royalist, and he bragged of his connection with Lord Bute, which enabled him in 1762 to get his son, William, then age 31, appointed royal governor of New Jersey.

Reluctantly, Franklin had to go back to Pennsylvania in 1762 in order to look after his post office, but he promised his friends in London that he would soon return and perhaps stay forever in England. After touring the post offices up and down North America, a trip of 1,780 miles, he had to deal with an uprising of some Scotch-Irish settlers in the Paxton region of western Pennsylvania who were angry at the Quaker assembly's unwillingness to finance military protection from the Indians on the frontier. After losing an election to the Pennsylvania Assembly in 1764, Franklin could hardly wait to get back to London. Deborah stayed in Philadelphia, and Franklin never saw her again.

He soon had to face the problems arising from the Stamp Act of 1765, which created a firestorm of opposition in America. Like other colonial agents, Franklin opposed Parliament's stamp tax, asserting that taxation ought to be the prerogative of the colonial legislatures. But once he saw that passage of the tax was inevitable, he sought to make the best of the situation. After all, he said, empires cost money. He ordered stamps for

his printing firm in Philadelphia and procured for his friend John Hughes the stamp agency for Pennsylvania. In the process, he almost ruined his position in American public life and nearly cost Hughes his life.

Franklin was shocked by the mobs that effectively prevented enforcement of the Stamp Act everywhere in North America. He told Hughes to remain cool in the face of the mob. "A firm Loyalty to the Crown and faithful Adherence to the Government of this Nation…," he said, "will always be the wisest Course for you and I to take, whatever may be the Madness of the Populace or their blind

An engraving of Benjamin Franklin, 1775.

Leaders." Only Franklin's four-hour testimony before Parliament denouncing the act in 1766 saved his reputation in America. The experience shook Franklin, and his earlier confidence in the wisdom of British officials became punctuated by doubts and resentments. He began to feel what he called his "Americanness" as never before.

During the next four or five years Franklin sought to bridge the growing gulf between the colonies and the British government. Between 1765 and 1775 he wrote 126 newspaper pieces, most of which tried to explain each side to the other. But, as he said, the English thought him too American, while the Americans thought him too English. He had not, however, given up his ambition of acquiring a position in the imperial hierarchy. But in 1771 opposition by Lord Hillsborough, who had just been appointed head of the new American Department, left Franklin depressed and dispirited; in a mood of frustration, nostalgia, and defiance, he began writing his *Autobiography*, which eventually became one of the most widely read autobiographies ever published.

In recounting the first part of his life, up to age 25—the best part of the *Autobiography*, most critics agree—Franklin sought to soothe his wounds and justify his apparent failure in British politics. Most important, in this beginning part of his *Autobiography*, he in effect

THE move backfired completely. On January 29, 1774, Franklin stood silent in an amphitheater near Whitehall while being viciously attacked by the British solicitor-general before the Privy Council and the court, most of whom were hooting and laughing. Two days later he was fired as deputy postmaster. He sailed for America in March 1775.

was telling the world (and his son) that, as a free man who had established himself against overwhelming odds as an independent and industrious artisan, he did not have to kowtow to some patronizing, privileged aristocrat.

When the signals from the British government shifted and Hillsborough was dismissed from the cabinet, Franklin dropped the writing of the *Autobiography*, which he would not resume until 1784 in France following the successful negotiation of the treaty establishing American independence. Franklin still thought he might be able to acquire an imperial office and work to hold the empire together. But he became involved in the affair of the Hutchinson letters—an affair that ultimately destroyed his position in England. In 1772 Franklin had sent back to Boston some letters written in the 1760s by Thomas Hutchinson, then lieutenant governor of Massachusetts, in which Hutchinson had made some indiscreet remarks about the need to abridge American liberties. Franklin naively thought that these letters would somehow throw blame for the imperial crisis on native officials such as Hutchinson and thus absolve the ministry in London of responsibility. This, Franklin believed, would allow his friends in the ministry, such as Lord Dartmouth, to settle the differences between the mother country and her colonies, with Franklin's help.

Although upon his arrival in Philadelphia Franklin was immediately elected to the Second Continental Congress, some Americans remained suspicious of his real loyalties. He had been so long abroad that some thought he might be a British spy. He was delighted that the Congress in 1776 sent him back to Europe as the premier agent in a commission seeking military aid and diplomatic recognition from France. He played on the French aristocracy's liberal sympathies for the oppressed Americans and extracted not only diplomatic recognition of the new republic but also loan after loan from an increasingly impoverished French government. His image as the democratic folk genius from the wilderness of America preceded him, and he exploited it brilliantly for the American cause. His face appeared everywhere—on medallions, on snuffboxes, on candy boxes, in rings, in statues, in prints; women even did their hair à la Franklin. Franklin played his role to perfection. In violation of all protocol, he dressed in a simple brown-and-white linen suit and wore a fur cap, no wig, and no sword to the court of Versailles, the most formal and elaborate court in all of Europe. And the French aristocracy and court loved it, caught up as they were with the idea of America.

Beset with the pain of gout and a kidney stone, and surrounded by spies and his sometimes clumsy fellow commissioners—especially Arthur Lee of Virginia and John Adams of Massachusetts, who disliked and mistrusted him—Franklin nonetheless succeeded marvelously. He first secured military and diplomatic alliances with France in 1778 and then played a crucial role in bringing about the final peace treaty with Britain in 1783. In violation of their instructions and the French alliance, the American peace commissioners signed a separate peace with Britain. It was left to Franklin to apologize to the comte de Vergennes, Louis XVI's chief minister, which he did in a beautifully wrought diplomatic letter.

No wonder the eight years in France were the happiest of Franklin's life. He was doing what he most yearned to do—shaping events on a world stage. At this point, in 1784, he resumed work on his *Autobiography*, writing the second part of it, which presumes human control over one's life.

LAST YEARS

In 1785 Franklin reluctantly had to come to America to die, even though all his friends were in France. Although he feared he would be "a stranger in my own country," he now knew that his destiny was linked to America.

Franklin's reception was not entirely welcoming. The family and friends of the Lees in Virginia and the Adamses in Massachusetts spread stories of his overweening love of France and his dissolute ways. The Congress treated him shabbily, ignoring his requests for some land in the West and a diplomatic appointment for his grandson. In 1788 he was reduced to petitioning the Congress with a pathetic "Sketch of the Services of B. Franklin to the United States," which the Congress never answered. Just before his death in 1790, Franklin retaliated by signing a memorial requesting that the Congress abolish slavery in the United States. This memorandum provoked some

UPON his death the Senate refused to go along with the House in declaring a month of mourning for Franklin. In contrast to the many expressions of French affection for Franklin, his fellow Americans gave him one public eulogy— and that was delivered by his inveterate enemy the Rev. William Smith, who passed over Franklin's youth because it seemed embarrassing.

congressmen into angry defenses of slavery, which Franklin exquisitely mocked in a newspaper piece published a month before he died. Franklin died on April 17, 1790, in Philadelphia.

Following the publication of the *Autobiography* in 1794, Franklin's youth was no longer embarrassing. In the succeeding decades, he became the hero of countless early 19th-century artisans and self-made businessmen who were seeking a justification of their rise and their moneymaking. They were the creators of the modern folksy image of Franklin, the man who came to personify the American dream.

ASSESSMENT

Franklin was not only the most famous American in the 18th century but also one of the most famous figures in the Western world of the 18th century; indeed, he is one of the most celebrated and influential Americans who has ever lived. Although one is apt to think of Franklin exclusively as an inventor, as an early version of Thomas Edison, which he was, his 18th-century fame came not simply from his many inventions but, more important, from his fundamental contributions to the science of electricity. If there had been a Nobel Prize for Physics in the 18th century, Franklin would have been a contender. Enhancing his fame was the fact that he was an American, a simple man from an obscure background who emerged from the wilds of America to dazzle the entire intellectual world. Most Europeans in the 18th century thought of America as a primitive, undeveloped place full of forests and savages and scarcely capable of producing enlightened thinkers. Yet Franklin's electrical discoveries in the mid-18th century had surpassed the achievements of the most sophisticated scientists of Europe. Franklin

became a living example of the natural untutored genius of the New World that was free from the encumbrances of a decadent and tired Old World—an image that he later parlayed into French support for the American Revolution.

Despite his great scientific achievements, however, Franklin always believed that public service was more important than science, and his political contributions to the formation of the United States were substantial. He had a hand in the writing of the Declaration of Independence, contributed to the drafting of the Articles of Confederation—America's first national constitution—and was the oldest member of the Constitutional Convention of 1787 that wrote the Constitution of the United States of America in Philadelphia. More important, as diplomatic representative of the new American republic in France during the Revolution, he secured both diplomatic recognition and financial and military aid from the government of Louis XVI and was a crucial member of the commission that negotiated the treaty by which Great Britain recognized its former 13 colonies as a sovereign nation. Since no one else could have accomplished all that he did in France during the Revolution, he can quite plausibly be regarded as America's greatest diplomat.

Equally significant perhaps were

Franklin's many contributions to the comfort and safety of daily life, especially in his adopted city of Philadelphia. No civic project was too large or too small for his interest. In addition to his lightning rod and his Franklin stove (a wood-burning stove that warmed American homes for more than 200 years), he invented bifocal glasses, the odometer, and the glass harmonica (armonica). He had ideas about everything—from the nature of the Gulf Stream to the cause of the common cold. He suggested the notions of matching grants and Daylight Saving Time. Almost single-handedly he helped to create a civic society for the inhabitants of Philadelphia. Moreover, he helped to establish new institutions that people now take for granted: a fire company, a library, an insurance company, an academy, and a hospital.

Probably Franklin's most important invention was himself. He created so many personas in his newspaper writings and almanac and in his posthumously published *Autobiography* that it is difficult to know who he really was. Following his death in 1790, he became so identified during the 19th century with the persona of his *Autobiography* and the Poor Richard maxims of his almanac—e.g., "Early to bed, early to rise, makes a man healthy, wealthy, and wise"—that he acquired the image of the self-made moralist obsessed with the getting and saving of money. Consequently, many imaginative writers, such as Edgar Allan Poe, Henry David Thoreau, Herman Melville, Mark Twain, and D.H. Lawrence, attacked Franklin as a symbol of America's middle-class moneymaking business values. Indeed, early in the 20th century the famous German sociologist Max Weber found Franklin to be the perfect exemplar of the "Protestant ethic" and the modern capitalistic spirit. Although Franklin did indeed become a wealthy tradesman by his early 40s, when he retired from his business, during his lifetime in the 18th century he was not identified as a self-made businessman or a budding capitalist. That image was a creation of the 19th century. But as long as America continues to be pictured as the land of enterprise and opportunity, where striving and hard work can lead to success, then that image of Franklin is the one that is likely to endure.

ALEXANDER HAMILTON (1755/57–1804)

Alexander Hamilton was a New York delegate to the Constitutional Convention (1787), major author of the *Federalist* papers, and first secretary of the Treasury of the United States (1789–1795). He was the foremost champion of a strong central government for the new United States.

EARLY LIFE

Hamilton was born January 11 in either 1755 or 1757, in Nevis, in the British West Indies. His father was James Hamilton, a drifting trader and son of Alexander Hamilton, the laird of Cambuskeith, Ayrshire, Scot.; his mother was Rachel Fawcett Lavine, the daughter of a French Huguenot physician and the wife of John Michael Lavine, a German or Danish merchant who had settled on the island of St. Croix in the Danish West Indies. Rachel probably began living with James Hamilton in 1752, but Lavine did not divorce her until 1758.

In 1765 James Hamilton abandoned his family. Destitute, Rachel set up a small shop, and at age 11 Alexander went to work, becoming a clerk in the countinghouse of two New York merchants who had recently established themselves at St. Croix. When Rachel died in 1768, Alexander became a ward of his mother's relatives, and in 1772 his ability, industry, and engaging manners won him advancement from bookkeeper to manager. Later, friends sent him to a preparatory school in Elizabethtown, New Jersey, and in the autumn of 1773 he entered King's College (later Columbia) in New York. Intensely ambitious, he became a serious and successful student, but his studies were interrupted by the brewing revolt against Great Britain. He publicly defended the Boston Tea Party, in which Boston colonists destroyed several tea cargoes in defiance of the tea tax. In 1774–1775 he wrote three influential pamphlets, which upheld the agreements of the Continental Congress on the nonimportation, nonconsumption, and nonexportation of British products and attacked British policy in Quebec. Those anonymous publications—one of them attributed to John Jay and John Adams, two of the ablest of American propagandists—gave the first solid evidence of Hamilton's precocity.

AMERICAN REVOLUTION

In March 1776, through the influence of friends in the New York legislature, Hamilton was commissioned a captain in the provincial artillery. He organized his own company and at the Battle of Trenton, when he and his men prevented the British under Lord Cornwallis from crossing the Raritan River and attacking

George Washington's main army, showed conspicuous bravery.

In February 1777 Washington invited Hamilton to become an aide-de-camp with the rank of lieutenant colonel. In his four years on Washington's staff he grew close to the general and was entrusted with his correspondence. He was sent on important military missions and, thanks to his fluent command of French, became liaison officer between Washington and the French generals and admirals.

Eager to connect himself with wealth and influence, Hamilton married Elizabeth, the daughter of General Philip Schuyler, the head of one of New York's most distinguished families. Meantime, having tired of the routine duties at headquarters and yearning for glory, he pressed Washington for an active command in the field. Washington refused, and in early 1781 Hamilton seized upon a trivial quarrel to break with the general and leave his staff. Fortunately, he had not forfeited the general's friendship, for in July Washington gave him command of a battalion. At the siege of Cornwallis's army at Yorktown in October, Hamilton led an assault on a British stronghold.

EARLY POLITICAL ACTIVITIES

In letters to a member of Congress and to Robert Morris, the superintendent of finance, Hamilton analyzed the financial and political weaknesses of the government. In November 1781, with the war virtually over, he moved to Albany, where he studied law and was admitted to practice in July 1782. A few months later the New York legislature elected him to the Continental Congress. He continued to argue in essays for a strong central government, and in Congress from November 1782 to July 1783 he worked for the same end, being convinced that the Articles of Confederation were the source of the country's weakness and disunion.

In 1783 Hamilton began to practice law in New York City. He defended unpopular loyalists who had remained faithful to the British during the Revolution in suits brought against them under a state law called the Trespass Act. Partly as a result of his efforts, state acts disbarring loyalist lawyers and disfranchising loyalist voters were repealed. In that year he also won election to the lower house of the New York legislature, taking his seat in January 1787. Meanwhile, the legislature had appointed him a delegate to the convention in Annapolis, Maryland, that met in September 1786 to consider the commercial plight of the Union. Hamilton suggested that the convention exceed its delegated powers and call for another meeting of representatives from all the states to discuss various problems confronting the nation. He drew up the draft of the address to the states from which emerged the Constitutional Convention that met in Philadelphia in May 1787. After persuading New York to send a delegation, Hamilton obtained a place for himself on the delegation.

Hamilton went to Philadelphia as an uncompromising nationalist who wished to replace the Articles of Confederation with a strong centralized government, but he did not take much part in the debates. He served on two important committees, one on rules in the beginning of the convention and the other on style at the end of the convention. In a long speech on June 18, he presented his own idea of what the national government should be. Under his plan, the national government would have had unlimited power over the states. Hamilton's plan had little impact on the convention; the delegates went ahead to frame a constitution that, while it gave strong power to a federal government, stood some chance of being accepted by the people. Since the other two delegates from New York, who were strong opponents of a Federalist constitution, had withdrawn from the convention, New York was not officially represented, and Hamilton had no power to sign for his state. Nonetheless, even though he knew that his state wished to go no further than a revision of the Articles of Confederation, he signed the new constitution as an individual.

HAMILTON wrote at least two-thirds of the essays in *The Federalist,* including some of the most important ones that interpreted the Constitution, explained the powers of the executive, the senate, and the judiciary, and expounded the theory of judicial review (for example, the power of the Supreme Court to declare legislative acts unconstitutional and, thus, void).

Opponents in New York quickly attacked the Constitution, and Hamilton answered them in the newspapers under the signature Caesar. Since the Caesar letters seemed not influential, Hamilton turned to another classical pseudonym, Publius, and to two collaborators, James Madison, the delegate from Virginia, and John Jay, the secretary of foreign affairs, to write *The Federalist,* a series of 85 essays in defense of the Constitution and republican government that appeared in newspapers between October 1787 and May 1788.

Although written and published in haste, *The Federalist* was widely read, had a great influence on contemporaries, became one of the classics of political literature, and helped shape American political institutions. In 1788 Hamilton was reappointed a delegate to the Continental Congress from New York. At the ratifying convention in June, he became the chief champion of the Constitution and, against strong opposition, won approval for it.

HAMILTON'S FINANCIAL PROGRAM

In 1789 when President Washington appointed Hamilton the first secretary of the Treasury, Congress asked him to draw up a plan for the "adequate support of the public credit." Envisaging himself as something of a prime minister in Washington's official family, Hamilton developed a bold and masterly program designed to build a strong union, one that would weave his political philosophy into the government. His immediate objectives were to establish credit at home and abroad and to strengthen the national government at the expense of the states. He outlined his program in four notable reports to Congress (1790–1791).

In the first two, *Reports on the Public Credit*, which he submitted on January 14,

1790, and December 13, 1790, he urged the funding of the national debt at full value, the assumption in full by the federal government of debts incurred by the states during the Revolution, and a system of taxation to pay for the assumed debts. His motive was as much political as economic. Through payment by the central government of the states' debts, he hoped to bind the men of wealth and influence, who had acquired most of the domestically held bonds, to the national government. But such powerful opposition arose to the funding and assumption scheme that Hamilton was able to push it through Congress only after he had made a bargain with Thomas Jefferson, who was then secretary of state, whereby he gained Southern votes in Congress for it in exchange for his own support in locating the future national capital on the banks of the Potomac.

Hamilton's third report, the *Report on a National Bank*, which he submitted on December 14, 1790, advocated a national bank called the Bank of the United States and modeled after the Bank of England. With the bank, he wished to solidify the partnership between the government and the business classes who would benefit most from it and further advance his program to strengthen the national government. After Congress passed the bank charter, Hamilton persuaded Washington to sign it

In the *Report on Manufactures*, the fourth and most farsighted of Hamilton's reports, submitted on December 5, 1791, he proposed to aid the growth of infant industries through various protective laws. Basic to it was his idea that the general welfare required the encouragement of manufacturers and that the federal government was obligated to direct the economy to that end.

into law. He advanced the argument that the Constitution was the source of implied as well as enumerated powers and that through implication the government had the right to charter a national bank as a proper means of regulating the currency. This doctrine of implied powers became the basis for interpreting and expanding the Constitution in later years.

In writing his report, Hamilton had leaned heavily on *The Wealth of Nations*, written in 1776 by the Scottish political economist Adam Smith, but he revolted against Smith's laissez-faire idea that the state must keep hands off the economic processes, which meant that it could provide no bounties, tariffs, or other aid. The report had greater appeal to posterity than to Hamilton's contemporaries, for Congress did nothing with it.

ESTABLISHMENT OF POLITICAL PARTIES

A result of the struggle over Hamilton's program and over issues of foreign policy was the emergence of national political parties. Like Washington, Hamilton had deplored parties, equating them with disorder and instability. He had hoped to establish a government of superior persons who would be above party. Yet he became the leader of the Federalist Party, a political organization in large part dedicated to the support of his policies. Hamilton placed himself at the head of that party because he needed organized political support and strong leadership in the executive branch to get his program through Congress. The political organization that challenged the Hamiltonians was the Republican Party (later Democratic-Republican Party) created by James Madison, a member of the House of Representatives, and Secretary of State Thomas Jefferson.

In foreign affairs the Federalists favored close ties with England, whereas the Republicans preferred to strengthen the old attachment to France. In attempting to carry out his program, Hamilton interfered in Jefferson's domain of foreign affairs. Detesting the French Revolution and the egalitarian doctrines it spawned, he tried to thwart Jefferson's policies that might aid France or injure England and to induce Washington to follow his own ideas in foreign policy. Hamilton went so far as to warn British officials of Jefferson's attachment to France and to suggest that they bypass the secretary of state and instead work through himself and the president in matters of foreign policy. This and other parts of Hamilton's program led to a feud with Jefferson in which the two men attempted to drive each other from the cabinet.

When war broke out between France and England in February 1793, Hamilton wished to use the war as an excuse for jettisoning the French alliance of 1778 and steering the United States closer to England, whereas Jefferson insisted that the alliance was still binding. Washington essentially accepted Hamilton's advice and in April issued a proclamation of neutrality that was generally interpreted as pro-British.

At the same time, British seizure of U.S. ships trading with the French West Indies and other grievances led to popular demands for war against Great Britain, which Hamilton opposed. He believed that such a war would be national suicide, for his program was anchored on trade with Britain and on the import duties that supported his funding system. Usurping the power of the State Department, Hamilton persuaded the president to send John Jay to London to negotiate a treaty. Hamilton wrote Jay's instructions, manipulated the negotiations, and defended the unpopular treaty Jay brought back in 1795, notably in a series of newspaper essays he wrote under the signature Camillus; the treaty kept the peace and saved his system.

OUT OF THE CABINET

Lashed by criticism, tired and anxious to repair his private fortune, Hamilton left the cabinet on January 31, 1795. His influence, as an unofficial adviser, however, continued as strong as ever. Washington and his cabinet consulted him on almost all matters of policy. When Washington decided to retire, he turned to Hamilton, asking his opinion as to the best time to publish his farewell. With his eye on the coming presidential election, Hamilton advised withholding the announcement until a few months before the meeting of the presidential electors. Following that advice, Washington gave his *Farewell Address* in September 1796.

Hamilton drafted most of the address, and some of his ideas were prominent in it. In the election, Federalist leaders passed over Hamilton's claims and nominated John Adams for the presidency and Thomas Pinckney for the vice presidency. Because Adams did not appear devoted to Hamiltonian principles, Hamilton tried to manipulate the electoral college so as to make Pinckney president. Adams won the election, and Hamilton's intrigue succeeded only in sowing distrust within his own party. Hamilton's influence in the government continued, however, for Adams retained Washington's cabinet, and

IN retaliation to Adams's resistance, Hamilton tried to prevent Adams's reelection. In October 1800 he privately circulated a personal attack on Adams, *The Public Conduct and Character of John Adams, Esq., President of the United States.* Aaron Burr of New York, the Republican candidate for vice president and Hamilton's political enemy, obtained a copy and had it published. Hamilton was then compelled to acknowledge his authorship and to bring his quarrel with Adams into the open, a feud that revealed an irreparable schism in the Federalist Party. Thomas Jefferson and Aaron Burr won the election, but, because both had received the same number of electoral votes, the choice between them for president was cast into the House of Representatives. Hating Jefferson, the Federalists wanted to throw the election to Burr. Hamilton helped to persuade them to select Jefferson instead. By supporting his old Republican enemy, who won the presidency, Hamilton lost prestige within his own party and virtually ended his public career.

its members consulted Hamilton on all matters of policy, gave him confidential information, and in effect urged his policies on the president.

When France broke relations with the United States, Hamilton stood for firmness, though not immediate war; however, after the failure of a peace mission that President Adams had sent to Paris in 1798, followed by the publication of dispatches insulting to U.S. sovereignty, Hamilton wanted to place the country under arms. He even believed that the French, with whom the United States now became engaged in an undeclared naval war, might attempt to invade the country. Hamilton sought command of the new army, though Washington would be its titular head. Adams resisted Hamilton's desires, but in September 1798 Washington forced him to make Hamilton second in command of the army, the inspector general, with the rank of major general. Adams never forgave Hamilton for this humiliation. Hamilton wanted to lead his army into Spain's Louisiana and the Floridas and other points south but never did. Through independent diplomacy, Adams kept the quarrel from spreading and at the order of Congress disbanded the provisional army. Hamilton resigned his commission in June 1800. In the meantime Adams had purged his cabinet of those he regarded as "Hamilton's spies."

THE BURR QUARREL

In 1801 Hamilton built a country house called the Grange on Manhattan island and helped found a Federalist newspaper, the *New York Evening Post*, the policies of which reflected his ideas. Through the *Post* he hailed the purchase of Louisiana in 1803, even though New England Federalists had opposed it. Some of them talked of secession and in 1804 began to negotiate with Burr for his support. Almost all the Federalists but Hamilton favored Burr's candidacy for the governorship of New York state. Hamilton urged the election of Burr's Republican opponent, who won by a close margin, but it is doubtful that Hamilton's influence decided the outcome. In any event, Hamilton and Burr had long been enemies, and Hamilton had several times thwarted Burr's ambitions. In June 1804, after the election, Burr demanded satisfaction for remarks Hamilton had allegedly made at a dinner party in April in which he said he held a "despicable opinion" of Burr. Hamilton held an aversion to dueling, but as a man of honor he felt compelled to accept Burr's challenge. The two antagonists met early in the morning of July 11 on the heights of Weehawken, New Jersey, where Hamilton's eldest son, Philip, had died in a duel three years before. Burr's bullet found its mark, and Hamilton fell. He died the following day in New York. Hamilton left his wife and seven children heavily in debt, which friends helped to pay off.

ASSESSMENT

Hamilton was a man both of action and of ideas, but all his ideas involved action and were directed toward some specific goal in statecraft. Unlike Benjamin Franklin or Thomas Jefferson, he did not have a broad inquisitive mind, nor was he speculative in his thinking in the philosophical sense of seeking intangible truths. He was ambitious, purposeful, a hard worker, and one of America's administrative geniuses. In foreign policy he was a realist, believing that self-interest should be the nation's polestar; questions of gratitude, benevolence, and moral principle, he held, were irrelevant.

What renders him fascinating to biographers are the streaks of ambition, jealousy, and impulsiveness that led him into disastrous personal clashes—the rupture with Washington in 1781, which luckily did him no harm; an adulterous affair in 1791, which laid him open to blackmail; the assault on Adams that doomed Federalist prospects in 1800; and perhaps even the duel in which he died. The union of a mind brilliantly tuned to the economic future with the temperament of a Hotspur is rare.

Most of all, Hamilton was one of America's first great nationalists. He believed in an indivisible nation where the people would give their loyalty not to any state but to the nation. Although a conservative, he did not fear change or experimentation. The conservatism that led him to denounce democracy as hostile to liberty stemmed from his fear that democracy tended to invade the rights of property, which he held sacred. His concern for property was a means to an end. He wished to make private property sacred because upon it he planned to build a strong central government, one capable of suppressing internal disorders and assuring tranquillity. His economic, political, military, and diplomatic schemes were all directed toward making the Union strong. Hamilton's most enduring monument was the Union, for much of it rested on his ideas.

PATRICK HENRY (1736–1799)

Patrick Henry was a brilliant orator and a major figure of the American Revolution, perhaps best known for his words "Give me liberty or give me death!" which he delivered in 1775. He was independent Virginia's first governor (serving 1776–1779, 1784–1786).

Henry was born May 29, 1736, in Studley, Virginia. He was the son of John Henry, a well-educated Scotsman who

An 1876 Currier & Ives representation of Patrick Henry (standing at left) delivering his famous "Give me liberty or give me death!" speech at the second Virginia Convention in Richmond on March 23, 1775.

served in the colony as a surveyor, colonel, and justice of the Hanover County Court. Before he was 10, Patrick received some rudimentary education in a local school, later reinforced by tutoring from his father, who was trained in the classics. As a youth, he failed twice in seven years as a storekeeper and once as a farmer; and during this period he increased his responsibilities by marriage, in 1754, to Sarah Shelton. The demands of a growing family spurred him to study for the practice of law, and in this profession he soon displayed remarkable ability. Within a few years after his admission to the bar in 1760 he had a large and profitable clientele. He was especially successful in criminal cases, where he made good use of his quick wit, his knowledge of human nature, and his forensic gifts.

Meanwhile, his oratorical genius had been revealed in the trial known as the Parson's Cause (1763). This suit grew out of the Virginia law, disallowed by King George III, that permitted payment of the Anglican clergy in money instead of tobacco when the tobacco crop was poor. Henry astonished the audience in the courtroom with his eloquence in invoking the doctrine of natural rights, the political theory that man is born with certain inalienable rights.

Two years later, at the capitol in Williamsburg, where he had just been seated as a member of the House of Burgesses (the lower house of the colonial legislature), he delivered a speech opposing the British Stamp Act. The act was a revenue law requiring certain colonial publications and documents to bear a legal stamp. Henry offered a series of resolutions asserting the right of the colonies to legislate independently of the British Parliament, and he supported these resolutions with great eloquence: "Caesar had his

CONVINCED that war with Great Britain was inevitable, Henry presented strong resolutions for equipping the Virginia militia to fight against the British and defended them in a fiery speech with the famed peroration, "I know not what course others may take, but as for me, give me liberty or give me death!"

The resolutions passed, and Henry was appointed commander of the Virginia forces, but his actions were curbed by the Committee of Safety; in reaction, he resigned on February 28, 1776. Henry served on the committee in the Virginia Convention of 1776 that drafted the first constitution for the state. He was elected governor the same year and was reelected in 1777 and 1778 for one-year terms, thereby serving continuously as long as the new constitution permitted. As wartime governor, he gave Gen. George Washington able support, and during his second term he authorized the expedition to invade the Illinois country under the leadership of George Rogers Clark.

Brutus, Charles the First his Cromwell, and George III..." Here he was interrupted by cries of "Treason! treason!" But he concluded, according to a likely version, "...may profit by their example. If this be treason, make the most of it."

During the next decade Henry was an influential leader in the radical opposition to the British government. He was a member of the first Virginia Committee of Correspondence, which aided intercolonial cooperation, and a delegate to the Continental Congresses of 1774 and 1775. At the second Virginia Convention, on March 23, 1775, in St. John's Church, Richmond, he delivered the speech that assured his fame as one of the great advocates of liberty.

After the death of his first wife, Henry married Dorothea Dandridge and retired to life on his estate in Henry county. He was recalled to public service as a leading member of the state legislature from 1780 to 1784 and again from 1787 to 1790. From 1784 to 1786 he served as governor. He declined to attend the Philadelphia Constitutional Convention of 1787 and in 1788 was the leading opponent of ratification of the U.S. Constitution at the Virginia Convention. This action, which has aroused much controversy ever since, resulted from his fear that the original document did not secure either the rights of the states or those of individuals, as well as from his suspicion that the North would abandon to Spain the vital right of navigation on the Mississippi River.

Henry was reconciled, however, to the new federal government, especially after the passage of the Bill of Rights, for which he was in great measure responsible. Because of family responsibilities and ill health, he declined a series of offers of high posts in the new federal government. In 1799, however, he consented to run again for the state legislature, where he wished to oppose the Kentucky and Virginia resolutions, which claimed that the states could determine the constitutionality of federal laws. During his successful electoral campaign, he made his last speech, a moving plea for American unity. On June 6, 1799, he died at his home, Red Hill, before he was to have taken the seat.

THOMAS JEFFERSON (1743–1826)

Thomas Jefferson earned his place in the Gallery of Greats as the draftsman of the Declaration of Independence. Afterward, he went on to serve as the country's first secretary of state (1789–1794), its second vice president (1797–1801), and its third president (1801–1809).

IN 1774 Jefferson wrote A *Summary View of the Rights of British America,* which was quickly published, though without his permission, and catapulted him into visibility beyond Virginia as an early advocate of American independence from Parliament's authority; the American colonies were tied to Great Britain, he believed, only by wholly voluntary bonds of loyalty to the king.

His reputation thus enhanced, the Virginia legislature appointed him a delegate to the Second Continental Congress in the spring of 1775. He rode into Philadelphia—and into American history—on June 20, 1775, a tall (slightly above 6 feet 2 inches) and gangly young man with reddish blond hair, hazel eyes, a burnished complexion, and rock-ribbed certainty about the American cause. In retrospect, the central paradox of his life was also on display, for the man who the following year was to craft the most famous manifesto for human equality in world history arrived in an ornate carriage drawn by four handsome horses and accompanied by three slaves.

EARLY YEARS

Jefferson was born on April 13, 1743, in Shadwell, Virginia, in Albermarle county, which lay in the foothills of the Blue Ridge Mountains in what was then regarded as a western province of the Old Dominion. His father, Peter Jefferson, was a self-educated surveyor who amassed a tidy estate that included 60 slaves. According to family lore, Jefferson's earliest memory was as a three-year-old boy "being carried on a pillow by a mounted slave" when the family moved from Shadwell to Tuckahoe. His mother, Jane Randolph Jefferson, was descended from one of the most prominent families in Virginia. She raised two sons, of whom Jefferson was the eldest, and six daughters. There is reason to believe that Jefferson's relationship with his mother was strained, especially after his father died in 1757, because he did everything he could to escape her supervision and had almost nothing to say about her in his memoirs. He boarded with the local schoolmaster to learn his Latin and Greek until 1760, when he entered the College of William and Mary in Williamsburg.

By all accounts he was an obsessive student, often spending 15 hours of the day with his books, three hours practicing his violin, and the remaining six hours eating and sleeping. The two chief influences on his learning were William Small, a Scottish-born teacher of mathematics and science, and George Wythe, the leading legal scholar in Virginia. From them Jefferson learned a keen appreciation of supportive mentors, a concept he later institutionalized at the University of Virginia. He read law with Wythe from 1762 to 1767, then left Williamsburg to practice, mostly representing small-scale planters from the western counties in cases involving land claims and titles. Although he handled no landmark cases and came across as a nervous and somewhat indifferent speaker before the bench, he earned a reputation as a formidable legal scholar. He was a shy and extremely serious young man.

In 1768 he made two important decisions: first, to build his own home atop an 867-foot-high mountain near Shadwell that he eventually named Monticello and, second, to stand as a candidate for the House of Burgesses. These decisions nicely embodied the two competing impulses that would persist throughout his life—namely, to combine an active career in politics with periodic seclusion in his own private haven. His political timing was also impeccable, for he entered the Virginia legislature just as opposition to the taxation policies of the British Parliament was congealing. Although he made few speeches and tended to follow the lead of the Tidewater elite, his support for resolutions opposing Parliament's authority over the colonies was resolute.

In the early 1770s his own character was also congealing. In 1772 he married Martha Wayles Skelton (Martha Jefferson), an attractive and delicate young widow whose dowry more than doubled his holdings in land and slaves.

DECLARING INDEPENDENCE

Jefferson's inveterate shyness prevented him from playing a significant role in the debates within the Congress. John Adams, a leader in those debates, remembered that Jefferson was silent even in committee meetings, though consistently staunch in his support for independence. His chief role was as a draftsman of resolutions. In that capacity, on June 11, 1776, he was appointed to a five-person committee, which also included Adams and Benjamin Franklin, to draft a formal statement of the reasons why a break with Great Britain was justified. Adams asked him to prepare the first draft, which he did within a few days. He later claimed that he was not striving for "originality of principle or sentiment," only seeking to provide "an expression of the American mind"; that is, putting into words those ideas already accepted by a majority of Americans. This accurately describes the longest section of the Declaration of Independence, which lists the grievances against George III. It does not, however, describe the following 55 words, which are generally regarded as the seminal statement of American political culture:

> We hold these truths to be self-evident; that all men are created equal; that they are endowed by their Creator with certain inalienable rights; that among these are life, liberty and the pursuit of happiness; that to secure these rights, governments are instituted among men, deriving their just powers from the consent of the governed.

On July 3–4 the Congress debated and edited Jefferson's draft, deleting and revising

fully one-fifth of the text. But they made no changes whatsoever in this passage, which over succeeding generations became the lyrical sanction for every liberal movement in American history. At the time, Jefferson himself was disconsolate that the Congress had seen fit to make any changes in his language. Nevertheless, he was not regarded by his contemporaries as the author of the Declaration, which was seen as a collective effort by the entire Congress. Indeed, he was not known by most Americans as the principal author until the 1790s.

He returned to Virginia in October 1776 and immediately launched an extensive project for the reform of the state's legal code to bring it in line with the principles of the American Revolution. Three areas of reform

THE American Revolution, as Jefferson saw it, was the first shot in what would eventually became a global battle for human liberation from despotic institutions and all coercive versions of government.

suggest the arc of his political vision: first, he sought and secured abolition of primogeniture, entail, and all those remnants of feudalism that discouraged a broad distribution of property; second, he proposed a comprehensive plan of educational reform designed to assure access at the lowest level for all citizens and state support at the higher levels for the most talented; third, he advocated a law prohibiting any religious establishment and requiring complete separation of church and state. The last two proposals were bitterly contested, especially the statute for religious freedom, which was not enacted until 1786.

Taken together, these legal reforms capture the essence of Jefferson's political philosophy, which was less a comprehensive body of thought than a visionary prescription. He regarded the past as a "dead hand" of encrusted privileges and impediments that must be cast off to permit the natural energies of individual citizens to flow freely.

At the end of what was probably the most creative phase of his public career, personal misfortune struck in two successive episodes. Elected governor of Virginia in 1779, he was caught off-guard by a surprise British invasion in 1780 against which the state was defenseless. His flight from approaching British troops was described in the local press, somewhat unfairly, as a cowardly act of abdication. (Critics would recall this awkward moment throughout the remainder of his long career.) Then, in September 1782, his wife died after a difficult delivery in May of their third daughter. These two disasters caused him to vow that he would never again desert his family for his country.

AMERICAN IN PARIS

The vow was sincere but short-lived. Jefferson agreed, albeit reluctantly, to serve as a delegate to the Continental Congress in December 1782, where his major contribution was to set forth the principle that territories in the West should not be treated as colonies but rather should enter the Union with status equal to the original states once certain conditions were met. Then, in 1784, recognizing the need to escape the memories of Martha that haunted the hallways at Monticello, he agreed to replace Franklin as American minister to France; or, as legend tells the story, he agreed to succeed Franklin, noting that no one could replace him.

During his five-year sojourn in Paris, Jefferson accomplished very little in any official sense. Several intractable conditions rendered his best diplomatic efforts futile: the United States was heavily in debt owing to the recent war, so few European nations were interested in signing treaties of amity and commerce with the infant American republic; the federal government created

A lithograph of Thomas Jefferson
by Stuart Gilbert, c. 1825.

under the Articles of Confederation was notoriously weak, so clear foreign policy directives proved impossible; Great Britain already enjoyed a monopoly, controlling more than 80 percent of America's foreign trade, so it had no incentive to negotiate commercial treaties on less favorable terms; and France was drifting toward a cataclysmic political crisis of its own, so relations with the upstart new nation across the Atlantic were hardly a high priority.

As a result, Jefferson's diplomatic overtures to establish a market for American tobacco and to reopen French ports to whale oil produced meagre results, his efforts to create an alliance of American and European powers to contest the terrorism of the Barbary pirates proved stillborn, and his vision of open markets for all nations, a world without tariffs, seemed excessively visionary. His only significant achievement was the negotiation of a $400,000 loan from Dutch bankers that allowed the American government to consolidate its European debts, but even that piece of diplomacy was conducted primarily by John Adams, then serving as American minister to the Court of St. James's in London.

But the Paris years were important to Jefferson for personal reasons and are important to biographers and historians for the new light they shed on his famously elusive personality. The dominant pattern would seem to be the capacity to live comfortably with contradiction. For example, he immersed himself wholeheartedly in the art, architecture, wine, and food of Parisian society but warned all prospective American tourists to remain in America so as to avoid the avarice, luxury, and sheer sinfulness of European fleshpots. He made a point of bringing along his elder daughter, Martha (called Patsy as a girl), and later sent for his younger daughter, Maria (called Polly), all as part of his genuine devotion as a single parent. But he then placed both daughters in a convent, wrote them stern lecturelike letters about proper female etiquette, and enforced a patriarchal distance that was in practice completely at odds with his theoretical commitment to intimacy.

With women in general his letters convey a message of conspicuous gallantry, playfully flirtatious in the manner of a male coquette. The most self-revealing letter he ever wrote, "a dialogue between the head and the heart," was sent to Maria Cosway, an Anglo-Italian beauty who left him utterly infatuated. Jefferson and Cosway, who was married to a prominent if somewhat degenerate English miniaturist, spent several months in a romantic haze, touring Parisian gardens, museums, and art shows together, but whether Jefferson's head or heart prevailed, either in the letter or in life, is impossible to know. Meanwhile, there is considerable evidence to suggest, but not to prove conclusively, that Jefferson initiated a sexual liaison with his attractive young mulatto slave Sally Hemings in 1788, about the time his torrid affair with Cosway cooled down— this despite his public statements denouncing blacks as biologically inferior and sexual relations between the races as taboo.

During the latter stages of Jefferson's stay in Paris, Louis XVI, the French king, was forced to convene the Assembly of Notables in Versailles to deal with France's deep financial crisis. Jefferson initially regarded the assembly as a French version of the Constitutional Convention, then meeting in Philadelphia. Much influenced by moderate leaders such as the Marquis de Lafayette, he expected the French Revolution to remain a bloodless affair that would culminate in a revised French government, probably a constitutional monarchy along English lines. He remained oblivious to the resentments and volatile energies pent up within French society that were about to explode in the Reign of Terror, mostly because he thought the French Revolution would follow the American model. He was fortunate to depart France late in 1789, just at the onset of mob violence.

SLAVERY AND RACISM

Even before his departure from France, Jefferson had overseen the publication of *Notes on the State of Virginia*. This book, the only one Jefferson ever published, was part travel guide, part scientific treatise, and part philosophical meditation. Jefferson had written it in the fall of 1781 and had agreed to a French edition only after learning that an unauthorized version was already in press. Notes contained an extensive discussion of slavery, including a graphic description of its horrific effects on both blacks and whites, a strong assertion that it violated the principles on which the American Revolution was based, and an apocalyptic prediction that failure to end slavery would lead to "convulsions which will probably never end but in the extermination of one or the other race." It also contained the most explicit assessment that Jefferson ever wrote of what he believed were the biological differences between blacks and whites, an assessment that exposed the deep-rooted racism that he, like most Americans and almost all Virginians of his day, harbored throughout his life.

To his critics in later generations, Jefferson's views on race seemed particularly virulent because of his purported relationship with Sally Hemings, who bore several children obviously fathered by a white man and some of whom had features resembling those of Jefferson. The public assertion of this relationship was originally made in 1802 by a disreputable journalist interested in injuring Jefferson's political career. His claim was corroborated, however, by one of Hemings's children in an 1873 newspaper interview and then again in a 1968 book by Winthrop Jordan revealing that Hemings became pregnant only when Jefferson was present at Monticello. Finally, in 1998, DNA samples were gathered from living descendants of Jefferson and Hemings. Tests revealed that Jefferson was almost certainly the father of some of Hemings's children. What remained unclear was the character of the relationship—consen-

sual or coercive, a matter of love or rape, or a mutually satisfactory arrangement. Jefferson's admirers preferred to consider it a love affair and to see Jefferson and Hemings as America's preeminent biracial couple. His critics, on the other hand, considered Jefferson a sexual predator whose eloquent statements about human freedom and equality were hypocritical.

In any case, coming as it did at the midpoint of Jefferson's career, the publication of *Notes* affords the opportunity to review Jefferson's previous and subsequent positions on the most volatile and therefore most forbidden topic in the revolutionary era. Early in his career Jefferson had taken a leadership role in pushing slavery onto the political agenda in the Virginia assembly and the federal Congress. In the 1760s and '70s, like most Virginia planters, he endorsed the end of the slave trade. (Virginia's plantations were already well stocked with slaves, so ending the slave trade posed no economic threat and even enhanced the value of the existent slave population.) In his original draft of the Declaration of Independence, he included a passage, subsequently deleted by the Continental Congress, blaming both the slave trade and slavery itself on George III. Unlike most of his fellow Virginians, Jefferson was prepared to acknowledge that slavery was an anomaly in the American republic established in 1776. His two most practical proposals came in the early 1780s: a gradual emancipation scheme by which all slaves born after 1800 would be freed and their owners compensated, and a prohibition of slavery in all the territories of the West as a condition for admission to the Union. By the time of the publication of *Notes*, then, Jefferson's record on slavery placed him among the most progressive elements of Southern society. Rather than ask how he could possibly tolerate the persistence of slavery, it is more historically correct to wonder how this member of Virginia's planter class had managed to develop such liberal convictions.

Dating the onset of a long silence is inevitably an imprecise business, but by the time of his return to the United States in 1789 Jefferson had backed away from a leadership position on slavery. The ringing denunciations of slavery presented in *Notes* had generated controversy, especially within the planter class of Virginia, and Jefferson's deep aversion to controversy made him withdraw from the cutting edge of the antislavery movement once he experienced the sharp feelings it aroused. Moreover, the very logic of his argument in *Notes* exposed the inherent intractability of his position. Although he believed that slavery was a gross violation of the principles celebrated in the Declaration of Independence, he also believed that people of African descent were biologically inferior to whites and could

never live alongside whites in peace and harmony. They would have to be transported elsewhere, back to Africa or perhaps the Caribbean, after emancipation. Because such a massive deportation was a logistical and economic impossibility, the unavoidable conclusion was that, though slavery was wrong, ending it, at least at present, was inconceivable. That became Jefferson's public position throughout the remainder of his life.

It also shaped his personal posture as a slave owner. Jefferson owned, on average, about 200 slaves at any point in time, and slightly over 600 over his lifetime. To protect himself from facing the reality of his problematic status as plantation master, he constructed a paternalistic self-image as a benevolent father caring for what he called "my family."

Believing that he and his slaves were the victims of history's failure to proceed along the enlightened path, he saw himself as the steward for those entrusted to his care until a better future arrived for them all. In the meantime, his own lavish lifestyle and all the incessant and expensive renovations of his Monticello mansion were wholly dependent on slave labor. Whatever silent thoughts he might have harbored about freeing his slaves never found their way into the record. (He freed only five slaves, all members of the Hemings family.) His mounting indebtedness rendered all such thoughts superfluous toward the end, because his slaves, like all his possessions, were mortgaged to his creditors and therefore not really his to free.

PARTY POLITICS

Jefferson returned to the United States in 1789 to serve as the first secretary of state under President George Washington. He was entering the most uncharted waters in American history. There had never been an enduring republican government in a nation as large as the United States, and no one was sure if it was possible or how it would work. The Constitution ratified in 1788 was still a work-in-progress, less a blueprint that provided answers than a framework for arguing about the salient questions. And because Jefferson had been serving in France when the constitutional battles of 1787–1788 were waged in Philadelphia and then in the state ratifying conventions, he entered the volatile debates of the 1790s without a clear track record of his constitutional convictions. In truth, unlike his friend and disciple James Madison, Jefferson did not think primarily in constitutional categories. His major concern about the new Constitution was the absence of any bill of rights. He was less interested in defining the powers of government than in identifying those regions where government could not intrude.

During his tenure as secretary of state (1790–1793), foreign policy was his chief responsibility. Within the cabinet a three-pronged division soon emerged over American policy toward the European powers. While all parties embraced some version of the neutrality doctrine, the specific choices posed by the ongoing competition for supremacy in Europe between England and France produced a bitter conflict. Washington and Adams, who was serving as vice president, insisted on complete neutrality, which in practice meant tacking back and forth between the two dominant world powers of the moment. Alexander Hamilton pushed for a pro-English version of neutrality—chiefly commercial ties with the most potent mercantile power in the world. Jefferson favored a pro-French version of neutrality, arguing that the Franco-American treaty of 1778 obliged the United States to honor past French support during the war for independence, and that the French Revolution embodied the "spirit of '76" on European soil. Even when the French Revolution spun out of control and began to devour its own partisans, Jefferson insisted that these bloody convulsions were only temporary excesses justified by the larger ideological issues at stake.

This remained his unwavering position throughout the decade. Even after he retired from office late in 1793, he issued directives from Monticello opposing the Neutrality Act (1793) and the Jay Treaty (1795) as pacts with the British harlot and betrayals of our French brethren. Serving as vice president during the Adams presidency (1797–1801), Jefferson worked behind the scenes to undermine Adams's efforts to sustain strict neutrality and blamed the outbreak of the "quasi-war" with France in 1797–1798 on what he called "our American Anglophiles" rather than the French Directory. His foreign-policy vision was resolutely moralistic and highly ideological, dominated by a dichotomous view of England as a corrupt and degenerate engine of despotism and France as the enlightened wave of the future.

Jefferson's position on domestic policy during the 1790s was a variation on the same ideological dichotomy. As Hamilton began to construct his extensive financial program—to include funding the national debt, assuming the state debts, and creating a national bank—Jefferson came to regard the consolidation of power at the federal level as a diabolical plot to subvert the true meaning of the American Revolution. As Jefferson saw it, the entire Federalist commitment to an energetic central government with broad powers over the domestic economy replicated the arbitrary policies of Parliament and George III, which the American Revolution had supposedly repudiated as monarchical and aristocratic practices, incompatible with the principles of republicanism. Jefferson

sincerely believed that the "principles of '76" were being betrayed by a Federalist version of the "court party," whose covert scheme was to install monarchy and a pseudo-aristocracy of bankers and "monocrats" to rule over the American yeomanry.

All the major events of the decade—the creation of a national bank, the debate over the location of a national capital, the suppression of the Whiskey Rebellion in western Pennsylvania, the passage of the Jay Treaty, and, most notoriously, the enforcement of the Alien and Sedition Acts—were viewed through this ideological lens. By the middle years of the decade two distinctive political camps had emerged, calling themselves Federalists and Republicans (later Democratic-Republicans). Not that modern-day political parties, with their mechanisms for raising money, selecting candidates, and waging election campaigns, were fully formed at this stage. (Full-blooded political parties date from the 1830s and '40s.) But an embryonic version of the party structure was congealing, and Jefferson, assisted and advised by Madison, established the rudiments of the first opposition party in American politics under the Republican banner.

The partnership between Jefferson and Madison, labeled by subsequent historians as "the great collaboration," deserves special attention. John Quincy Adams put it nicely when he observed that "the mutual influence of these two mighty minds on each other is a phenomenon, like the invisible and mysterious movements of the magnet in the physical world." Because the notion of a legitimate opposition to the elected government did not yet exist, and because the term party remained an epithet that was synonymous with faction, meaning an organized effort to undermine the public interest, Jefferson and Madison were labeled as traitors by the Federalist press. They were, in effect, inventing a modern form of political behavior before there was any neutral vocabulary for talking about it. Jefferson's own capacity to live comfortably with contradictions served him well in this context, since he was creating and leading a political party while insisting that parties were evil agents. In 1796 he ran for the presidency against Adams, all the while claiming not to know that he was even a candidate. Most negative assessments of Jefferson's character date from this period, especially the charge of hypocrisy and duplicity.

The highly combustible political culture of the early republic reached a crescendo in the election of 1800, one of the most fiercely contested campaigns in American history. The Federalist press described Jefferson as a pagan and atheist, a treasonable conspirator against the duly elected administrations of Washington and Adams, a utopian dreamer with anarchistic tendencies toward the role of government, and a cunning behind-the-scenes manipulator of Republican propaganda. All these charges were gross exaggerations, save the last. Always operating through intermediaries, Jefferson paid several journalists to libel Adams, his old friend but current political enemy, and offered the vice presidency to Aaron Burr in return for delivering the electoral votes of New York. In the final tally the 12 New York votes made the difference, with the tandem of Jefferson and Burr winning 73 to 65. A quirk in the Constitution, subsequently corrected in the Twelfth Amendment, prevented electors from distinguishing between their choice of president and vice president, so Jefferson and Burr tied for the top spot, even though voter preference for Jefferson was incontestable. The decision was thrown into the House of Representatives where, after several weeks of debate and backroom wheeling and dealing, Jefferson was elected on the 36th ballot.

PRESIDENCY

There was a good deal of nervous speculation whether the new American nation could survive a Jefferson presidency. The entire thrust of Jefferson's political position throughout the 1790s had been defiantly negative, rejecting as excessive the powers vested in the national government by the Federalists. In his Virginia Resolutions of 1798, written in protest of the Alien and Sedition Acts, he had described any projection of federal authority over the domestic policy of the states as a violation of "the spirit of '76" and therefore a justification for secession from the Union. (This became the position of the Confederacy in 1861.)

JEFFERSON'S inaugural address was conciliatory. Its most famous line—"We are all republicans: we are all federalists"—suggested that the scatological party battles of the previous decade must cease. He described his election as a recovery of the original intentions of the American Revolution, this after the hostile takeover of those "ancient and sacred truths" by the Federalists, who believed in a powerful central government.

His Federalist critics wondered how he could take an oath to preserve, protect, and defend the Constitution of the United States if his primary goal as president was to dismantle the federal institutions created by that very document. As he rose to deliver his inaugural address on March 4, 1801, in the still-unfinished Capitol of the equally unfinished national capital on the Potomac, the mood was apprehensive. The most rabid alarmists had already been proved wrong, since the first transfer of power from one political regime to another had occurred peacefully, even routinely. But it was still very much an open question whether, as Lincoln later put it, "any nation so conceived and so dedicated could long endure" in the absence of a central government along Federalist lines.

In Jefferson's truly distinctive and original formulation, the coherence of the American republic did not require the mechanisms of a powerful state to survive or flourish. Indeed, the health of the emerging American nation was inversely proportional to the power of the federal government, for in the end the sovereign source of republican government was voluntary popular opinion, "the people," and the latent energies these liberated individuals released when unburdened by government restrictions.

In 1804 Jefferson was easily reelected over Federalist Charles Cotesworth Pinckney, winning 162 electoral votes to Pinckney's 14. Initially, at least, his policies as president reflected his desire for decentralization, which meant dismantling the embryonic federal government, the army and navy, and all federal taxation programs, as well as placing the national debt, which stood at $112 million, on the road to extinction. These reforms enjoyed considerable success for two reasons. First, the temporary cessation of the war between England and France for European supremacy permitted American merchants to trade with both sides and produced unprecedented national prosperity. Second, in selecting Albert Gallatin as secretary of the Treasury, Jefferson placed one of the most capable managers of fiscal policy in the most strategic location. Gallatin, a Swiss-born prodigy with impeccable Republican credentials, dominated the cabinet discussions alongside Madison, the ever-loyal Jefferson disciple who served as secretary of state.

Actually there were very few cabinet discussions because Jefferson preferred to do the bulk of business within the executive branch in writing. Crafting language on the page was his most obvious talent, and he required all cabinet officers to submit drafts of their recommendations, which he then edited and returned for their comments. The same textual approach applied to his dealings with Congress. All of his annual messages were delivered in writing rather than in person. Indeed, apart from his two inaugural addresses, there is no record of Jefferson delivering any public speeches whatsoever. In part this was a function of his notoriously inadequate abilities as an orator, but it also reflected his desire to make the office of the presidency almost invisible. His one gesture at visibility was to schedule weekly dinners when Congress was in session, which became famous for the quality of the wine, the pell-mell seating arrangements, and informal approach to etiquette—a clear defiance of European-style decorum.

The major achievement of his first term was also an act of defiance, though this time it involved defying his own principles. In 1803 Napoleon decided to consolidate his resources for a new round of the conflict with England by selling the vast Louisiana region, which stretched from the Mississippi Valley to the Rocky Mountains.

If the Louisiana Purchase was the crowning achievement of Jefferson's presidency, it also proved to be the high point from which events moved steadily in the other direction. Although the Federalist Party was dead as a national force, pockets of Federalist opposition still survived, especially in New England. Despite his eloquent testimonials to the need for a free press, Jefferson was outraged by the persistent attacks on his

ALTHOUGH the asking price—$15 million—was a stupendous bargain, assuming the cost meant substantially increasing the national debt. More significantly, what became known as the Louisiana Purchase violated Jefferson's constitutional scruples. Indeed, many historians regard it as the boldest executive action in American history. But Jefferson never wavered, reasoning that the opportunity to double the national domain was too good to miss. The American West always triggered Jefferson's most visionary energies, seeing it, as he did, as America's future, the place where the simple republican principles could be constantly renewed. In one fell swoop he removed the threat of a major European power from America's borders and extended the life span of the uncluttered agrarian values he so cherished. Even before news that the purchase was approved reached the United States in July 1803, Jefferson dispatched his private secretary, Meriwether Lewis, to lead an expedition to explore the new acquisition and the lands beyond, all the way to the Pacific.

policies and character from those quarters, and he instructed the attorneys general in the recalcitrant states to seek indictments, in clear violation of his principled commitment to freedom of expression. He was equally heavy-handed in his treatment of Aaron Burr, who was tried for treason after leading a mysterious expedition into the American Southwest allegedly designed to detach that region from the United States with Burr crowned as its benevolent dictator. The charges were never proved, but Jefferson demanded Burr's conviction despite the lack of evidence. He was overruled in the end by Chief Justice John Marshall, who sat as the judge in the trial.

But Jefferson's major disappointment had its origins in Europe with the resumption of the Napoleonic Wars, which resulted in naval blockades in the Atlantic and Caribbean that severely curtailed American trade and pressured the U.S. government to take sides in the conflict. Jefferson's response was the Embargo Act (1807), which essentially closed American ports to all foreign imports and American exports. The embargo assumed that the loss of American trade would force England and France to alter their policies, but this fond hope was always an illusion, since the embryonic American economy lacked the size to generate such influence and was itself wrecked by Jefferson's action. Moreover, the enforcement of the Embargo Act required the exercise of precisely those coercive powers by the federal government that Jefferson had previously opposed. By the time he left office in March 1809, Jefferson was a tired and beaten man, anxious to escape the consequences of his futile efforts to preserve American neutrality and eager to embrace the two-term precedent established by Washington.

RETIREMENT

During the last 17 years of his life Jefferson maintained a crowded and active schedule. He rose with the dawn each day, bathed his feet in cold water, then spent the morning on his correspondence (one year he counted writing 1,268 letters) and working in his garden. Each afternoon he took a two-hour ride around his grounds. Dinner, served in the late afternoon, was usually an occasion to gather his daughter Martha and her 12 children, along with the inevitable visitors. Monticello became a veritable hotel during these years, on occasion housing 50 guests. The lack of privacy caused Jefferson to build a separate house on his Bedford estate about 90 miles from Monticello, where he periodically fled for seclusion.

Three architectural projects claimed a considerable share of his attention. Throughout his life Monticello remained a work-in-progress that had the appearance of a construction site. Even during his retirement years, Jefferson's intensive efforts at completing the renovations never quite produced the masterpiece of neoclassical design he wanted to achieve and that modern-day visitors to Monticello find so compelling. A smaller but more architecturally distinctive mansion at Bedford, called Poplar Forest, was completed on schedule. It too embodied neoclassical principles but was shaped as a perfect octagon. Finally there was the campus of the University of Virginia at Charlottesville, which Jefferson called his "academical village." Jefferson surveyed the site, which he could view in the distance from his mountaintop, and chose the Pantheon of Rome as the model for the rotunda, the centerpiece flanked by two rows of living quarters for students and faculty. Even the "interior" design of the University of Virginia embodied Jeffersonian principles, in that he selected all the books for the library, defined the curriculum, picked the faculty, and chaired the Board of Visitors. Unlike every other American college at the time, "Mr. Jefferson's university" had no religious affiliation and imposed no religious requirement on its students. As befitted an institution shaped by a believer in wholly voluntary and consensual networks of governance, there were no curric-ular requirements, no mandatory code of conduct except the self-enforced honor system, no president or administration. Every aspect of life at the University of Virginia reflected Jefferson's belief that the only legitimate form of governance was self-governance.

In 1812 his vast correspondence began to include an exchange with his former friend and more recent rival John Adams. The reconciliation between the two patriarchs was arranged by their mutual friend Benjamin Rush, who described them as "the North and South poles of the American Revolution." That description suggested

THE exchange of 158 letters between Jefferson and Adams between 1812 and 1826 permitted the two sages to pose as philosopher-kings and create what is arguably the most intellectually impressive correspondence between statesmen in all of American history.

Beyond the elegiac tone and almost sculpted serenity of the letters, the correspondence exposed the fundamental contradictions that the American Revolution managed to contain. As Adams so poignantly put it, "You and I ought not to die before we have explained ourselves to each other." And because of Adams's incessant prodding, Jefferson was frequently forced to clarify his mature position on the most salient issues of the era.

more than merely geographic symbolism, since Adams and Jefferson effectively, even dramatically, embodied the twin impulses of the revolutionary generation. As the "Sage of Monticello," Jefferson represented the Revolution as a clean break with the past, the rejection of all European versions of political discipline as feudal vestiges, the ingrained hostility toward all mechanisms of governmental authority that originated in faraway places. As the "Sage of Quincy (Massachusetts)," Adams resembled an American version of Edmund Burke, which meant that he attributed the success of the American Revolution to its linkage with past practices, most especially the tradition of representative government established in the colonial assemblies. He regarded the constitutional settlement of 1787–1788 as a shrewd compromise with the political necessities of a nation-state exercising jurisdiction over an extensive, eventually continental, empire, not as a betrayal of the American Revolution but an evolutionary fulfillment of its promise.

These genuine differences of opinion made Adams and Jefferson the odd couple of the American Revolution and were the primary reasons why they had drifted to different sides of the divide during the party wars of the 1790s.

One issue that even Adams and Jefferson could not discuss candidly was slavery. Jefferson's mature position on that forbidden subject represented a further retreat from any leadership role in ending the "peculiar institution." In 1819, during the debate in Congress over the Missouri Compromise, he endorsed the expansion of slavery into all the western territories, precisely the opposite of the position he had taken in the 1780s. Though he continued to insist that slavery was a massive anomaly, he insisted even more strongly that it was wrong for the federal government to attempt any effort at emancipation. In fact he described any federal intrusion in the matter as a despotic act analogous to George III's imperial interference in colonial affairs or Hamilton's corrupt scheme to establish a disguised form of monarchy in the early republic. His letters to fellow Virginians during his last years reflect a conspiratorial mentality toward the national government and a clear preference for secession if threatened with any mandatory plan for abolition.

Apart from slavery, the other shadow that darkened Monticello during Jefferson's twilight years was debt. Jefferson was chronically in debt throughout most of his life, in part because of obligations inherited from his father-in-law in his wife's dowry, mostly because of his own lavish lifestyle, which never came to terms with the proverbial bottom line despite careful entries in his account books that provided him with only the illusion of control. In truth, by the 1820s the interest on his debt was compounding at a faster rate than any repayment schedule could meet. By the end, he was more than $100,000—in modern terms several million dollars—in debt. An exception was made in Virginia law to permit a lottery that Jefferson hoped would allow his heirs to retain at least a portion of his property. But the massiveness of his debt overwhelmed all such hopes. Monticello, including land, mansion, furnishings, and the vast bulk of the slave population, was auctioned off the year after his death, and his surviving daughter, Martha, was forced to accept charitable contributions to sustain her family.

Before that ignominious end, which Jefferson never lived to see, he managed to sound one last triumphant note that projected his most enduring and attractive message to posterity. In late June 1826 Jefferson was asked to join the Independence Day celebrations in Washington, D.C., on the 50th anniversary of the defining event in his and the nation's life. He declined, explaining that he was in no condition to leave his mountaintop. But he mustered up one final surge of energy to draft a statement that would be read in his absence at the ceremony. He clearly intended it as his final testament. Though some of the language, like the language of the Declaration itself, was borrowed from others, here was the vintage Jeffersonian vision:

May it be to the world, what I believe it will be, (to some parts sooner, to others later, but finally to all,) the signal of arousing men to burst the chains under which monkish ignorance and superstition had persuaded them to bind themselves, and to assume the blessings and security of self-government.... All eyes are opened or opening to the rights of men. The general spread of the light of science has already laid open to every view the palpable truth, that the mass of mankind has not been born with saddles on their backs, nor a favored few, booted and spurred, ready to ride them legitimately by the grace of God. These are grounds of hope for others; for ourselves, let the annual return of this day forever refresh our recollections of these rights, and an undiminished devotion to them.

Even as these words were being read in Washington, Jefferson went to his maker in his bed at Monticello at about half past noon on July 4, 1826. His last conscious words, uttered the preceding evening, were "Is it the Fourth?" Always a man given to Herculean feats of self-control, he somehow managed to time his own death to coincide with history.

More remarkably, up in Quincy on that same day his old rival and friend also managed to die on schedule. John Adams passed away later in the afternoon. His last words— "Thomas Jefferson still lives"—were wrong at the moment but right for the future, since Jefferson's complex legacy was destined to become the most resonant and controversial touchstone in all of American history.

JAMES MADISON (1751–1836)

James Madison served as the fourth president of the United States (1809–1817). Before that, he played an instrumental role at the Constitutional Convention (1787), influencing the planning and ratification of the U.S. Constitution and collaborating with Alexander Hamilton and John Jay in the publication of the Federalist papers. As a member of the new House of Representatives, he sponsored the first 10 amendments to the Constitution, commonly called the Bill of Rights.

EARLY LIFE AND POLITICAL ACTIVITIES

Madison was born on March 16, 1751, in Port Conway, Virginia, at the home of his maternal grandmother. The son and namesake of a leading Orange county landowner and squire, he maintained his lifelong home in Virginia at Montpelier, near the Blue Ridge Mountains. In 1769 he rode horseback to the College of New Jersey (Princeton University), selected for its hostility to episcopacy. He completed the four-year course in two years, finding time also to demonstrate against England and to lampoon members of a rival literary society in ribald verse. Overwork produced several years of epileptoid hysteria and premonitions of early death, which thwarted military training but did not prevent home study of public law, mixed with early advocacy of independence (1774) and furious denunciation of the imprisonment of nearby dissenters from the established Anglican Church. Madison never became a church member, but in maturity he expressed a preference for Unitarianism.

His health improved, and he was elected to Virginia's 1776 Revolutionary convention, where he drafted the state's guarantee of religious freedom. In the convention-turned-legislature he helped Thomas Jefferson disestablish the church but lost reelection by refusing to furnish the electors with free whiskey. After two years on the governor's council, he was sent to the Continental Congress in March 1780.

Defending Virginia's charter title to the

FIVE feet four inches tall and weighing about 100 pounds, small boned, boyish in appearance, and weak of voice, Madison waited six months before taking the floor, but strong actions belied his mild demeanour. He rose quickly to leadership against the devotees of state sovereignty and enemies of Franco-U.S. collaboration in peace negotiations.

vast Northwest against states that had no claim to western territories and whose major motive was to validate barrel-of-rum purchases from Indian tribes, Madison defeated the land speculators by persuading Virginia to cede the western lands to Congress as a national heritage.

Following the ratification of the Articles of Confederation in 1781, Madison undertook to strengthen the Union by asserting implied power in Congress to enforce financial requisitions upon the states by military coercion.

This move failing, he worked unceasingly for an amendment conferring power to raise revenue and wrote an eloquent address adjuring the states to avert national disintegration by ratifying the submitted article. The Chevalier de la Luzerne, French minister to the United States, wrote that Madison was "regarded as the man of the soundest judgment in Congress."

THE FATHER OF THE CONSTITUTION

Reentering the Virginia legislature in 1784, Madison defeated Patrick Henry's bill to give financial support to "teachers of the Christian religion." To avoid the political effect of his extreme nationalism, he persuaded the states-rights advocate John Tyler to sponsor the calling of the Annapolis Convention of 1786, which, aided by Madison's influence, produced the Constitutional Convention of 1787.

There his Virginia, or large-state, Plan, put forward through Governor Edmund Randolph, furnished the basic framework and guiding principles of the Constitution, earning him the title of father of the Constitution. Madison believed keenly in the value of a strong government in which power was well controlled because it was well balanced among the branches. Delegate William Pierce of Georgia wrote that, in the management of every great question, Madison "always comes forward the best informed Man of any point in debate." Pierce called him "a Gentleman of great modesty—with a remarkable sweet temper. He is easy and unreserved among his acquaintances, and has a most agreeable style of conversation."

Madison took day-by-day notes of debates at the Constitutional Convention, which furnish the only comprehensive history of the proceedings. To promote ratification he collaborated with Alexander Hamilton and John Jay in newspaper publication of the Federalist papers (Madison wrote 29 out of 85), which became the standard commentary on the Constitution.

His influence produced ratification by Virginia and led John Marshall to say that, if eloquence included "persuasion by convincing, Mr. Madison was the most eloquent man I ever heard."

Elected to the new House of Representatives, Madison sponsored the first 10 amendments to the Constitution—the Bill of Rights—placing emphasis in debate on freedom of religion, speech, and press. His leadership in the House, which caused the Massachusetts congressman Fisher Ames to call him "our first man," came to an end when he split with Secretary of the Treasury Hamilton over methods of funding the war debts. Hamilton's aim was to strengthen the

national government by cementing men of wealth to it; Madison sought to protect the interests of Revolutionary War veterans.

Hamilton's victory turned Madison into a strict constructionist of the congressional power to appropriate for the general welfare. He denied the existence of implied power to establish a national bank to aid the Treasury. Later, as president, he asked for and obtained a bank as "almost [a] necessity" for that purpose, but he contended that it was constitutional only because Hamilton's bank had gone without constitutional challenge. Unwillingness to admit error was a lifelong characteristic. The break over funding split Congress into Madisonian and Hamiltonian factions, with Fisher Ames now calling Madison a "desperate party leader" who enforced a discipline "as severe as the Prussian." (Madisonians turned into Jeffersonians after Jefferson, having returned from France, became secretary of state.)

In 1794 Madison married a widow, Dolley Payne Todd, a handsome, buxom, vivacious Quaker 17 years his junior, who rejected church discipline and loved social activities. Her first husband had died in the yellow fever epidemic the previous year. She periodically served as official hostess for President Jefferson, who was a widower. As Madison's wife, she became a fixture at soirées, usually wearing a colorful feathered

DURING eight years as Jefferson's secretary of state (1801–1809), Madison used the words "The President has decided" so regularly that his own role can be discovered only in foreign archives. British diplomats dealing with Madison encountered "asperity of temper and fluency of expression." Senators John Adair and Nicholas Gilman agreed in 1806 that he "governed the President," an opinion held also by French minister Louis-Marie Turreau.

The "Wednesday drawing rooms" that she instituted for the public added to her popularity. She earned the nation's undying gratitude for rescuing a Gilbert Stuart portrait of George Washington in 1814 just ahead of the British troops who put the torch to the White House in the War of 1812.

Madison left Congress in 1797, disgusted by John Jay's treaty with England, which frustrated his program of commercial retaliation against the wartime oppression of U.S. maritime commerce. The Alien and Sedition Acts of 1798 inspired him to draft the Virginia Resolutions of that year, denouncing those statutes as violations of the First Amendment of the Constitution and affirming the right and duty of the states "to interpose for arresting the progress of the evil." Carefully worded to mean less legally than they seemed to threaten, they forced him to spend his octogenarian years combating South Carolina's interpretation of them as a sanction of state power to nullify federal law.

MADISON'S PRESIDENCY

Although he was accused of weakness in dealing with France and England, Madison won the presidency in 1808 by publishing his vigorous diplomatic dispatches. Faced with a senatorial cabal on taking office, he made a senator's lackluster brother, Robert

turban and an elegant dress ornamented with jewelry and furs. She may be said to have created the role of First Lady as a political partner of the president, although that label did not come into use until much later. An unpretentious woman, she ate heartily, gambled, rouged her face lavishly, and took snuff.

A lithograph of James Madison
by Stuart Gilbert, c. 1828.

Smith, secretary of state and wrote all important diplomatic letters for two years before replacing him with James Monroe. Although he had fully supported Jefferson's wartime shipping embargo, Madison reversed his predecessor's policy two weeks after assuming the presidency by secretly notifying both Great Britain and France, then at war, that, in his opinion, if the country addressed should stop interfering with U.S. commerce and the other belligerent continued to do so, "Congress will, at the next ensuing session, authorize acts of hostility...against the other."

An agreement with England providing for repeal of its Orders in Council, which limited trade by neutral nations with France, collapsed because the British minister violated his instructions; he concealed the requirements that the United States continue its trade embargo against France, renounce wartime trade with Britain's enemies, and authorize England to capture any U.S. vessel attempting to trade with France. Madison expelled the minister's successor for charging, falsely, that the president had been aware of the violation.

Believing that England was bent on permanent suppression of American commerce, Madison proclaimed nonintercourse with England on November 2, 1810, and notified France on the same day that this would "necessarily lead to war" unless England stopped its impressment of American seamen and seizure of American goods and vessels. One week earlier, unknown to Congress (in recess) or the public, he had taken armed possession of the Spanish province of West Florida, claimed as part of the Louisiana Purchase. He was reelected in 1812, despite strong opposition and the vigorous candidacy of DeWitt Clinton.

As wartime commander in chief Madison was hampered by the refusal of Congress to heed pleas for naval and military development and made the initial error of entrusting army command to aging veterans of the Revolution. The small U.S. Navy sparkled, but on land defeat followed defeat.

By 1814, however, Madison had lowered the average age of generals from 60 to 36 years; victories resulted, ending a war the principal cause of which had been removed by revocation of the Orders in Council the day before the conflict began. Contemporary public opinion in the United States, Canada, England, and continental Europe proclaimed the result a U.S. triumph. Still the country would never forget the ignominy of the president and his wife having to flee in the face of advancing British troops bent on laying waste Washington, D.C., including setting afire the executive mansion, the Capitol, and other public buildings.

The Federalist Party was killed by its opposition to the war, and the president was lifted to a pinnacle of popularity. Madison's greatest fault was delay in discharging incompetent subordinates, including Secretary of War John Armstrong, who had scoffed at the president's repeated warnings of a coming British attack on Washington and ignored presidential orders for its defense.

On leaving the presidency, Madison was eulogized at a Washington mass meeting for having won national power and glory "without infringing a political, civil, or religious right." Even in the face of sabotage of war operations by New England Federalists, he had lived up to the maxim he laid down in 1793 when he had said:

If we advert to the nature of republican government we shall find that the censorial power is in the people over the government, and not in the government over the people.

LATER LIFE

Never again leaving Virginia, Madison managed his 5,000-acre farm for 19 years, cultivating the land by methods regarded today as modern innovations. As president of the Albemarle Agricultural Society, he warned that human life might be wiped out by upsetting the balance of nature, including invisible organisms. He hated slavery, which held him in its economic chains, and worked to abolish it through government purchase of slaves and their resettlement in Liberia, financed by sale of public lands. When his personal valet ran away in 1792 and was recaptured—a situation that usually meant sale into the yellow fever-infested West Indies—Madison set him free and hired him. Another slave managed one-third of the Montpelier farmlands during Madison's years in federal office.

Madison participated in Jefferson's creation of the University of Virginia (1819) and later served as its rector. Excessive hospitality, chronic agricultural depression, the care of aged slaves, and the squandering of $40,000 by and on a wayward stepson made him land-poor in old age. His last years were spent in bed; he was barely able to bend his rheumatic fingers, which nevertheless turned out an endless succession of letters and articles combating nullification and secession—the theme of his final "Advice to My Country." He finally succumbed to death on June 28, 1836, in Montpelier, Virginia. Henry Clay called him, after George Washington, "our greatest statesman."

JOHN MARSHALL (1755–1835)

John Marshall was the fourth chief justice of the United States and the principal founder of the U.S. system of constitutional law. As perhaps the Supreme Court's most influential chief justice, Marshall was responsible for constructing and defending both the foundation of judicial power and the principles of American federalism. The first of his great cases in more than 30 years of service was *Marbury v. Madison* (1803), which established the Supreme Court's right to expound constitutional law and exercise judicial review by declaring laws unconstitutional. During his tenure as chief justice, Marshall participated in more than 1,000 decisions, writing more than 500 of them himself.

YOUTH

Born on September 24, 1755, in a log cabin near Germantown (now Midland), Virginia, Marshall was the eldest of 15 children of Thomas Marshall, a sheriff, justice of the peace, and land surveyor who came to own some 200,000 acres of land in Virginia and Kentucky and who was a leading figure in Prince William county (from 1759 Fauquier county), Virginia, and Mary Keith Marshall, a clergyman's daughter whose family was related to both the Randolphs and the Lees (two of Virginia's most prominent families). Marshall's childhood and youth were spent in the near-frontier region of Fauquier county, and he later lived in the Blue Ridge mountain area where his father had acquired properties. His schooling was primarily provided by his parents, supplemented only by the instruction afforded by a visiting clergyman who lived with the family for about a year and by a few months of slightly more formal training at an academy in Westmoreland county.

EARLY CAREER

When political debate with England was followed by armed clashes in 1775, Marshall, as lieutenant, joined his father in a Virginia regiment of minutemen and participated in the first fighting in that colony. Joining the Continental Army in 1776, Marshall served under George Washington for three years in New Jersey, New York, and Pennsylvania, his service including the harsh winter of 1777–1778 at Valley Forge. He eventually rose to the rank of captain, and when the term of service of his Virginia troops expired in 1779, Marshall returned to Virginia and thereafter saw little active service prior to his discharge in 1781.

Marshall's only formal legal training was a brief course of lectures he attended in 1780 at William and Mary College given by George Wythe, an early advocate of judicial review. Licensed to practice law in August 1780, Marshall returned to Fauquier county and was elected to the Virginia House of Delegates in 1782 and 1784. Attending the sessions of the legislature in the state capital at Richmond, he established a law practice there and made the city his home after his marriage to Mary Ambler in January 1783.

For the next 15 years Marshall's career was marked by increasing stature at the bar of Virginia and within Virginia politics. Although by 1787 he had not achieved a public position that would have sent him as a delegate to the Constitutional Convention in Philadelphia, he was an active, if junior, proponent of the new Constitution of the United States in the closely contested fight for ratification. That year Marshall was elected to the legislature that would take the first step toward ratification by issuing a call for a convention in Virginia to consider ratifying; he was also elected a delegate to the convention. His principal effort on the floor of the convention was, perhaps prophetically, a defense of the judiciary article. He then used his acknowledged popularity to gain or build the narrow margin by which Virginia's ratification of the Constitution was won.

Shortly after the new constitution came into force, President Washington offered Marshall appointment as U.S. attorney for Virginia, a post Marshall declined. In 1789, however, he sought and obtained a further term in Virginia's House of Delegates as a supporter of the national government. As party lines emerged and became defined in the 1790s, Marshall was recognized as one of the leaders of the Federalist Party in Virginia. In 1795 Washington tendered him an appointment as attorney general. This, too, was declined, but Marshall returned to the state legislature as a Federalist leader.

In 1797 Marshall accepted an appointment by President John Adams to serve as a member of a commission, with Elbridge Gerry and Charles C. Pinckney, that unsuccessfully sought to improve relations with the government of France. After the mission, reports were published that disclosed that certain intermediaries, some shadowy figures known as X, Y, and Z, had approached the commissioners and informed them that they would not be received by the French government unless they first paid large bribes; the reports further revealed that these advances had been rebuffed in a memorandum prepared by Marshall.

THE XYZ affair subsequently made Marshall a popular figure, and the conduct of his mission was applauded by one of the earliest American patriotic slogans, "Millions for defense, but not one cent for tribute."

Upon his return from France, Marshall declined appointment to the Supreme Court to succeed James Wilson, but he was persuaded by Washington to run for Congress and was elected in 1799 as a Federalist. His service in the House of Representatives was brief, however. His chief accomplishment

there was the effective defense of the president against a Republican attack for having honored a British request under the extradition treaty for the surrender of a seaman charged with murder on a British warship on the high seas.

In May 1800 President Adams requested the resignation of his secretary of war and offered the post to Marshall, and again Marshall declined. Adams then dismissed his secretary of state and offered Marshall the vacant position. In an administration harassed by dissension and with uncertain prospects in the forthcoming election, the appeal of the invitation must have been addressed principally to Marshall's loyalty. After some initial hesitation, Marshall accepted. In the autumn of 1800, Chief Justice Oliver Ellsworth resigned because of ill health. Adams, defeated in the November election, tendered reappointment to John Jay, the first chief justice, but Jay declined. Adams then turned to Marshall, and in January 1801 Adams sent to the Senate the nomination of John Marshall to be chief justice. The last Federalist-controlled Senate confirmed the nomination on January 27, 1801. On February 4, Marshall was sworn in, but at Adams's request Marshall continued to act as secretary of state for the last month of the Adams presidential administration. (Marshall also served briefly, at Jefferson's request, as secretary of state in Jefferson's administration.)

CHIEF JUSTICE OF THE UNITED STATES

Under Marshall's leadership for more than 34 years—the longest tenure for any chief justice—the Supreme Court set forth the main structural lines of the government. Initially, there was no consensus as to whether the Constitution had created a federation or a nation, and although judicial decisions could not alone dispel differences of opinion, they could create a body of coherent, authoritative, and disinterested doctrine around which opinion could mass and become effective. To the task of creating such a core of agreement Marshall brought qualities that were admirably adapted for its accomplishment. His own mind had apparently a clear and well-organized concept of the effective government that he believed was needed and was provided by the Constitution. He wrote with a lucidity, a persuasiveness, and a vigour that gave to his judicial opinions a quality of reasoned inevitability that more than offset an occasional lack in precision of analysis. His tenure gave opportunity for the development of a unified body of constitutional doctrine. It was the first aspect of Marshall's accomplishment that he and the court he headed

did not permit this opportunity to pass unrecognized.

Marshall distinguished himself from his colleagues by wearing a plain black robe, in stark contrast to the scarlet and ermine robes worn by the other justices. Prior to Marshall's appointment, it had been the custom of the Supreme Court, as it was in England, for each justice to deliver an opinion in each significant case. This method may be effective where a court is dealing with an organized and existing body of law, but with a new court and a largely unexplored body of law, it created an impression of tentativeness, if not of contradiction, which lent authority neither to the court nor to the law it expounded. With Marshall's appointment—and presumably at his insti-

MARBURY v. *Madison* (1803) was the first of Marshall's great cases and the case that established for the court its power to invalidate federal laws and acts found to be in conflict with the Constitution.

gation—this practice changed. Thereafter, for some years, it became the general rule that there was only a single opinion from the Supreme Court. Indeed, Marshall's term was marked by great consensus and stability on the court; Marshall only dissented formally once during his tenure, and between 1811 and 1823 the Supreme Court's personnel did not change—the longest such period in history. This change of practice alone would have contributed to making the court a more effective institution. And when the opinions were cast in the mold of Marshall's clear and compelling statement, the growth of the court's authority was assured.

The foundation of *Marbury* v. *Madison* (1803) and the significance of its ruling must be understood within the historical and strategic context of the time. Shortly before the expiration of President Adams's term, the Federalist-controlled Congress created and Adams filled a number of federal judicial positions. The commissions of the judges had been signed and the seal of the United States affixed in the office of the secretary of state (Marshall's office), but some of them, including that of William Marbury, remained undelivered. (Ironically, Marshall, as secretary of state, was responsible for delivering these appointments.) Offended by what he perceived to be a Federalist court-packing plan, President Jefferson ordered

his secretary of state, James Madison, to halt delivery of the remaining commissions.

Marbury unsuccessfully petitioned the Department of State for his commission, and subsequently he instituted suit in the Supreme Court against Madison. Although the matter was not beyond question, the court found that Congress had, under the authority of Section 13 of the Judiciary Act of 1789, authorized that such suits be started in the Supreme Court rather than in a lower court. The court faced a dilemma of historic proportions. If it issued a writ of mandamus ordering Madison to deliver the commission, it was clear that such a command would be ignored, thereby undermining the court's influence for generations, but if it failed to issue the writ the Supreme Court would be seen as cowering in the face of presidential power. Under Marshall's direction, the Supreme Court altered the issue at hand, and, speaking through Marshall, the court held that Article III of the Constitution did not permit this expansion of the court's original jurisdiction and that the court could not follow a statute that was in conflict with the Constitution. It thereby confirmed for itself its most controversial power—the function of judicial review, of finding and expounding the law of the Constitution.

Throughout Marshall's tenure as chief justice, the Supreme Court held only one term each year, lasting about seven or eight weeks (slightly longer after 1827). Each justice, however, also conducted a circuit court—Marshall in Richmond, Virginia, and Raleigh, North Carolina. Marshall's conflict with the Jefferson administration erupted once more in 1807 in Richmond, where Marshall presided at the treason trial of former Vice President Aaron Burr, successfully frustrating President Jefferson's efforts toward a runaway conviction; as a result, Burr was freed. With hardly more than three months annually engaged in judicial duties (at that time, the court's docket was much smaller than it is today), Marshall had much time to devote to personal endeavours. In 1807 he completed the five-volume *The Life of George Washington*. He also served (1812) as chair of a commission charged with finding a land and water route to link eastern and western Virginia, and in 1829 he was part of the Virginia state constitutional convention.

Once the power of judicial review had been established, Marshall and the court followed with decisions that assured that it would be exercised and that the whole body of federal law would be determined, in a unified judicial system with the Supreme Court at its head. *Martin v. Hunter's Lessee* (1816) and *Cohens v. Virginia* (1821) affirmed the Supreme Court's right to review and

overrule a state court on a federal question, and in *McCulloch v. Maryland* (1819) the Supreme Court asserted the doctrine of "implied powers" granted Congress by the Constitution (in this instance, that Congress could create a bank of the United States, even though such a power was not expressly given by the Constitution).

McCulloch v. Maryland well illustrated that judicial review could have an affirmative aspect as well as a negative; it may accord an authoritative legitimacy to contested government action no less significant than its restraint of prohibited or unauthorized action. The ruling, which nearly precipitated a constitutional crisis, upheld the authority of the federal government and denied to the states the right to impose a tax on the federal government. Faced with the daunting task of explaining where the authority of the Congress to create a bank is located in the Constitution, Marshall turned to Article I, Section 8, Paragraph 18, which grants to the federal government the power to "make all laws which shall be necessary and proper" for carrying out the powers it was explicitly granted in the Constitution. The ruling infuriated states' rights advocates, leading several, including judges Spencer Roane and William Brockenbrough, to admonish Marshall and the court through the press. In an unprecedented move, Marshall replied under an assumed name, writing as "A Friend to the Constitution."

In commerce law Marshall led the court in deciding a number of cases brought in response to the emerging American economy and the government's attempts to regulate it. *Fletcher* v. *Peck* (1810) and the Dartmouth College case (1819) established the inviolability of a state's contracts, and *Gibbons* v. *Ogden* (1824) affirmed the federal government's right to regulate interstate commerce and to override state law in doing so. Many of Marshall's decisions dealing with specific restraints upon government have turned out to be his less-enduring ones, however, particularly in later eras of increasing governmental activity and control; indeed, it has been in this area that judicial review has evoked its most vigorous critics.

Outside the court, Marshall spent much of his time caring for an invalid wife. He also enjoyed companionship, drinking, and debating with friends in Richmond. In general, for the first 30 years of his service as chief justice, his life was largely one of contentment. In late 1831, at age 76, Marshall underwent the rigours of surgery for the removal of kidney stones and appeared to make a rapid and complete recovery. But the death of his wife on Christmas of that year was a blow from which his spirits did not so readily recover. In 1835 his health declined

rapidly, and on July 6 he died in Philadelphia. He was buried alongside his wife in Shockoe Cemetery in Richmond.

GEORGE MASON (1725–1792)

George Mason, born in 1725 in Fairfax county, Virginia was an American patriot and statesman who insisted on the protection of individual liberties in the composition of both the Virginia and U.S. Constitutions (1776, 1787). Despite his Southern roots, he was ahead of his time in opposing slavery and in rejecting the constitutional compromise that perpetuated it.

As a landowner and near neighbor of George Washington, Mason took a leading part in local affairs. He also became deeply interested in Western expansion and was active in the Ohio Company, organized in 1749 to develop trade and sell land on the upper Ohio River. At about the same time, Mason helped to found the town of Alexandria, Virginia. Because of ill health and family problems, he generally eschewed public office, though he accepted election to the House of Burgesses in 1759. Except for his membership in the Constitutional Convention at Philadelphia, this was the highest office he ever held—yet

An undated portrait of George Mason.

few men did more to shape U.S. political institutions.

A leader of the Virginia patriots on the eve of the American Revolution (1775–1783), Mason served on the Committee of Safety and in 1776 drafted the state constitution, his declaration of rights being the first authoritative formulation of the doctrine of inalienable rights. Mason's work was known to Thomas Jefferson and influenced his drafting of the Declaration of Independence. The model was soon followed by most of the states and was also incorporated in diluted form in the federal Constitution. He served as a member of the Virginia House of Delegates from 1776 to 1788.

As a member of the Constitutional Convention, Mason strenuously opposed the compromise permitting the continuation of the slave trade until 1808. Although he was a Southerner, Mason castigated the trade as "disgraceful to mankind"; he favored manumission and education for bondsmen and supported a system of free labor. Because he also objected to the large and indefinite powers vested in the new government, he joined several other Virginians in opposing adoption of the new document. A Jeffersonian Republican, he believed that local government should be kept strong and central government weak. His criticism helped bring about the adoption of the Bill of Rights to the Constitution.

Soon after the Convention, Mason retired to his home, Gunston Hall. He died on October 7, 1792, in Fairfax county.

CHAPTER 5

FOUNDING "MOTHERS"

THAT ALL OF THE INDIVIDUALS WHO SIGNED THE Declaration of Independence and the Constitution were men did not preclude women from making their imprint on the winning of American independence or on the founding of the new republic.

Indeed, women such as Abigail Adams, who famously told her husband John not to forget the "ladies," and Dolley Madison, who became the model for first ladies for more than a century, and the others profiled here are but a few of the women in colonial and republican America who worked tirelessly for the cause of liberty. Their stories help to provide a framework for understanding a history that has often gone unwritten.

ABIGAIL ADAMS (1744–1818)

Abigail Adams served as America's first lady from 1797 to 1801, during her husband John's administration, and was the mother of John Quincy Adams, sixth president of the United States. She was a prolific letter writer whose correspondence gives an intimate and vivid portrayal of life in the young republic.

Born Abigail Smith on November 22, 1744, in Weymouth, Massachusetts, to William Smith, a Congregational minister, and Elizabeth Quincy Smith, Abigail was the second of four children. Educated entirely at home, she read widely in her father's large library, and the constant flow of interesting, intelligent, and well-educated guests at the Smith home turned her into a learned, witty

young woman. For her introduction to great literature, she credited her brother-in-law, Richard Cranch.

Abigail's plans to marry John Adams, a Harvard-educated lawyer nine years her senior, did not gain the immediate approval of Smith, who considered a lawyer's prospects inadequate.

WHEN Abigail and John Adams married on October 25, 1764, the bride's father, who performed the ceremony, amused the guests by citing a passage from the Book of Luke: "John came neither eating bread nor drinking wine and some say he has a devil in him."

During the first 10 years of their marriage Abigail gave birth to five children, including a daughter who died in infancy and John Quincy Adams. She managed the second decade of her marriage on her own, as John participated in the colonial struggle for independence as a member of the Continental

Congress and later as a representative of his country in France. Their correspondence during these years, especially when added to the spirited letters penned earlier during their courtship, provides a rich account of their activities and thinking as well as their love and devotion to each other. It is from these letters that historians, including the Adamses' grandson Charles Francis Adams, have concluded that Abigail played a significant role in her husband's career, particularly in managing the family farm and his business affairs. Because of her, the Adamses avoided the financial ruin that befell some other early presidents, such as Thomas Jefferson, after they left office.

As the revolutionary spirit swept through the colonies, Abigail firmly supported the movement for independence. In March 1776, when her husband prepared to gather with his colleagues to write a statement of principles that would soon be adopted by the Continental Congress as the Declaration of Independence, she asked him to "remember the ladies and be more generous and favorable to them than your ancestors." Although this letter has often been cited, correctly, as evidence of her fervent desire for women's rights, she did not champion, then or later, the right of women to vote, a position virtually unheard of at the time. She did, however, strongly support a woman's right to education,

and in 1778 she wrote her husband that "you need not be told how much female education is neglected, nor how fashionable it has been to ridicule female learning." She also favored the abolition of slavery.

In 1784 Abigail joined her husband in Europe, when he began serving as American minister to Britain. Her letters from Paris and London contain descriptive musings on British royalty, French customs, and the superiority of the quiet life of an American farmer. She wrote in early 1788 that she much preferred her "own little farm" to "the court of Saint James's where I seldom meet with characters so inoffensive as my Hens and chickings." Later that year the Adamses returned to the United States; when John assumed the vice presidency in 1789, Abigail divided her time between the capital city (first New York City and then, in 1790, Philadelphia) and the family home in Massachusetts. She missed her husband's presidential inauguration in March 1797 in order to care for his sick mother, and during his presidency she often stayed in Massachusetts to look after family matters.

As first lady, she kept a rigorous daily schedule, rising at 5:00 AM to manage a busy household and receive callers for two hours each day. Unlike Martha Washington, who had been a gracious hostess but avoided all political discussions, Abigail involved herself in the most interesting debates of the day. As the two major political factions, the Federalists and the Anti-Federalists, developed into political parties in the 1790s, she pointed out her husband's friends and foes in both groups. About Alexander Hamilton, who along with Adams was a leading Federalist, she wrote that she saw in his eyes "the very devil...lasciviousness itself." She judged Albert Gallatin, a Republican opponent of her husband, "sly, artfull...insidious." Her critics objected that the wife of the president should not insinuate herself in political discussions; Gallatin wrote, "She is Mrs. President not of the United States but of a faction....It is not right."

In November 1800, just as the election that denied John Adams a second term as president was being held, Abigail oversaw the Adamses' move from Philadelphia to the newly constructed presidential mansion in Washington, D.C. Her letters to family members showed her displeasure at finding the building roughly finished and unfurnished, but she warned her daughter not to reveal her thoughts, since people would think her ungrateful. On New Year's Day 1801 she opened the mansion, soon to be known as the White House, to visitors, continuing a tradition begun by the Washingtons and maintained by every subsequent first lady until 1933.

After leaving office, Abigail and John retired to their home in Massachusetts. She continued a lively correspondence with many people and even resumed writing to Thomas Jefferson, from whom she had been estranged as a result of political differences. She died on October 28, 1818, in Quincy and was buried in the First Church of Quincy; her husband, who died in 1826, was buried beside her.

Until the 20th century few first ladies shared Abigail Adams's interest in politics or in the treatment of government leaders by the press. She vigorously objected to what she considered inaccurate reporting on her husband and son. But she was not altogether surprised by the "lies [and] Falshoods," writing in 1797 to her sister that she "expected to be vilified and abused, with my whole family." Although her approach to the office of first lady was in many ways advanced, her fame rests primarily on her thousands of letters, which form an eloquent and evocative description of her life and times.

MARGARET CORBIN (1751–1800)

Margaret Corbin, born Margaret Cochran on November 12, 1751, in western Pennsylvania in what is now Franklin county, was an American Revolutionary War heroine whose valor and sacrifice were so great that they were recognized by the new United States government. Having lost both her parents in an Indian raid when she was five, she grew up with relatives and, in 1772, married John Corbin. When he enlisted in the First Company of Pennsylvania Artillery for service in the Revolution, she followed him east. (According to some historians, she held a paid position as an enlisted soldier.) On November 16, 1776, Corbin was manning a gun on a ridge near Fort Washington, New York, when he was killed during a Hessian advance. Observing from nearby, Margaret immediately leaped to the gun and continued to serve in her husband's stead until she was felled by grapeshot wounds. Upon the surrender of the American position she was not taken among the prisoners. She made her way to Philadelphia and there, completely disabled, came to the attention of the state's Executive Council, by which she was granted temporary relief in June 1779. The next month the Continental Congress approved the granting of a lifetime soldier's half-pay

pension to her. She was thereafter included on military rolls and in April 1783 was formally mustered out of the Continental Army. She lived in Westchester County, New York, until her death on January 16, 1800. Her story has sometimes been confused with that of Mary McCauley ("Molly Pitcher").

DOLLEY MADISON (1768–1849)

Dolley (or Dolly) Madison, the wife of Pres. James Madison, served as America's first lady from 1809 to 1817. Raised in the plain style of her Quaker family, she was renowned for her charm, warmth, and ingenuity. Her popularity as manager of the White House made that task a responsibility of every first lady who followed.

Dolley Madison was born Dolley Payne on May 20, 1768, one of eight children of John Payne, a merchant, and Mary Coles Payne. Soon after her birth, her father's business fell on hard times and the family moved to eastern Virginia, where they were active members of the Society of Friends. When she was 15 her family moved to Philadelphia, where Dolley married a young lawyer, John Todd, in 1790. The couple had two children, but in 1793 her youngest son and husband died during an epidemic of yellow fever, widowing Dolley at 25.

A few months later Aaron Burr, then a U.S. senator from New Jersey, introduced Dolley to James Madison, who was 17 years her senior; though a small man physically he was a towering political figure. There was a mutual, immediate, and strong attraction between James and Dolley, and they wed on September 15, 1794, at her sister's home in Virginia. Because her husband was Episcopalian, however, the Quakers disowned her. Soon after their marriage, accompanied by her son, the Madisons moved to Philadelphia, then the nation's capital, where James served as a member of the House of Representatives. During the presidency of John Adams (1797–1801), the Madisons lived on James's estate, Montpellier (now Montpelier), in Virginia. Soon after the election of Thomas Jefferson in 1800, they relocated to Washington, D.C., where James served as secretary of state and Dolley assisted the widowed Jefferson as hostess at official events, giving her ample preparation for her future role as first lady.

The first president's wife to preside over the White House for any significant amount of time, Dolley Madison set many precedents. She established the tradition that the mansion would reflect the first lady's tastes and ideas about entertaining. With the help of Benjamin Latrobe, architect and surveyor of public buildings, she decorated and furnished the house so that it was both elegant and comfortable. Unfortunately, not many Americans had the chance to see it before the British burned the mansion in August 1814 during the War of 1812. Dolley underscored the first lady's responsibility for caring for the mansion and its contents when she directed the removal and safe storage of precious holdings, including the famous Gilbert Stuart portrait of George Washington that still hangs in the East Room.

As hostess, Dolley Madison carefully balanced two competing traditions in the new nation: the democratic emphasis on equal treatment and the elitist notion that the president's house was the province of the privileged few. At weekly receptions she opened the doors to virtually anyone who wanted to come and then moved among the guests, greeting all with charming ease. In her stylish turbans and imported clothes, she became enormously popular and much imitated. Although most Americans approved, she did have her critics, including Elijah Mills, a senator from Massachusetts, who complained that she mixed "all classes of people...greasy boots and silk stockings."

Although she eschewed taking public stands on controversial issues, Dolley had a shrewd political sense and cultivated her husband's enemies as carefully as his friends. When President Madison dismissed his secretary of state, Robert Smith, she invited him to dinner; when he failed to accept she went to call on him personally. In the election of 1812, when many Americans complained that Madison had led them into an unnecessary war, she used her invitation lists to win him favor and a second term, according to some historians.

She insisted on visiting the household of every new representative or senator, a task that proved very time-consuming as the nation grew and the number of congressmen increased. Since many representatives chose to bring their families to Washington, dozens of households expected a call from the president's wife. Her successors found the practice too burdensome and stopped it.

When James's second term ended in 1817, he and Dolley moved back to Montpellier, where they lived until his death in 1836. James's last decades were not prosperous, and the debts of young Payne Todd depleted the family's resources. To supplement Dolley's income after James's death, a sympathetic and grateful Congress appropriated $30,000 to purchase the Madison papers.

In 1837 Dolley moved back to Washington. Living in a home opposite the White House, she was the nation's most prestigious hostess. Presidents and social leaders

DOLLEY Madison enjoyed a happy marriage; different as she and her husband were in personality, they doted on each other. However, her relationship with her son, John Payne Todd, was a different matter. He spent money recklessly and expected his mother to cover his debts and losses.

called on her, and she was a frequent White House guest. But her profligate son continued to try her patience and deplete her purse. In 1842 she traveled to New York City to arrange a loan from the wealthy fur magnate John Jacob Astor, and Congress came to her aid once more by agreeing to buy the remaining Madison papers for $25,000, but only on the condition that the money be placed in trust so that her son could not get it.

When Dolley Madison died in Washington on July 12, 1849, she was one of the most popular figures in Washington and the nation's favorite first lady. At her funeral President Zachary Taylor, his cabinet, the diplomatic corps, and members of Congress lined up to pay their respects. She was buried beside James Madison at a family plot near Montpelier.

ELIZABETH MONROE (1768–1830)

Elizabeth Monroe, wife of Pres. James Monroe, served as America's first lady from 1817 to 1825. Although she was noted for her beauty and elegance, her aloofness made her unpopular.

Born Elizabeth Kortright on June 30, 1768, in New York, New York, she was the daughter of Lawrence Kortright, a wealthy merchant who lost much of his fortune during the American Revolutionary War, and Hannah Aspinwall Kortright. With a reputation as a petite beauty, Elizabeth met James Monroe while she was still in her teens and he was serving as a congressional representative of his native Virginia in New York City, then the nation's capital. They married in New York on February 16, 1786, and moved to Fredericksburg, Virginia, where he practiced law.

In 1794 James Monroe was named American minister to France, and Elizabeth accompanied him to Paris on her first trip to Europe. In Paris her charm, beauty, and flair for fashion made her very popular, and she was dubbed *la belle americaine*. In a dramatic gesture, she used her popularity to save the life of Marie-Adrienne Lafayette, the wife of the marquis de Lafayette, the French revolutionary leader who assisted the United States during the American Revolution. Lafayette had been imprisoned when her husband fled France, and the Monroes hoped to show their gratitude to him by obtaining his wife's freedom. Riding through the streets of Paris to the prison where Madame Lafayette was being held under a death sentence for treason, Elizabeth requested a visit, and the two women embraced in public; soon afterward Lafayette was released.

This attitude affected her reputation as first lady. Her refusal to follow the practice of her predecessor, Dolley Madison, by initiating social calls on legislators' wives as they arrived in Washington, D.C., was so insulting to the women that they prevailed on their husbands to bring the matter to the president's attention. It was resolved in Elizabeth's favor at a meeting of the cabinet in December 1817, but she soon faced other problems. When her younger daughter married in 1820, she insisted on keeping the event private, thereby annoying Washington society. Moreover, Elizabeth often fled the capital, saying she was ill, to stay with her

AFTER six years in Virginia (1797–1803), the Monroes returned to Europe, where they lived in Paris and London for the next four years. Elizabeth's experiences abroad during this period influenced her greatly but also harmed her image among the American public, which came to regard her as too European and elitist. Elizabeth, for her part, preferred to distance herself from people she considered unsophisticated.

daughters. Washingtonians reacted by boycotting the few parties that she hosted, and they lamented the loss of the egalitarian atmosphere that prevailed in the White House under the Madisons.

Elizabeth Monroe is best remembered for her role in choosing new furniture for the presidential mansion when it was rebuilt in 1817 (after its destruction by the British during the War of 1812). Elizabeth had developed a great appreciation for French style and workmanship, and she and the president instructed an agent in Paris to spend a special congressional appropriation there. When the White House was refurbished in the early 1960s, these purchases were considered some of its finest holdings.

After leaving Washington, the Monroes retired to their estate in Oak Hill, Virginia, where Elizabeth died on September 23, 1830. She and James, who survived her by less than one year, were buried beside each other in Richmond, Virginia.

MOLLY PITCHER (1754–1832)

Molly Pitcher, the nickname of Mary Ludwig Hays McCauly, is best known in American lore as the heroine of the Battle of Monmouth Court House during the American Revolution.

She was born in 1754 near Trenton, New Jersey. According to legend, at the Battle of Monmouth on June 28, 1778, Mary Hays, wife of artilleryman William Hays, carried water to cool both the cannon and the soldiers in her husband's battery—hence the nickname "Molly Pitcher." Legend also

The Heroine on Monmouth, an idealized lithograph of Molly Pitcher at the Battle of Monmouth by Currier & Ives, c. 1876; the dead soldier at Pitcher's feet is her husband.

asserts that when William Hays collapsed or was wounded, she took her husband's place in the gun crew for the rest of the battle.

Patriotic prints and literature depicting the alleged event initially referred to "Captain Molly." The less martial and more nurturing "Molly Pitcher" did not appear as a cognomen until the mid-19th century. Neither image was identified with a specific person until 1876, when the citizens of Carlisle claimed a woman buried there was the literal heroine of Monmouth. Military

records indicate that a William Hays did enlist in the artillery in 1776 and died about 1789. His wife Mary remarried and eventually applied for a pension as a soldier's widow. Instead, on February 21, 1822, Pennsylvania awarded her an annual grant of $40 "for services she rendered." The services were unspecified, though the wording of the pension bill suggests that she may have played some kind of direct role in the Revolution. Whether she was this particular woman or not, monuments near the Monmouth battle site and at Mary Hays's grave recognize Molly Pitcher's contribution to American independence. She died on January 22, 1832, in Carlisle, Pennsylvania.

BETSY ROSS (1752–1836)

Betsy Ross is famed as the seamstress who, according to legend, fashioned the first flag of the United States.

Born Elizabeth Griscom on January 1, 1752, in Philadelphia, she was brought up a Quaker and educated in Quaker schools. On her marriage to John Ross, an Episcopalian, in 1773, she was disowned by the Society of Friends. Her husband was killed in 1776 while serving in the militia, and Ross took over the upholstering business he had founded.

According to her grandson, William Canby, in a paper presented before the Historical Society of Pennsylvania in 1870, Ross was visited in June 1776 by George Washington, Robert Morris, and George Ross, her late husband's uncle. The story is that they asked her to make a flag for the new nation that would declare its independence the following month. A rough sketch presented to her was redrawn by Washington incorporating her suggestions. Betsy Ross then fashioned the flag in her back parlor—again, according to the legend. She is supposed also to have suggested the use of the five-pointed star rather than the six-pointed one chosen by Washington. On June 14, 1777, a day now recognized as Flag Day, the Continental Congress adopted the Stars and Stripes as the national flag of the United States.

Ross married Joseph Ashburn in 1777, and, after his death in a British prison in 1782, she was married for a third time, in 1783, to John Claypoole. She continued the

It is known that Betsy Ross made flags for the navy of Pennsylvania, but there is no firm evidence in support of the popular tale about her and the national flag. There is, however, no conflicting testimony or evidence, either, and the story is now indelibly a part of American legend.

upholstering business, which became very profitable, until 1827, when she turned it over to her daughter. She died on January 30, 1836, in Philadelphia. The Philadelphia house in which Betsy Ross lived and from which she ran her upholstery business still stands; it has been restored and is open to the public.

Then, now, and forever!, a painting by Percy Moran showing Betsy Ross sewing a flag while George Washington looks on, c. 1908.

MERCY OTIS WARREN (1728–1814)

Mercy Otis Warren was an American poet, dramatist, and historian whose proximity to political leaders and events of her day gives particular value to her writing on the American Revolutionary period.

Born Mercy Otis on September 25, 1728, in Barnstable, Massachusetts, she was the sister of the political activist James Otis, who was early involved in events leading to the American Revolution. She received no formal schooling but managed to absorb something of an education from her brothers' tutors. In 1754 she married James Warren, a Massachusetts political leader. Knowing most of the leaders of the Revolution personally, Warren was continually at or near the center of events from 1765 to 1789. She combined her vantage point with a talent for writing to become both a poet and a historian of the Revolutionary era. She wrote several plays, including the satiric *Adulateur* (1772). Directed against Governor Thomas Hutchinson of Massachusetts, the play foretold the War of Revolution.

The Defeat, also featuring the character based on Hutchinson, followed, and in 1775 Warren published *The Group*, a satire conjecturing what would happen if the British king abrogated the Massachusetts charter of rights. The anonymously published *The Blockheads* (1776) and *The Motley Assembly* (1779) are also attributed to her. In 1788 she published *Observations on the New Constitution*, whose ratification she opposed.

Warren corresponded with her friend Abigail Adams on her belief that the relegation of women to minor concerns reflected not their inferior intellect but the inferior opportunities offered them to develop their capacities. In 1790 she published *Poems, Dramatic and Miscellaneous*, a collection of her works. In 1805 she completed a three-volume history titled *A History of the Rise, Progress, and Termination of the American Revolution*, which remains especially useful for its knowledgeable comments on the important personages of the day. The book's sharp comments on John Adams led to a heated correspondence and a breach in her friendship with the Adamses that lasted until 1812. She died on October 19, 1814, in Plymouth, Massachusetts.

MARTHA WASHINGTON (1731–1802)

Martha Washington, wife of President George Washington, was America's first first lady from 1789 to 1797. She set many of the standards and customs for the proper behaviour and treatment of the president's wife.

Born Martha Dandridge on June 2, 1731, in New Kent County, Virginia, she was the daughter of farmers John and Frances Jones Dandridge. Martha grew up among the wealthy plantation families of the Tidewater region of eastern Virginia, and she received an education traditional for young women of her class and time, one in which domestic skills and the arts far outweighed science and mathematics. In 1749, at age 18, she married Daniel Parke Custis, who was 20 years her senior and an heir to a neighboring plantation. During their life together she bore four children, two of whom died in infancy. Her husband's death in July 1757 made her one of the wealthiest widows in the region.

In the spring of the following year George Washington, then a young plantation owner and commander of the Virginia forces in the French and Indian War, began to court her, and their attachment grew increasingly deep. The couple married at Martha's home on January 6, 1759, and she and her children joined Washington at Mount Vernon, his

An uncredited portrait of Martha Washington, 1800.

plantation on the Potomac River. Washington later resented suggestions, which were undoubtedly true, that his wife's considerable property had eased his life in the early years of their marriage.

At Mount Vernon Martha became known for her graciousness and hospitality. After George was chosen to command the American forces in the Revolutionary War, Martha spent winters with him at his various military quarters, where she lived simply and encouraged other officers' wives to help in the war effort by economizing and assisting their husbands. After the war, during which her only surviving son died, Martha virtually adopted two of her grandchildren, and they substituted in many ways for the children she and George never had.

In 1789, shortly after her husband's inauguration as president of the United States, Martha joined him in New York City, then the national capital. Martha was widely

As wife of the first president of the United States, Martha Washington had no examples to follow. Although she was reluctant to assume a public role, her willingness to do so contributed to the eventual strength and influence of the position of first lady.

hailed and often feted along the route, and she became known to Americans as "Lady Washington."

The couple's rented home on Broadway also served as the president's office, exposing her to her husband's callers and drawing her into political discussions more than would have been the case had home and office been separated. When Philadelphia became the seat of government in 1790 and the Washingtons moved to a house on High Street, Martha's hospitality became even more elaborate. The first lady took no stands on public issues, but she was criticized by some for entertaining on a scale too opulent for a republican government, and she

was only too glad to retire to Mount Vernon after her husband completed his second term of office in 1797.

Following George's death in 1799, Martha continued to reside at Mount Vernon. In 1800 Congress granted her a lifetime franking privilege, which it continued to grant to any president's widow who applied for it. After Martha died on May 22, 1802, at Mount Vernon, there was considerable discussion in Congress about burying the Washingtons in the capital city that bore their name, but instead she was buried beside George in a family tomb at Mount Vernon.

PHILLIS WHEATLEY (1753–1784)

Phillis Wheatley was the first black woman poet of note in the United States. She was born in about 1753, probably in present-day Senegal, in West Africa. Her work was frequently cited by abolitionists to combat the charge of innate intellectual inferiority among blacks and to promote educational opportunities for African Americans.

The young girl who was to become Phillis Wheatley was kidnapped and taken to Boston on a slave ship in 1761 and purchased by a tailor, John Wheatley, as a personal servant for his wife. She was treated kindly in the Wheatley household, almost as a third child. The Wheatleys soon recognized her talents and gave her privileges unusual for a slave, allowing her to learn to read and write. In less than two years, under the tutelage of Mrs. Wheatley and her daughter, Phillis had mastered English; she went on to learn Greek and Latin and caused a stir among Boston scholars by translating a tale from Ovid. From age 14 she wrote exceptionally mature, if conventional, poetry that was largely concerned with morality and piety.

Wheatley's better-known pieces include "To the University of Cambridge in New England," "To the King's Most Excellent Majesty," "On the Death of Rev. Dr. Sewall," and "An Elegiac Poem, on the Death of the Celebrated Divine...George Whitefield," the last of which was the first of her poems to be published, in 1770. She was escorted by Mr. Wheatley's son to London in 1773, and there her first book, *Poems on Various Subjects, Religious and Moral*, was published. Her personal qualities, even more than her literary talent, contributed to her great social success in London. She returned to Boston shortly thereafter because of the illness of her mistress. Both Mr. and Mrs. Wheatley died soon thereafter, and Phillis was freed. In 1778 she married John Peters, a free black man who eventually abandoned her. At the end of her life Wheatley was working as a servant, and she died in poverty on December 5, 1784, in Boston.

Two books issued posthumously were *Memoir* and *Poems of Phillis Wheatley* (1834) and *Letters of Phillis Wheatley, the Negro Slave-Poet of Boston* (1864).

CHAPTER 6

BROTHERHOOD OF FOUNDERS

T HERE IS NO COMPREHENSIVE, UNIVERSALLY AGREED LIST of Founding Fathers. Thus, this chapter provides a mere snapshot of some of the men who helped win American independence and foster the survival and development of the American republic.

The first person profiled in this chapter, Crispus Attucks, would not live to see American independence, nor would he see how his country would relegate most black people like him to slavery and servitude until the Civil War was fought that would emancipate his people. Attucks (who is also thought to have had some Native American ancestry) was one of the first heroes of the American Revolution, though he died six years before the actual revolution began. Through Attucks's story, and those of the other men profiled in this chapter, it becomes obvious that though there is one history of the United States, there are disparate lives and voices that help comprise the American story.

CRISPUS ATTUCKS (1723?–1770)

Crispus Attucks was an American hero and martyr of the Boston Massacre. His life prior to the day of his death is still shrouded in mystery. He is estimated to have been born around 1723, though historians are unsure where. His father is thought to be Prince Yonger, who was a slave brought to America, while his mother is thought to be Nancy Attucks, a Natick Indian. In the *Boston Gazette* on October 2, 1750, William Brown,

a resident of Framingham, Massachusetts, advertised for the recovery of a runaway slave named Crispus (spelled Crispas in the advertisement)—usually thought to be the Crispus in question. That advertisement, which proclaimed that Crispus had run away, described him as 27 years old and 6 feet 2 inches.

In the 20-year interval between his escape from slavery and his death at the hands of British soldiers, Attucks probably spent a good deal of time aboard whaling ships. All that is definitely known about him concerns the Boston Massacre on March 5, 1770.

A portrait of Crispus Attucks, c. 1897.

Toward evening that day, a crowd of colonists gathered and began taunting a small group of British soldiers. Tension mounted rapidly, and when one of the soldiers was struck the others fired their muskets, killing three of the Americans instantly and mortally wounding two others. Attucks was the first to fall, thus becoming one of the first men to lose his life in the cause of American independence. His body was carried to Faneuil Hall, where it lay in state until March 8, when all five victims were buried in a common grave. Attucks was the only victim of the Boston Massacre whose name was widely remembered. In 1888 the Crispus Attucks monument was unveiled in the Boston Common.

JOHN BLAIR
(1732–1800)

John Blair was born in Williamsburg, Virginia, in 1732. A member of one of Virginia's most prominent landed families and a close friend of George Washington, Blair studied law at the Middle Temple in London and, in 1766, was elected to represent William and Mary College in the Virginia House of Burgesses. He served in the Burgesses until 1770, and then for five years he was clerk of the royal governor's Council.

In 1776 he took part in the convention to frame a constitution and plan of government for the new commonwealth of Virginia and was elected to the state Privy Council. In 1778 he was elected one of the judges of the state General Court and later became its chief justice. He subsequently served as a judge of the High Court of Chancery and was a judge of the Court of Appeals when it heard the case of *Commonwealth of Virginia* v. *Caton* in 1782. He sided with the majority when it laid down the principle that a court can annul a law deemed to conflict with the constitution. Blair took part in the Constitutional Convention of 1787 and, in 1789, was appointed by President Washington to the U.S. Supreme Court (taking his oath of office the following year). He was a judicial conservative and served on the court until his retirement in 1796. He died on August 31, 1800, in Williamsburg.

AARON BURR
(1756–1836)

Aaron Burr was America's third vice president, serving from 1801 to 1805. His turbulent career included the killing of his political rival, Alexander Hamilton, in a duel in 1804. In 1807 he was arrested for treason.

Born on February 6, 1756, in Newark, New Jersey, Burr, the son of Aaron Burr and Esther Edwards, came from a prominent New Jersey family and was a grandson of the theologian Jonathan Edwards. He studied law and served on the staff of Gen. George Washington during the American Revolution (1775–1783) but was transferred after antagonizing him.

In 1782 Burr was admitted to the New York state bar, and his law practice in New York City soon flourished. In 1784 and 1785 he was elected to the state assembly, and in 1789 he was appointed attorney general by Governor George Clinton. By 1791 he had built a successful political coalition against Gen. Philip Schuyler, father-in-law of Alexander Hamilton (then secretary of the treasury), and won election to the United States Senate, incurring the enmity of Hamilton. Burr failed to win reelection in 1797 and spent the next two years in state politics.

In 1800 Burr won the vice presidential nomination on the Jeffersonian Republican ticket. He carried New York state and thus helped bring about a national victory for his party. Under the electoral college procedures then prevailing, the electors had cast their votes for both Thomas Jefferson and Burr without indicating which should be president and which vice president.

Both men had an equal number of electoral votes, and the Federalist-controlled House of Representatives had to break the tie. Although Burr maintained that he would not challenge Jefferson—an assertion that Jefferson did not wholly accept—Hamilton's determined opposition to Burr was a strong factor in Jefferson's election after 36 ballots. (In 1804 the Twelfth Amendment to the United States Constitution was adopted, requiring electors to cast separate ballots for president and vice president.)

In February 1804 Burr's friends in the New York legislature nominated him for the governorship. Hamilton helped to contribute to Burr's defeat by disseminating letters containing derogatory comments about Burr, and shortly thereafter Clinton replaced him as the Republican vice presidential candidate. Once again Burr felt himself to be the political victim of Hamilton's animosity, and he challenged him to a duel (July 11, 1804) at Weehawken, New Jersey, in which Hamilton was killed.

Arrest warrants were issued for Burr, whom many now viewed as a murderer, and he fled to Philadelphia, where he contacted his friend General James Wilkinson, a United States Army officer secretly in the pay of Spain. Expecting war to break out between the United States and Spain over boundary disputes, Wilkinson and Burr planned an invasion of Mexico in order to establish an independent government there. Possibly—the record is inconclusive—they also discussed a plan to foment a secessionist movement in the West and, joining it to Mexico, to found an empire on the Napoleonic model. In any event, Wilkinson became alarmed and betrayed Burr to President Jefferson. Trying to escape to Spanish territory, Burr was arrested and returned for trial in the Circuit Court in Richmond, Virginia (May 1807), before Chief Justice John Marshall.

Although the evidence showed only that Burr had planned an illegal attack upon Spanish territory, he was tried for treason, and though he was acquitted, he remained under a cloud of suspicion and distrust. He soon left for Europe, where he tried in vain to enlist the aid of Napoleon in a plan to conquer Florida. Burr remained abroad for four years, living in customary indebtedness. He returned to New York in 1812 and practiced law. He married a wealthy widow, Elizabeth Brown Jumel, in 1833, though he frittered away much of her wealth within a year. Eventually she sued for divorce on grounds of adultery, and a divorce decree was granted on September 14, 1836, the day he died in Port Richmond, New York.

CHARLES CARROLL (1737–1832)

Charles Carroll was an American patriot leader, who had the distinction of being the longest surviving signer of the Declaration of Independence. He was the only Roman Catholic to sign that document.

Charles Carroll was born on September 19, 1737, in Annapolis, Maryland. Until 1765 Carroll attended Jesuit colleges in Maryland and France and studied law in France and England. Before and during the American Revolution, he served on committees of correspondence and in the Continental Congress (1776–1778), where he was an important member of the board of war. In 1776, with Benjamin Franklin, Samuel Chase, and his cousin, the Rev. John Carroll, he was sent to Canada in a fruitless effort to persuade Canadians to join the cause of the 13 colonies. He was elected again to the Continental Congress in 1780, but he decided not to serve.

Carroll was a state senator in Maryland (1777–1800) and concurrently a U.S. Senator (1789–1792). He retired from the latter position when Maryland passed a law forbidding members of the state Senate to serve in the U.S. Congress. When political parties were formed in the United States, he became a Federalist. After leaving the state Senate, he lived a fairly quiet life, though he did partici-pate in the forming of the Baltimore & Ohio Railroad Company. He died on November 14, 1832, in Baltimore, Maryland.

SAMUEL CHASE (1741–1811)

Samuel Chase, a signer of the Declaration of Independence, went on to serve as asso-ciate justice of the U.S. Supreme Court. His acquittal in an impeachment trial (1805) inspired by President Thomas Jefferson for political reasons strengthened the indepen-dence of the judiciary.

Samuel Chase was born on April 17, 1741, in Princess Anne, Maryland. He served as a member of the Maryland assembly (1764–1784) and in the Continental Congress (1774–1778, 1784–1785). As a member of the latter, he was a signer of the Declaration of Independence. He then went on to serve as a judge of the Baltimore crim-inal court (1788) and then as chief judge of the Maryland General Court from 1791 to 1796, when President George Washington appointed him to the U.S. Supreme Court. In *Ware v. Hylton* (1796), an important early test of nationalism, he upheld the primacy of U.S. treaties over state statutes. In *Calder v.*

Bull (1798), he asserted that legislative power over liberty and property is limited by "cer-tain vital principles in our free Republican governments"; later courts read these prin-ciples into the "due process of law" clauses of the Fifth and Fourteenth Amendments to the Constitution.

During the struggle between the Federalist and Jeffersonian Republican parties, Chase, a Federalist, conducted his circuit court in a partisan manner. In 1804, the House of Representatives, encouraged by Jefferson, charged Chase with improper actions in treason and sedition trials and with a political address to a grand jury. In March 1805 the Senate, acting as trial court, found him not guilty. His acquittal, by establishing the principle that federal judges could be removed only for indictable criminal acts, clarified the constitutional provision (Article III, Section 1) that judges shall hold office during good behavior. Some scholars believe that if Chase had been found guilty, the Jefferson administration would have proceeded against other Federalist justices, particularly Chief Justice John Marshall, a leading opponent of Jefferson. He retained his seat until his death, on June 19, 1811, in Washington, D.C.

ABRAHAM CLARK
(1726–1794)

Abraham Clark was an American patriot and signer of the Declaration of Independence. He was born on February 15, 1726, in Elizabethtown, New Jersey. Though he had little formal education, Clark became a surveyor and managed transfers of property. He had a gift for politics and served in many public offices in New Jersey, including as sheriff of Essex county. He served in New Jersey's colonial legislature in 1775–1776, championing the cause of the colonies and in 1776 was elected to the Continental Congress, where he voted for separation from Great Britain and signed the Declaration of Independence. He was reelected to the Continental Congress several times and was also a delegate to the Annapolis Convention (1786). He was chosen to be a delegate to the federal Constitutional Convention (1787) but was unable to attend because of illness. Clark opposed the adoption of the new U.S. Constitution until he was assured that a bill of rights would be added to it. He served in the U.S. House of Representatives from 1791 until his death. He died on September 15, 1794, in Elizabeth, New Jersey.

JONATHAN DAYTON
(1760–1824)

Jonathan Dayton was the youngest member of the U.S. Constitutional Convention, speaker of the U.S. House of Representatives, and developer of large tracts in what later became the state of Ohio.

Dayton was born on October 16, 1760, in Elizabeth, New Jersey, the son of Elias Dayton. Immediately following graduation from the College of New Jersey (Princeton University) in 1776, Dayton enlisted in the New Jersey militia. He fought in the New York and New Jersey campaigns, rose to the rank of captain, was at Yorktown in 1781, and returned to civilian life two years later.

Dayton then studied law and was admitted to the bar, but his future lay more in public service than in private law practice. He served in the New Jersey Assembly, 1786-87, then—at age 27—became the youngest delegate at the Constitutional Convention. Dayton was a frequent participant in the debates and opposed several aspects of the Constitution. He nonetheless signed the final document.

Elected to a seat in the first Congress, Dayton instead served in the New Jersey Council (1789) and Assembly (1790), where he served as speaker. But when elected once again to the U.S. House in 1790, he joined that body and remained there until his fourth term expired in 1799. As a congressman he backed Hamilton's financial program, pressed for suppression of the Whiskey Rebellion, and supported the Jay Treaty with Great Britain (1794). During his last two terms he was speaker of the House.

Dayton was elected to the Senate, where he served for the term of 1799–1805. As a loyal Federalist he opposed Jefferson's administration by voting against the repeal of the Judiciary Act of 1801, against the Twelfth Amendment (specifying separate votes for president and vice president), and for the acquittal of Supreme Court Justice Samuel Chase. But he favored the Louisiana Purchase of 1803.

After Dayton left the Senate in 1805, he held public office just once more in his life—a term in the New Jersey legislature (1814–1815). Most of his time he devoted to developing his large landholdings (250,000 acres) in Ohio. (The city of Dayton, Ohio, is named for him.) He apparently played some role in Aaron Burr's western conspiracy of 1807 but—though indicted for high treason—was never prosecuted. He died on October 9, 1824, in Elizabeth.

JOHN DICKINSON (1732–1808)

John Dickinson was an American statesman often referred to as the "penman of the Revolution." He was born on November 8, 1732, in Talbot county, Maryland, and moved with his family to Dover, Delaware, in 1740. He studied law in London at the Middle Temple and practiced law in Philadelphia (1757–1760) before entering public life. He represented Pennsylvania in the Stamp Act Congress (1765) and drafted its declaration of rights and grievances. He won fame in 1767–1768 as the author of the *Letters from a Farmer in Pennsylvania, to the Inhabitants of the British Colonies*, which appeared in many colonial newspapers. The letters helped turn opinion against the Townshend Acts (1767), under which new duties were collected to pay the salaries of royal officials in the Colonies. He also denounced the establishing of the American Board of Customs Commissioners at Boston to enforce the acts.

Dickinson was a delegate from Pennsylvania in the Continental Congress (1774–1776) and was the principal author of the "Declaration…Setting Forth the Causes and Necessity of Their Taking Up Arms." He helped prepare the first draft of the Articles of Confederation (1776–1777) but voted against the Declaration of Independence

(1776) because he still hoped for conciliation with the British. Although he was accused of being a loyalist, he later served in the Pennsylvania militia, rising to the rank of brigadier-general.

In 1781 he served as president of the state of Delaware and then from 1782 to 1785 as the president of Pennsylvania before returning to Delaware. As a delegate from Delaware to the Federal Constitutional Convention (1787), Dickinson signed the U.S. Constitution and worked for its adoption. He later defended the document in a series of letters signed "Fabius." He died on February 14, 1808, in Wilmington, Delaware.

Dickinson College at Carlisle, Pennsylvania, chartered in 1783, was named in his honor.

ELBRIDGE GERRY (1744–1814)

Elbridge Gerry, a signer of the American Declaration of Independence, was the fifth vice president of the United States, serving from 1813 to 1814, during the second term of President James Madison. He is perhaps best known for having the term gerrymander derived from his name.

Gerry, born July 17, 1744, in Marblehead, Massachesetts, was the son of Thomas Gerry,

a merchant, and Elizabeth Greenleaf. He graduated from Harvard in 1762 and entered his father's business. He was a member of the Massachusetts legislature and General Court (1772–1773), served on a Committee of Correspondence, was a member of the Massachusetts Provincial Congress (1774–1775), and was a delegate to the Continental Congress in Philadelphia (1776–1780), where he was an early advocate of independence. He was also a member of Congress (1783–1785) under the Articles of Confederation and was a delegate to the Constitutional Convention in Philadelphia (1787). He was an outspoken opponent of ratification of the United States

An engraved portrait of Elbridge Gerry, 1847.

IN 1797 President John Adams sent Elbridge Gerry, John Marshall, and Charles Cotesworth Pinckney to France on the mission that resulted in the XYZ Affair. The mission, an unsuccessful attempt to negotiate a treaty to settle several long-standing disputes, ended early because of the duplicitous treatment of the American negotiators by the French foreign minister, Charles-Maurice de Talleyrand, and his subordinates. After the French agents demanded bribes, Marshall and Pinckney departed in disgust; however, Gerry remained in Paris in the vain hope that Talleyrand might offer him, a known friend of France, terms that had been refused to Marshall and Pinckney. This action brought a storm of abuse and censure from Federalist partisans, from which Gerry never fully cleared himself.

Constitution, fearing that it might give way to aristocratic or monarchical rule. However, he gave it his full support after its ratification, helping to draft the Bill of Rights and serving as a representative in Congress for two terms (1789–1793).

After four attempts to win election as governor of Massachusetts, Gerry succeeded in 1810 and was reelected in 1811. His administration was notable for its use of what became known as gerrymandering, the division of electoral districts for partisan political advantage.

In 1812 Gerry, an ardent supporter of war with Great Britain in the War of 1812, was elected vice president of the United States on the Jeffersonian Republican ticket with Madison. In 1813, while presiding over the Senate, Gerry, who along with Madison was in ill health, refused to yield his chair at the close of the legislative session, thus preventing William Giles, a senator from Virginia and an advocate of peace with Britain, from becoming president pro tempore of the Senate and thereby second in line (after the vice president) to succeed the president under the Presidential Succession Act of 1792. Gerry suffered a hemorrhage of the lungs on his way to the Senate and died on November 23, 1814, in Washington, D.C.

BUTTON GWINNETT (1735–1777)

Button Gwinnett was a merchant, an American patriot, and a signer of the Declaration of Independence. Born 1735 in Gloucester, England, he emigrated to Georgia sometime before 1765. In Savannah he pursued commercial interests as a trader and in 1769 was elected to the Georgia Commons House of Assembly. Suffering from financial distress, he left political life in 1773. In January 1776, however, he reentered politics and was elected a delegate from that colony to the Continental Congress and, as such, signed the Declaration. Returning to Georgia, he was elected speaker of the provincial assembly and was a member of the convention to frame a new state constitution. In 1777 he was appointed acting president and commander-in-chief of Georgia after his predecessor, Archibald Bulloch, died. He was then unsuccessful in his attempt to win election as governor of Georgia. He died on May 16, 1777, on St. Catherine's Island, off

TODAY, Button Gwinnett is perhaps best known chiefly because his autographs are extremely rare, and collectors have forced their value to a high figure. In 2001 one of his 36 autographs sold at public auction for $110,000.

Savannah, Georgia, from wounds received in a duel with Lachlan McIntosh, a Continental general, whose brother Gwinnett had arrested.

NATHAN HALE (1755–1776)

Nathan Hale was an American Revolutionary officer who attempted to spy on the British and was hanged. He was born on June 6, 1755, in Coventry, Connecticut. He attended Yale University, from which he graduated in 1773, and became a schoolteacher, first in East Haddam and then in New London. He

NATHAN Hale is regarded by American Revolutionary tradition as a hero and a martyr. He is supposed to have said before his death, "I only regret that I have but one life to lose for my country," a remark similar to one in Joseph Addison's play *Cato*. In the diary entry of one of the British officers made on the day of Hale's execution, it said: "He behaved with great composure and resolution, saying he thought it the duty of every good Officer, to obey any orders given him by his Commander-in-Chief; and desired the Spectators to be at all times prepared to meet death in whatever shape it might appear."

joined a Connecticut regiment in 1775, served in the siege of Boston, and was commissioned a captain (1776). He went to New York with William Heath's brigade and is said to have participated in the capture of a provision sloop from under the guns of a British man-of-war. Hale was captured on September 21, 1776, by the British while attempting to return to his regiment, having penetrated the British lines on Long Island to obtain information. He was hanged on Manhattan Island without trial the next day.

JOHN HANCOCK (1737–1793)

John Hancock was a leader of the American Revolutionary effort and the first signer of the U.S. Declaration of Independence.

He was born on January 12, 1737, in Braintree (now Quincy), Massachusetts. After graduating from Harvard (1754), Hancock entered a mercantile house in Boston owned by his uncle Thomas Hancock, who later left him a large fortune. In 1765 he became a selectman of Boston and from 1769 to 1774 was a member of the Massachusetts General Court. He was chairman of the Boston town committee formed immediately after the Boston Massacre in 1770 to demand the removal of British troops from the city.

In 1774 and 1775 Hancock was president of the first and second provincial congresses, and he shared with Samuel Adams the leadership of the Massachusetts Patriots. With Adams he was forced to flee Lexington for Philadelphia when warned in April 1775 that he was being sought by General Thomas Gage's troops, approaching from Boston. Hancock was a member of the Continental Congress from 1775 to 1780; he served as its president from May 1775 to October 1777. He hoped to become commander in chief of the Continental Army, but George Washington was selected instead.

Hancock was a member of the Massachusetts Constitutional Convention of 1780 and in the same year was elected governor of the state. He served in Congress under the Articles of Confederation in 1785–1786 and then returned to the governorship. He presided over the Massachusetts Convention of 1788 that ratified the federal Constitution, although he had been unfriendly at first toward the document. Hancock died on October 8, 1793, in Quincy while serving his ninth term as governor.

A portrait of John Hancock
by John Singleton Copley, c.1912

FRANCIS HOPKINSON (1737–1791)

Francis Hopkinson was a lawyer, musician, and author, who served in the Continental Congress and signed the Declaration of Independence.

Hopkinson, born on October 2, 1737, in Philadelphia, was educated at the College of Philadelphia (later the University of Pennsylvania), graduating in 1757, and also studied law. After a brief business career, he launched a successful legal practice in New

Jersey, being admitted to the bar in 1761. During the 1760s he was secretary of a commission that finalized a treaty between Native Americans and Pennsylvania and served as a customs collector in Salem, New Jersey, and New Castle, Delaware.

In 1774 Hopkinson, who had restarted his law practice in Bordentown, New Jersey, was appointed to the governor's council, and in 1776 he represented New Jersey in the Continental Congress. He signed the Declaration of Independence and later served in several minor offices in the new American government. From 1779 to 1789 he was judge

An undated portrait of Francis Hopkinson.

of the admiralty court for Pennsylvania, and from 1789 to his death he was U.S. district judge for eastern Pennsylvania. An ardent backer of the Constitution, he was a member of the convention that approved it and wrote several effective articles that contributed to its ratification effort in Pennsylvania. From 1789 to 1791 he served as U.S. district court judge in Pennsylvania.

Hopkinson was an accomplished player of the harpsichord and a composer of both religious and secular songs. In addition, he wrote poetry and literary essays. During the Revolution, he ridiculed the British and their loyalist sympathizers with pointed political satires. After the Revolution, he maintained a steady correspondence with Benjamin Franklin, George Washington, and Thomas Jefferson.

Among his varied pursuits, Hopkinson was also an artist. He designed the seal of the American Philosophical Society, the seal for the State of New Jersey, and seals for various departments of the U.S. government. There is strong evidence to support the view that he helped design the American flag; the U.S. Congress, however, turned down his petition for payment, asserting that others had contributed to the design. He died on May 9, 1791, in Philadelphia.

JOHN JAY
(1745–1829)

John Jay served the United States in both law and diplomacy, establishing important judicial precedents as first chief justice of the United States (1789–1795) and negotiating the Jay Treaty of 1794, which settled major grievances with Great Britain and promoted commercial prosperity.

Jay was born on December 12, 1745, in New York City. He graduated from King's College (now Columbia University) in 1764, was admitted to the bar in 1768, and established himself as a successful attorney in New York. He deplored the growing estrangement between the colonies and the mother country, fearing that independence might stir up violence and mob rule. Nevertheless, once the revolution was launched, he became one of its staunchest supporters. As a delegate to the First Continental Congress (1774) in Philadelphia, he drafted *The Address to the People of Great Britain*, stating the claims of colonists. He helped assure the approval of the Declaration of Independence (1776) in New York, where he was a member of the provincial Congress. The following year he helped draft New York's first constitution, was elected the state's first chief justice, and in 1778 was chosen president of the Continental Congress.

In 1779 Jay was appointed minister plenipotentiary to Spain, which had joined France in openly supporting the revolutionaries against Britain. His mission—to borrow money and to gain access to the Mississippi River—proved abortive, and he was sent in May 1782 to join Benjamin Franklin in Paris as joint negotiator for peace with Great Britain. In undercover talks with the British he won surprisingly liberal terms, which were later included essentially intact in the Treaty of Paris (September 3, 1783), which concluded the war.

John Jay in a detail from a lithograph titled *The Chief Justices of the United States*, c. 1894

On his return from abroad, Jay found that Congress had elected him secretary for foreign affairs (1784–1790). Frustrated by the limitations on his powers in that office, he became convinced that the nation needed a more strongly centralized government than was provided for by the Articles of Confederation, and he plunged into the fight for ratification of the new federal Constitution, framed in 1787. Using the pseudonym Publius, he collaborated with Alexander Hamilton and James Madison by writing five essays for *The Federalist*—the classic defense of the new governmental structure. In 1789 President George Washington appointed Jay the country's first chief justice, in which capacity he was instrumental in shaping Supreme Court procedures in its formative years. His most notable case was *Chisholm v. Georgia* (1793), in which Jay and the court affirmed the subordination of the states to the federal government. Unfavorable reaction to the decision led to adoption of the Eleventh Amendment, denying federal courts authority in suits by citizens against a state.

In 1794 Washington sent Jay as a special envoy to Great Britain to help avert war over accumulated grievances. The commercial agreement, called the Jay Treaty (November 19), aroused a storm of protest among the Jeffersonian Republicans, who denounced it as a sellout by pro-British Federalists. Mobs burned Jay in effigy, and opponents denounced him as a traitor. Before the negotiations, Jay at one time had been considered a leading candidate to succeed Washington, but the unpopular treaty ruined whatever chances he had for the presidency. New York Federalists, however, elected him governor (1795–1801), an office from which he retired to spend the remainder of his life on his farm. (In 1800 Jay declined John Adams's offer for reappointment as chief justice.) He died on May 17, 1829, in Bedford, New York.

RUFUS KING (1755–1827)

Rufus King helped frame the federal Constitution and effect its ratification. An active Federalist senator and able diplomat, he ran unsuccessfully for vice president (1804, 1808) and for president (1816).

King was born on March 24, 1755, in Scarborough, Massachusetts. After graduating from Harvard in 1777, he began a career in law, being admitted to the bar in 1780. He served in the state legislature (1783–1784) and in the Continental Congress (1784–1787), where he introduced the resolution

(February 21, 1787) calling for a convention at Philadelphia to draft a new Constitution. An eloquent advocate of a strong central government, he signed the new document and contributed substantially to its acceptance in Massachusetts. In the Continental Congress he introduced a resolution (1785) that would prohibit slavery in the Northwest Territory—a provision included permanently in the Ordinance of 1787, which set the pattern for future standards in the territories.

In 1788 King moved to New York where, after a year in the state assembly, he was elected one of its first U.S. senators (1789–1796) and became a recognized Federalist leader in Congress. Sharing the Anglophile sentiments of his party, King went on to represent the new nation with tact yet firmness as ambassador to Great Britain for eight years (1796–1803) and again in 1825–1826. During the period of domination by the (Jeffersonian) Democratic-Republican Party, King served once more in the Senate (1813–1825) but received only a modest proportion of electoral votes for the nation's highest offices on three different occasions.

He died on April 29, 1827, in Jamaica, New York.

RICHARD HENRY LEE (1732–1794)

Richard Henry Lee was born on January 20, 1732, in Stratford, Virginia. Educated in England at Wakefield Academy, Lee returned to America in 1751 and served as a justice of the peace in Westmoreland country, Virginia. He then served in the Virginia House of Burgesses (1758–1775). He opposed arbitrary British policies at the time of the Stamp Act and the Townshend Acts, and, with Patrick Henry and Thomas Jefferson, he originated a plan for intercolonial committees of correspondence (March 1777).

Lee was an active member of the First Continental Congress, where admirers of his oratory compared him with Cicero. In the Second Continental Congress he introduced three resolutions: (1) for declaring independence; (2) for forming foreign alliances; and (3) for preparing a plan of confederation. His first resolution was adopted on July 2, and the Declaration of Independence followed two days later. He remained active in Congress until forced to resign in 1779 because of poor health. In 1777, 1780, and 1785 he served in the Virginia House of Delegates and in 1784 was back in Congress, where he remained until 1787, acting as its president in 1784. He opposed ratification of the federal Constitution because it created a "consolidated" government and lacked a bill of rights. He served, nonetheless, as senator from Virginia in the first Congress from 1789 to 1792, when he retired from public life. He died on June 19, 1794, in Chantilly, Virginia.

ROBERT R. LIVINGSTON (1746–1813)

Robert R. Livingston was an early American leader who served as a delegate to the Continental Congress, first secretary of the Department of Foreign Affairs (1781–1783), and minister to France (1801–1804).

Born on November 27, 1746, in New York into a wealthy and influential family, Livingston graduated from King's College (now Columbia University) in 1765 and was admitted to the bar in 1770. Devoted to the idea of independence from Britain, he worked on numerous committees of the Continental Congress at Philadelphia (1775–1776, 1779–1781, 1784–1785), especially in the areas of finance and foreign and judicial affairs. He was a member of the committee that drafted the Declaration of Independence, and, after helping to draft New York state's first constitution (1777),

he served as the state's first chancellor, a judicial office (1777–1801).

With the inauguration of the federal government under the Articles of Confederation (1781), Livingston was appointed secretary of the Department of Foreign Affairs, in which post he established vital administrative precedents and organized the conduct of foreign affairs on a businesslike basis. He insisted on greater independence for American delegates to the Paris Peace Conference (1782–1783) but reprimanded them for negotiating without the full concurrence of France.

On April 30, 1789, under the new Constitution, Chancellor Livingston administered the oath of office in New York City to the nation's first president, George Washington. During the 1790s he gradually associated himself with the anti-Federalists and in 1801 was appointed by President Thomas Jefferson to represent the United States in France. In that capacity he rendered his most distinguished service by helping effect the Louisiana Purchase (1803)—one of the country's greatest diplomatic coups.

In retirement Livingston became enthusiastically involved with steam-navigation experiments, and in partnership with the inventor Robert Fulton, he received a steamboat monopoly in New York waters. Their first successful steam vessel, operating on the Hudson River in 1807, was named the *Clermont* after Livingston's ancestral home. He died on February 26. 1813, in Clermont, New York.

ARTHUR MIDDLETON (1742–1787)

Arthur Middleton was a British American planter and legislator who signed the Declaration of Independence and was one of the leaders in the controversies leading up to the American Revolution (1775–1783).

He was born on June 26, 1742, near Charleston, South Carolina. After completing his education in England at various places, including at St. John's College, Cambridge, Middleton returned to South Carolina. In 1765 he became justice of the peace for Berkeley county and also was elected to the colonial legislature, serving 1765–1768 and 1772–1775. In 1775–1776 he was a member of the Council of Safety, a committee that directed leadership for the colony's preparations for revolution. He served on the legislative committee that drafted the South Carolina state constitution and was a delegate to the Continental Congress (1776–1777), where he signed the Declaration of Independence.

At the siege of Charleston (1780) he served in the militia, was taken prisoner when the city fell to the British, and was sent to St. Augustine, Florida, as a prisoner of war. After being exchanged in July 1781, he was a member of the Continental Congress (1781–1782), the South Carolina legislature (1785–1786), and on the original board of trustees of the College of Charleston. He died on January 1, 1787, in Goose Creek, South Carolina.

JAMES MONROE (1758–1831)

James Monroe was the fifth president of the United States (1817–1825). During his presidency, he made an important contribution to U.S. foreign policy in the Monroe Doctrine, a warning to European nations against intervening in the Western Hemisphere. The period of his administration has been called the Era of Good Feelings.

EARLY LIFE AND CAREER

Monroe was born on April 28, 1758, in Westmoreland county, Virginia. His father, Spence Monroe, was of Scottish descent, and his mother, Elizabeth Jones Monroe, of Welsh descent. The family were owners of a modest 600 acres in Virginia. At age 16 Monroe entered the College of William and Mary but in 1776 left to fight in the American Revolution. As a lieutenant he crossed the Delaware with General George Washington for what became the Battle of Trenton. Suffering a near fatal wound in the shoulder, Monroe was carried from the field. Upon recovering, he was promoted to captain for heroism, and he took part in the Battles of Brandywine and Germantown. Advanced to major, he became aide-de-camp to Gen. William Alexander (Lord Stirling) and with him shared the suffering of the troops at Valley Forge in the cruel winter of 1777–1778. Monroe was a scout for Washington at the Battle of Monmouth and served as Lord Stirling's adjutant general.

In 1780, having resigned his commission in the army, he began the study of law under Thomas Jefferson, then governor of Virginia, and between the two men there developed an intimacy and a sympathy that had a powerful influence upon Monroe's later career. Jefferson also fostered a friendship between Monroe and James Madison.

Monroe was elected to the Virginia House of Delegates in 1782 and was chosen a member of the governor's council. From 1783 to 1786 he served in the Congress under the Articles of Confederation, the first constitution of the new nation. During his term he vigorously insisted on the right of the United States to navigate the Mississippi River, then controlled by the Spanish, and attempted, in 1785, to secure for the weak Congress the power to regulate commerce, thereby removing one of the great defects in the existing central government. In 1786 Monroe, 27 years old, and Elizabeth Kortright of New York, 17 years old, were married. They had two daughters, Eliza Kortright and Maria Hester, and a son who died in infancy. Eliza often was at her father's side as official hostess when he was president, substituting for her ailing mother. Maria's marriage to a cousin, Samuel L. Gouverneur, in 1820 was the first wedding performed in the President's House, as the White House was then called.

Retiring from Congress in 1786, Monroe began practicing law at Fredericksburg, Virginia. He was chosen a member of the Virginia House of Delegates in 1787 and in 1788 a member of the state convention at which Virginia ratified the new federal Constitution. In 1790 he was elected to the U.S. Senate, where he vigorously opposed President George Washington's administration; nevertheless, in 1794 Washington nominated him as minister to France.

MINISTER TO FRANCE

It was the hope of the administration that Monroe's well-known French sympathies would secure for him a favorable reception and that his appointment would also conciliate France's friends in the United States.

His warm welcome in France and his enthusiasm for the French Revolution, which he regarded as a natural successor to the American Revolution, displeased the Federalists (the party of Alexander Hamilton, which encouraged close ties not to France but to England) at home.

Monroe did nothing, moreover, to reconcile the French to the Jay Treaty, which regulated commerce and navigation between the United States and Great Britain during the French Revolutionary wars.

Without real justification, the French regarded the treaty as a violation of the French-American treaty of commerce and amity of 1778 and as a possible cause for war. Monroe led the French government to believe that the Jay Treaty would never be ratified by the United States, that the administration of George Washington would be overthrown as a result of the obnoxious treaty, and that better things might be expected after the election in 1796 of a new president, perhaps Thomas Jefferson. Washington, though he did not know of this intrigue, sensed that Monroe was unable to represent his government properly and, late in 1796, recalled him.

Monroe returned to America in the spring of 1797 and in the following December published a defense of his course in a pamphlet of 500 pages entitled *A View of the Conduct of the Executive, in the Foreign Affairs of the United States*. Washington seems never to have forgiven Monroe for this stratagem, though Monroe's opinion of Washington and Jay underwent a change in his later years. In 1799 Monroe was chosen governor of Virginia and was twice reelected, serving until 1802.

THE LOUISIANA PURCHASE

There was much uneasiness in the United States when Spain restored Louisiana to France by the Treaty of San Ildefonso in October 1800 (confirmed March 1801). The Spanish district administrator's subsequent withdrawal of the United States' "right of deposit" at New Orleans—the privilege of storing goods there for later reshipment—greatly increased this feeling and led to much talk of war. Resolved to settle the matter by peaceful measures, President Jefferson in January 1803 appointed Monroe envoy extraordinary and minister plenipotentiary to France to aid Robert R. Livingston, the resident minister, in purchasing the territory at the mouth of the Mississippi—including the island of New Orleans—authorizing him at the same time to cooperate with Charles Pinckney, the minister at Madrid, in securing from Spain the cession of East and West Florida. On April 18 Monroe was further commissioned as the regular minister to Great Britain.

Monroe joined Livingston in Paris on April 12, after the latter's negotiations were well under way, and the two ministers, on finding Napoleon willing to dispose of the entire province of Louisiana, decided to exceed their instructions and effect its purchase. Accordingly, on May 2, 1803, they signed a treaty and two conventions (antedated to April 30) whereby France sold Louisiana to the United States. The fact that Monroe signed the treaty along with Livingston did not hurt his political career at home, but he is not entitled to much credit for the diplomatic achievement.

In July 1803 Monroe left Paris and entered upon his duties in London, and in the autumn of 1804 he proceeded to Madrid to assist Pinckney in his efforts to define the Louisiana boundaries and acquire the Floridas. After negotiating until May 1805 without success, Monroe returned to London and resumed his negotiations concerning the impressment of American seamen and the seizure of American vessels. As the British ministry was reluctant to discuss these vexing questions, little progress was made, and in May 1806 Jefferson ordered William Pinkney of Maryland to assist Monroe.

The result of the deliberations was a treaty signed on December 31, 1806, which contained no provision against impressments and provided no indemnity for the seizure of goods and vessels. Accompanying its signature was a British reservation maintaining freedom of action to retaliate against imminent French maritime decrees. In passing over these matters Monroe and Pinkney had disregarded their instructions, and Jefferson was so displeased with the treaty that he returned it to England for revision.

Monroe returned to the United States in December 1807. He was elected to the Virginia House of Delegates in the spring of 1810. In the following winter he was again chosen governor, serving from January to November 1811, when he resigned to become secretary of state under James Madison, a position he held until March 1817. The direction of foreign affairs in the troubled period immediately preceding and during the War of 1812, with Great Britain, thus fell upon him. On September 27, 1814, after the capture of Washington, D.C., by the British, he was appointed secretary of war and discharged the duties of this office, in addition to those of the Department of State, until March 1815.

THE "principles of President Monroe," as the message was referred to in Congress, consisted of three openly proclaimed dicta: no further European colonization in the New World, abstention of the United States from the political affairs of Europe, and nonintervention of Europe in the governments of the American hemisphere. In the diplomatic correspondence preceding the proclamation of these principles in the president's message was a fourth dictum not publicly associated with the doctrine until 1869: the United States opposed the transfer of any existing European colonies from one European sovereign to another.

PRESIDENCY

In 1816 Monroe was elected president of the United States as the Republican candidate, defeating Rufus King, the Federalist candidate; Monroe received 183 electoral votes and King, 34. By 1820, when he was reelected, receiving all the electoral votes but one, the Federalists had ceased to function as a party. The chief events of his calm and prosperous administration, which has been called the Era of Good Feelings, were the First Seminole War (1817–1818); the acquisition of the Floridas from Spain (1819–1821); the Missouri Compromise (1820), by which the first conflict over slavery under the Constitution was peacefully settled; recognition of the new Latin American states, former Spanish colonies, in Central and South America (1822); and— most intimately connected with Monroe's name—the enunciation, in the presidential message of December 2, 1823, of the Monroe Doctrine, which has profoundly influenced the foreign policy of the United States.

Not until 1848 when James K. Polk was president did the first reference to Monroe's statement as a "Doctrine" appear. The phrase Monroe Doctrine came into common use in the 1850s.

It is generally concluded that Secretary of State John Quincy Adams was the sole author of the noncolonization principle of the doctrine; the principle of abstention from European wars and politics was common to all the fathers of American independence, inherited and expressed by the younger Adams all his professional life; in cabinet meetings, Adams also urged the dictum of nonintervention in the affairs of the nations of the Western Hemisphere. But Adams had no idea of proclaiming these dicta to the world. Monroe took responsibility for embodying them in a presidential message that he drafted himself. Modern historical judgment considers the Monroe Doctrine to be appropriately named.

President Monroe and his wife remained smitten by France after their sojourn there and with their daughters often spoke French together when they were in the White House. Elizabeth Monroe clothed herself in Paris creations and insisted on French etiquette and French cuisine at her table. Given the opportunity to refurnish the executive mansion when it was rebuilt after its destruction in 1814, the Monroes spent lavishly on gilded furniture, silverware, and various objets d'art imported from France. Some items that the president had purchased from impoverished French noble families while he was minister he now lent or sold to the government for use in the President's House at prices some considered suspiciously high, although Monroe was later cleared of impropriety.

The first lady, who was always in fragile health, suffered from an unidentified malady. She was often away from Washington for months at a time visiting her married daughters. To the considerable irritation of Washington society, she discontinued Dolley Madison's practice of paying courtesy calls on Washington hostesses. Still, Elizabeth Monroe was not without ardor; shortly after her arrival in France, during the Reign of Terror, she had helped to rescue Madame Lafayette, wife of the marquis de Lafayette, from prison and perhaps save her from the guillotine.

On the expiration of his second term Monroe retired to his home at Oak Hill, Virginia. In 1826 he became a regent of the University of Virginia and in 1829 was a

AFTER Liberia was created in 1821 as a haven for freed slaves, its capital city was named Monrovia in honor of the American president, who had supported the repatriation of blacks to Africa.

A portrait of James Monroe by Gilbert Stuart, c.1817

member of the convention called to amend the state constitution. Having neglected his private affairs and incurred large expenditures during his missions to Europe and his presidency, he was deeply in debt and felt compelled to ask Congress to reimburse him. In 1826 Congress finally authorized the payment to him of $30,000. Almost immediately, adding additional claims, he went back to Congress seeking more money. Congress paid him another $30,000 in 1831, but he still did not feel satisfied. After his death Congress appropriated a small amount for the purchase of his papers from his heirs. Monroe died on July 4, 1831—like Jefferson and Adams before

him on the Fourth of July—in New York City at the home of his daughter, Maria, with whom he was living after the death of his wife the year before. In 1858, the centennial year of his birth, his remains were reinterred with impressive ceremonies at Richmond, Virginia.

Thomas Jefferson, James Madison, John Quincy Adams, and many other prominent statesmen of Monroe's time all spoke loudly in his praise, but he suffers by comparison with the greater men of his time. Possessing none of their brilliance, he had, nevertheless, to use the words of John Quincy Adams, "a mindsound in its ultimate judgments, and firm in its final conclusions." Some of Monroe's popularity undoubtedly stemmed from the fact that he was the last of the Revolutionary War generation, and he reminded people of those heady times when the struggle for independence was in the balance. Tall and stately in appearance, he still wore the knee britches, silk stockings, and cocked hat of those days, and many of his admirers said that he resembled George Washington.

GOUVERNEUR MORRIS (1752–1816)

Gouverneur Morris was an American statesman, diplomat, and financial expert who helped plan the U.S. decimal coinage system.

Morris was born on January 31, 1752, in Morrisania house in Manhattan, New York. He graduated from King's College (later Columbia University) in 1768, studied law, and was admitted to the bar in 1771. An extreme conservative in his political views, he distrusted the democratic tendencies of colonists who wanted to break with England, but his belief in independence led him to join their ranks. He served in the New York Provincial Congress (1775–1777), where he led a successful fight to include a provision for religious toleration in the first state constitution. He also served as a lieutenant colonel in the New York state militia. He then sat in the Continental Congress (1778–1779) and was a signer of the Articles of Confederation.

Following his defeat for reelection to Congress in 1779, Morris settled in Philadelphia as a lawyer. His series of essays on finance (published in the *Pennsylvania Packet*, 1780) led to his appointment, under the Articles of Confederation, as assistant to the superintendent of finance, Robert Morris (to whom he was not related). During his tenure (1781–1785) he proposed the decimal coinage system that, with some modifications by Thomas Jefferson, forms the basis of the present U.S. monetary system. During the Constitutional Convention (1787), Morris advocated a strong central government, with life tenure for the president and presidential appointment of senators. As a member of the Committee of Style, he was largely responsible for the final wording of the Constitution.

Morris was appointed minister to France in 1792; he openly disapproved of the French Revolution and sought to aid King Louis XVI in fleeing the country. His hostility led the French Revolutionary government to request his recall in 1794. After a brief term in the U.S. Senate (1800–1803), he ended his public career. Unsympathetic to the forces of republicanism, he allied himself with the extreme Federalists, who hoped to create a northern confederation during the War of 1812. From 1810 he was chairman of the commission in charge of the construction of the Erie Canal.

He died on November 6, 1816, in Morrisania house.

ROBERT MORRIS (1734–1806)

Robert Morris was an American merchant and banker who came to be known as the financier of the American Revolution.

Morris was born on January 31, 1734, in Liverpool, England. He left England to join his father in Maryland in 1747 and then entered a mercantile house in Philadelphia. During the war, Morris was vice president

An undated engraving of Robert Morris.

where Lord Cornwallis surrendered (1781). Morris had borrowed from the French, requisitioned from the states, and also advanced money from his own pocket. That same year, in Philadelphia, Morris established the Bank of North America. After the war he served as superintendent of finance under the Articles of Confederation (1781–1784) and then as a member of the Pennsylvania state assembly (1785–1787). He was a delegate to the Constitutional Convention (1787) and served in the U.S. Senate (1789–1795). Meanwhile, he had disposed of his mercantile and banking investments and had plunged heavily into land speculation. When returns from his lands slowed, he fell into bankruptcy and was confined in a debtors' prison for more than three years before his release in 1801. He died on May 8, 1806, in Philadelphia.

of the Pennsylvania Committee of Safety (1775–1776) and was a member of both the Continental Congress (1775–1778) and the Pennsylvania legislature (1778–1779, 1780–1781, 1785–1786). Because he was hoping for reconciliation with Britain, he did not sign the Declaration of Independence until several weeks after its adoption.

As chairman or member of various committees of the Continental Congress, Morris practically controlled the financial operations of the war from 1776 to 1778. He raised the funds that made it possible for Gen. George Washington to move his army from the New York area to Yorktown,

THOMAS PAINE (1737–1809)

Thomas Paine was an English American writer and political pamphleteer whose "Common Sense" and "Crisis" papers were important influences on the American Revolution. Other works that contributed to his reputation as one of the greatest political propagandists in history were *Rights*

A portrait of Thomas Paine by
John Wesley Jarvis, c. 1805.

of Man, a defense of the French Revolution
and of republican principles; and *The Age of
Reason*, an exposition of the place of religion
in society.

LIFE IN ENGLAND AND AMERICA

Paine was born on January 29, 1737, in
Thetford in Norfolk, England, of a Quaker
father and an Anglican mother. His formal
education was meagre, just enough to enable
him to master reading, writing, and arith-

metic. At 13 he began work with his father as
a corset maker and then tried various other
occupations unsuccessfully, finally becoming
an officer of the excise. His duties were to
hunt for smugglers and collect the excise taxes
on liquor and tobacco. The pay was insuffi-
cient to cover living costs, but he used part of
his earnings to purchase books and scientific
apparatus.

Paine's life in England was marked by
repeated failures. He had two brief marriages.
He was unsuccessful or unhappy in every job
he tried. He was dismissed from the excise
office after he published a strong argument in
1772 for a raise in pay as the only way to end
corruption in the service. Just when his situation appeared hopeless, he met Benjamin
Franklin in London, who advised him to seek
his fortune in America and gave him letters
of introduction.

Paine arrived in Philadelphia on November 30, 1774. His first regular employment
was helping to edit the *Pennsylvania Magazine*.
In addition Paine published numerous articles and some poetry, anonymously or under
pseudonyms. One such article was "African
Slavery in America," a scathing denunciation
of the African slave trade, which he signed
"Justice and Humanity."

Paine had arrived in America when the
conflict between the colonists and England
was reaching its height. After blood was

"*THE* American Crisis. Number I," published by Thomas Paine on December 19, 1776, when George Washington's army was on the verge of disintegration, opened with the flaming words: "These are the times that try men's souls." Washington ordered the pamphlet read to all the troops at Valley Forge.

spilled at the Battle of Lexington and Concord, April 19, 1775, Paine argued that the cause of America should not be just a revolt against taxation but a demand for independence.

He put this idea into "Common Sense," which came off the press on January 10, 1776. The 50-page pamphlet sold more than 500,000 copies within a few months. More than any other single publication, "Common Sense" paved the way for the Declaration of Independence, unanimously ratified July 4, 1776.

During the war that followed, Paine served as volunteer aide-de-camp to General Nathanael Greene. His great contribution to the patriot cause was the 16 "Crisis" papers issued between 1776 and 1783, each one signed "Common Sense."

In 1777 Congress appointed Paine secretary to the Committee for Foreign Affairs. He held the post until early in 1779, when he became involved in a controversy with Silas Deane, a member of the Continental Congress, whom Paine accused of seeking to profit personally from French aid to the United States. But in revealing Deane's machinations, Paine was forced to quote from secret documents to which he had access as secretary of the Committee for Foreign Affairs. As a result, despite the truth of his accusations, he was forced to resign his post.

Paine's desperate need of employment was relieved when he was appointed clerk of the General Assembly of Pennsylvania on November 2, 1779. In this capacity he had frequent opportunity to observe that American troops were at the end of their patience because of lack of pay and scarcity of supplies. Paine took $500 from his salary and started a subscription for the relief of the soldiers. In 1781, pursuing the same goal, he accompanied John Laurens to France. The money, clothing, and ammunition they brought back with them were important to the final success of the Revolution. Paine also appealed to the separate states to cooperate for the well-being of the entire nation. In "Public Good" (1780) he included a call for a national convention to remedy the ineffectual Articles of Confederation and establish a strong central government under "a continental constitution."

At the end of the American Revolution, Paine again found himself poverty-stricken. His patriotic writings had sold by the hundreds of thousands, but he had refused to accept any profits in order that cheap editions might be widely circulated. In a petition to Congress endorsed by Washington, he pleaded for financial assistance. It was buried by Paine's opponents in Congress, but Pennsylvania gave him £500 and New York a farm in New Rochelle. Here Paine devoted his time to inventions, concentrating on an iron bridge without piers and a smokeless candle.

IN EUROPE: "RIGHTS OF MAN"

In April 1787 Paine left for Europe to promote his plan to build a single-arch bridge across the wide Schuylkill River near Philadelphia. But in England he was soon diverted from his engineering project. In December 1789 he published anonymously a warning against the attempt of Prime Minister William Pitt to involve England in a war with France over Holland,

WHAT began as a defense of the French Revolution evolved into an analysis of the basic reasons for discontent in European society and a remedy for the evils of arbitrary government, poverty, illiteracy, unemployment, and war. Thomas Paine spoke out effectively in favor of republicanism as against monarchy and went on to outline a plan for popular education, relief of the poor, pensions for aged people, and public works for the unemployed, all to be financed by the levying of a progressive income tax.

reminding the British people that war had "but one thing certain and that is increase of taxes." But it was the French Revolution that now filled Paine's thoughts. He was enraged by Edmund Burke's attack on the uprising of the French people in his

Reflections on the Revolution in France, and, though Paine admired Burke's stand in favor of the American Revolution, he rushed into print with his celebrated answer, *Rights of Man* (March 13, 1791). The book immediately created a sensation. At least eight editions were published in 1791, and the work was quickly reprinted in the U.S., where it was widely distributed by the Jeffersonian societies. When Burke replied, Paine came back with *Rights of Man, Part II*, published on February 17, 1792.

To the ruling class Paine's proposals spelled "bloody revolution," and the government ordered the book banned and the publisher jailed. Paine himself was indicted for treason, and an order went out for his arrest. But he was en route to France, having been elected to a seat in the National Convention, before the order for his arrest could be delivered. Paine was tried in absentia, found guilty of seditious libel, and declared an outlaw, and *Rights of Man* was ordered permanently suppressed.

In France Paine hailed the abolition of the monarchy but deplored the terror against the royalists and fought unsuccessfully to save the life of King Louis XVI, favoring banishment rather than execution. He was to pay for his efforts to save the King's life when the radicals under Robespierre took power. Paine was imprisoned from December 28, 1793,

to November 4, 1794, when, with the fall of Robespierre, he was released and, though seriously ill, readmitted to the National Convention.

While in prison, the first part of Paine's *Age of Reason* was published (1794), and it was followed by Part II after his release (1796). Although Paine made it clear that he believed in a Supreme Being and as a deist opposed only organized religion, the work won him a reputation as an atheist among the orthodox. The publication of his last great pamphlet, "Agrarian Justice" (1797), with its attack on inequalities in property ownership, added to his many enemies in establishment circles.

Paine remained in France until September 1, 1802, when he sailed for the United States. He quickly discovered that his services to the country had been all but forgotten and that he was widely regarded only as the world's greatest infidel. Despite his poverty and his physical condition, worsened by occasional drunkenness, Paine continued his attacks on privilege and religious superstitions. He died in New York City on June 8, 1809, and was buried in New Rochelle on the farm given to him by the state of New York as a reward for his Revolutionary writings. Ten years later, William Cobbett, the political journalist, exhumed the bones and took them to England, where he hoped to give

Paine a funeral worthy of his great contributions to humanity. But the plan misfired, and the bones were lost, never to be recovered.

ASSESSMENT

At Paine's death most U.S. newspapers reprinted the obituary notice from the *New York Citizen*, which read in part: "He had lived long, did some good and much harm." This remained the verdict of history for more than a century following his death, but in recent years the tide has turned: on January 30, 1937, *The Times* of London referred to him as "the English Voltaire," and on May 18, 1952, Paine's bust was placed in the New York University Hall of Fame.

WILLIAM PATERSON (1745–1806)

Irish-born jurist William Paterson was one of the framers of the U.S. Constitution, a U.S. senator (1789–1790), and governor of New Jersey (1790–1793). He also served as an associate justice of the U.S. Supreme Court from 1793 to 1806.

Paterson, born on December 24, 1745, in County Antrim, Ireland, immigrated to America with his family in 1747. They came to Pennsylvania and then eventually settled in Princeton, New Jersey. He graduated in 1763 from the College of New Jersey (now Princeton University), studied law, and began to practice in 1769. He served twice in the provincial congress (1775–1776), was a delegate to the state constitutional convention (1776), and from 1776 to 1783 was attorney general of New Jersey. In 1787 Paterson headed the New Jersey delegation to the federal Constitutional Convention, where he played a leading role in the opposition of the small states to representation according to population in the federal legislature. As an alternative to the Virginia (or large-state) Plan, Paterson submitted the New Jersey (or small-state) Plan, also called the Paterson Plan, which advocated an equal vote for all states. The issue was finally resolved with the compromise embodied in the bicameral Congress—representation by population in the House of Representatives, and equality of states in the Senate.

Paterson was instrumental in securing ratification of the final document in New Jersey and was elected one of the state's first two U.S. senators. Resigning his seat in 1790, he served as governor of New Jersey until 1793, when he was named an associate justice of the U.S. Supreme Court. He died on September 9, 1806, in Albany, New York. The city of Paterson, New Jersey, was named for him.

CHARLES PINCKNEY (1757–1824)

Charles Pinckney was an American political leader and diplomat whose proposals for a new government—called the Pinckney plan—were largely incorporated into the Federal Constitution drawn up in 1787.

He was born on October 26, 1757, in Charleston, South Carolina. During the American Revolution, Pinckney was captured and held prisoner by the British. He was admitted to the bar in 1779 and began a legal practice. Serving in the Continental Congress for three years (1784–1787), he played a leading role in calling a national convention to revise and strengthen the Articles of Confederation.

As a South Carolina delegate to the Constitutional Convention at Philadelphia, he submitted a detailed plan of government, which, although the original draft was not preserved, is known to have contained a number of provisions that were incorporated into the new Constitution. Pinckney possibly had as large a share in determining the style, form, and content of the document as any other individual. At home he supported ratification, presided over the convention that remodeled the South Carolina Constitution in 1790, and as governor (1789–1792) guided the adjustment between the state and federal governments.

Pinckney began his political career as a Federalist but in 1791 transferred his allegiance to the Jeffersonian Republican Party. He served in the state legislature (1792–1796, 1810–1814) and as governor (1796–1798, 1806–1808), U.S. senator (1798–1801), and representative (1819–1821). He supported amendments to the state constitution that gave greater representation to the back country and extended suffrage to all white men. By opposing Federalist policies, especially in 1798, he estranged his two politically active cousins, Charles Cotesworth Pinckney and Thomas Pinckney—favorite-son pillars of South Carolina federalism. His efforts in getting South Carolina's

An 1896 portrait of Charles Pinckney by Charles Balthazar Julien Févret de Saint-Mémin.

electors to vote for Jefferson in 1800 were decisive to the election. Reflecting his Southern background, he bitterly assailed the proposed restrictions on slavery contained in the Missouri Compromise of 1820.

His fidelity to his party was rewarded by appointment as U.S. minister to Spain (1801–1805), where he negotiated an agreement providing for a joint tribunal to settle spoliation claims (arising from the seizure of a ship's papers when confiscated for suspected smuggling, carrying contraband of war, or being an enemy ship) and the restoration to U.S. shippers of the right of deposit (temporary storage of goods) at the port of New Orleans. He also won Spain's reluctant consent to Napoleon's sale of Louisiana to the United States, but failed to achieve the U.S. acquisition of Florida. He died on October 29, 1824, in Charleston.

CHARLES COTESWORTH PINCKNEY (1746–1825)

Charles Cotesworth Pinckney was a soldier, statesman, and diplomat who represented South Carolina at the Constitutional Convention (1787) and who participated

in the XYZ Affair, an unsavory diplomatic incident with France in 1798.

Pinckney was born on February 25, 1746, in Charleston, South Carolina. He entered public service in 1769 as a member of the South Carolina Assembly. He served in the first South Carolina Provincial Congress (1775) and later in both houses of the South Carolina legislature. During the American Revolution he was an aide to General George Washington at Brandywine and Germantown, Pennsylvania (both 1777), and later commanded a regiment at Savannah, Georgia; he was promoted to brigadier general in 1783. He took part in the Constitutional Convention of 1787, along with his cousin Charles Pinckney.

Pinckney was appointed minister to France (1796) but was refused recognition by the French Directory and left Paris for Amsterdam. He returned to Paris the following year as a member of a commission that included John Marshall and Elbridge Gerry. When one of the group of French negotiators (later referred to in the correspondence as "X,Y, and Z") suggested that the U.S. representatives offer a gift, Pinckney is said to have replied, "No! No! Not a sixpence!" No treaty was negotiated, and an undeclared war with France ensued. Upon his return home Pinckney was made a major general. An unsuccessful Federalist candidate for vice president in 1800 and for president in 1804 and 1808, Pinckney spent his later years in law practice. He died on August 16, 1825, in Charleston.

CAESAR RODNEY (1728–1784)

Caesar Rodney was a delegate to the Continental Congress (1774–1776, 1777–1778) and a key signer of the Declaration of Independence.

Rodney was born on October 7, 1728, in Dover, Delaware. Rodney had served as high sheriff of Kent county, Delaware (1755), and as a delegate to the Stamp Act Congress (1765). He served in the Delaware assembly from 1762 to 1769 and from 1769 to 1777 as an associate justice of the Delaware Supreme Court. One of Delaware's three delegates to the Continental Congress, Rodney had been away in Delaware when he got word of the impending vote on the resolution for independence. Hurrying back to Philadelphia on horseback, he arrived in time to break the tie in his delegation and cast Delaware's deciding vote for independence.

In 1777 he was made commander of the Delaware militia with the rank of brigadier general. From 1778 to 1782 he served as

A portrait of Caesar Rodney, 1800.

president of Delaware. In 1783 he was elected to the legislature but died the following year, on June 26, 1784, in Dover.

JOHN RUTLEDGE (1739–1800)

John Rutledge was a delegate to the Constitutional Convention of 1787, where he strongly supported the protection of slavery and the concept of a strong central government, a position then possible, but paradoxical in later times when slavery's defenders sheltered behind the bastion of states' rights.

Rutledge was born in September 1739 in Charleston, South Carolina. After studying in England, Rutledge returned to Charleston to practice law. Reflecting views acceptable to both planters and merchants in his area, he was chosen as a delegate to the Stamp Act Congress (1765) and to the Continental Congress (1774–1777, 1782–1783). After chairing the committee that framed the South Carolina constitution (1776), he was elected president of the state's General Assembly, but he resigned in 1778 when the constitution was amended to include provisions he considered too democratic. In 1779 he was elected South Carolina's governor, and, after the state was invaded by the British in that year, he held the skeleton colonial government together until the end of the war.

At the Constitutional Convention in 1787, Rutledge spoke for Southern planters by supporting slavery. He argued in favor of dividing society into classes as a basis for representation and also postulated high property qualifications for holding office. As chairman of the Committee on Detail, he recommended the granting of indefinite powers of legislation to the national government for the purpose of promoting the general welfare.

From 1789 to 1791 he served as an associate justice of the U.S. Supreme Court and for the next four years as chief justice of the South Carolina Supreme Court. Nominated Chief Justice of the United States in 1795, he failed to win Senate confirmation because of his outspoken opposition to the Jay Treaty of the previous year.

His brother Edward Rutledge was a signer of the Declaration of Independence (1776), fought against the British in South Carolina during the American Revolution, and served in the South Carolina legislature (1782–1798) and as governor (1798–1800) of the state. He died on July 18, 1800, in Charleston.

ROGER SHERMAN (1721–1793)

Roger Sherman was the author of the Connecticut, or Great, Compromise, which helped break the deadlock over representation of small and large states at the U.S. Constitutional Convention of 1787.

Sherman was born on April 19, 1721, in Newton, Massachusetts. After learning shoemaking, he moved to Connecticut in 1743, joining a brother two years after his father had died, and became surveyor of New Haven county. He then studied law and was admitted to the bar in 1754. He

A John Weir portrait of Roger Sherman, c. 1902.

signed the Declaration of Independence and helped draft the Articles of Confederation. From 1777 to 1779 he served on Connecticut's council of safety, and in 1784 he was elected mayor of New Haven.

Sherman's greatest service was rendered at the Constitutional Convention called to remedy the deficiencies of the Articles of Confederation. A critical difference appeared between larger states advocating congressional representation on the basis of population and smaller states desiring equal representation regardless of size. Sherman promoted what came to be known as the Connecticut (or Great) Compromise, providing for a bicameral legislature using a dual system of representation. His plan helped save the convention from disintegrating and established the basis of the present system of federal government.

Sherman served in Congress under the new Constitution, first as a representative (1789–1791) and then as a senator (1791–1793), supporting Alexander Hamilton's program for assumption of state debts, establishment of a national bank, and enactment of a tariff. He died in New Haven on July 23, 1793.

held numerous public offices, including several terms in the Connecticut legislature between 1755 and 1766. In 1755 he became a justice of the peace in Litchfield county and eventually rose to serve as a judge of the superior court, a post he held into the 1780s. Although a staunch conservative, he was an early supporter of American independence from Britain. As a delegate to the Second Continental Congress at Philadelphia, he

JAMES WILSON (1742–1798)

James Wilson was a colonial lawyer and political theorist who signed the Declaration of Independence and was a delegate to the Constitutional Convention of 1787.

Wilson was born on September 14, 1742, in Fife, Scot. Immigrating to North America in 1765, Wilson taught Greek and rhetoric in the College of Philadelphia and then studied law under John Dickinson, statesman and delegate to the First Continental Congress. Wilson's fame spread with publication in 1774 of his treatise *Considerations on the Nature and Extent of the Legislative Authority of the British Parliament*. In this work he set out a scheme of empire in which the British colonies would have the equivalent of dominion status. In 1774 he became a member of the Committee of Correspondence in Cumberland county, Pennsylvania, and he served as a delegate to the Second Continental Congress. In 1779 he was appointed advocate general for France and represented that country in cases rising out of its alliance with the American colonies. He became a champion of the Bank of North America and an associate of merchant-banker Robert Morris in his struggle for currency reform after 1781. As a member of the federal Congress (1783; 1785–1786), he pressed for an amendment to the Articles of Confederation to permit Congress to levy a general tax.

During the Constitutional Convention in 1787, Wilson helped to draft the U.S. Constitution; he then led the fight for ratification in Pennsylvania. In 1790 he engineered the drafting of Pennsylvania's new constitution and delivered a series of lectures that are landmarks in the evolution of American jurisprudence. He was appointed an associate justice of the U.S. Supreme Court (1789–1798), where his most notable decision was that on *Chisholm v. Georgia* (1793). In the winter of 1796–1797 financial ruin brought on by unwise land speculation shattered his health and ended his career. He died on August 21, 1798, in Edenton, North Carolina.

JOHN WITHERSPOON (1723–1794)

John Witherspoon was a Scottish American Presbyterian minister who was the only clergyman to sign the Declaration of Independence.

Witherspoon was born on February 15, 1723, in Gifford, East Lothian, Scotland. After completing his theological studies at the University of Edinburgh (1743), he was called to the parish of Beith in 1745 and in 1757 became pastor at Paisley. A conservative churchman, he frequently involved himself in ecclesiastical controversies, in which he proved himself a keen dialectician and an effective speaker. In 1768 he left Paisley to assume the presidency of the College of New Jersey. He was warmly received by the American Presbyterian Church and contributed significantly to its revitalization and growth. He was a vigorous college president, expanding the curriculum, providing scientific equipment, and working to increase the endowment and enrollment.

From his arrival, Witherspoon was an enthusiast about America, and in the dispute with the mother country he ranged himself uncompromisingly on the side of the colonists. He presided over the Somerset County Committee of Correspondence (1775–1776), was a member of two provincial congresses, and was a delegate to the Continental Congress (1776–1779, 1780–1782), where in 1776 he was a persuasive advocate of adopting a resolution of independence.

Witherspoon wrote extensively on religious and political topics. His works include *Ecclesiastical Characteristics* (1753), *Considerations on the Nature and Extent of the Legislative Authority of the British Parliament* (1774), as well as numerous essays, sermons, and pamphlets.

He died on November 15, 1794, in Tusculum, New Jersey.

OLIVER WOLCOTT (1726–1797)

Oliver Wolcott, born on November 20, 1726, in Windsor, Connecticut, was descended from an old Connecticut family long active in public affairs. He was the son of Roger Wolcott, who was the colonial governor in 1750–1754. Settling in Litchfield county, where he practiced law and was made sheriff (1751), he became a member of the Connecticut council (1771–1786) and a delegate to the Continental Congress in Philadelphia. At the beginning of the Revolution, Wolcott signed the Declaration of Independence, then returned home to raise a state militia, which he commanded in defense of New York City (August 1776). The following year he organized more Connecticut volunteers and took part in the successful campaign against General John Burgoyne. In 1779 he commanded Continental troops during the British invasion of his home state.

Wolcott had been appointed a commissioner for northern Indian affairs in 1775. After the war he helped negotiate the Second Treaty of Fort Stanwix, which redrew the western boundaries of the Six (Iroquois) Nations. He went on to serve as Connecticut's lieutenant governor (1787–1796) and governor (1796–1797), as well as a member of the Connecticut convention that ratified the new federal Constitution.

His son, Oliver Wolcott (1760–1833), continued the family tradition of public service as U.S. secretary of the Treasury (1795–1800) and governor of Connecticut (1817–1827). He died on December 1, 1797, in Litchfield.

GEORGE WYTHE (1726–1806)

George Wythe was one of the first U.S. judges to state the principle that a court can invalidate a law considered to be unconstitutional. He also was probably the first great American law teacher, whose pupils included such well-known figures as Thomas Jefferson, John Marshall, and Henry Clay.

Wythe was born in 1726 in Elizabeth City county, Virginia. Admitted to the bar in 1746, Wythe was a member (1754–1755, 1758–1768) and clerk (1769–1775) of the Virginia House of Burgesses. In 1764 he drew up a forceful remonstrance from Virginia to the British House of Commons against the Stamp Act. In 1776 Wythe, as a delegate to the Continental Congress, signed the Declaration of Independence. Also in that year he was appointed, with Jefferson, Edmund Pendleton, and George Mason, to revise the laws of Virginia. He was a member of the Constitutional Convention (1787) and of the Virginia convention (1788) that ratified the federal Constitution.

A chancery judge from 1778, Wythe became sole chancellor of Virginia in 1788. As an *ex officio* member of the state supreme court, Wythe, in the case of *Commonwealth v. Caton* (1782), asserted the power of courts to refuse to enforce unconstitutional laws.

The future President Jefferson studied law in Wythe's office, at Williamsburg, Virginia, in the 1760s. Appointed through Jefferson's influence, Wythe held (1779–1789), at the College of William and Mary, the first U.S. professorship of law. One of his students there in 1780 was John Marshall, later chief justice of the United States. Wythe's appointment as chancellor of Virginia required him to resign from the college and move to Richmond, where he opened a private school of law. Among his pupils in Richmond, and clerk of his court, was the future U.S. senator Henry Clay.

Wythe died on June 8, 1806, in Richmond, Virginia, of poisoning. A grandnephew and heir, George Wythe Sweeney, was acquitted of the murder in a trial in which the only witness was, as an African American, disqualified from testifying.

CHAPTER 7

FOUNDING DOCUMENTS

THE AMERICAN STORY SHAPED BY THE MEN AND WOMEN profiled in the preceding chapters still lives in the documents that they wrote and the speeches that they gave. Through reading them, we are able to transport ourselves back into the lives of the Founding Fathers by reading the voluminous literature they left behind, from Thomas Paine's "Common Sense" pamphlet, which exerted great influence on the American Revolution, to George Washington's "Farewell Address," which urges the United States to avoid excessive entanglements with foreign nations, to James Monroe's doctrine, which was a cornerstone of American foreign policy into the 20th century.

THOUGH considered by generations of Americans as the ultimate patriots, the Founders were engaging in treasonous behavior, and their words and actions would have resulted in their execution had their endeavours not succeeded. Indeed, at the signing of the Declaration of Independence in Philadelphia in 1776, Ben Franklin recognized this discomfiting thought, advising his fellow delegates that "We must all hang together, or assuredly we shall all hang separately."

Though more than two centuries old, these documents are also very much alive in today's politics, as groups on both sides of the political divide attempt to co-opt them in the political battles that dominate Washington. Although the documents of the Founding Fathers could occupy several volumes on their own, what follows is but a small sample— the Declaration of Independence, which announced America's separation from Great Britain; the Articles of Confederation, the country's first Constitution; the Constitution of the United States, a landmark document in the Western world that is the world's oldest constitution still in force; and Federalist 1 and 10, which helped secure the ratification of the Constitution.

DECLARATION OF INDEPENDENCE

The Declaration of Independence was approved by the Continental Congress on July 4, 1776, and announced the separation of 13 North American British colonies from Great Britain. It explained why the Congress on July 2 "unanimously" by the votes of 12 colonies (with New York abstaining) had resolved that "these United Colonies are, and of right ought to be Free and Independent States." Accordingly, the day on which final separation was officially voted was July 2, although the 4th, the day on which the

Declaration of Independence was adopted, has always been celebrated in the United States as the great national holiday—the Fourth of July, or Independence Day.

TOWARD INDEPENDENCE

On April 19, 1775, when armed conflict began between Britain and the 13 colonies (the nucleus of the future United States), the Americans claimed that they sought only their rights within the British Empire. At that time few of the colonists consciously desired to separate from Britain. As the American Revolution proceeded during 1775–1776 and Britain undertook to assert its sovereignty by means of large armed forces, making only a gesture toward conciliation, the majority of Americans increasingly came to believe that they must secure their rights outside the empire. The losses and restrictions that came from the war greatly widened the breach between the colonies and the mother country; moreover, it was necessary to assert independence in order to secure as much French aid as possible.

On April 12, 1776, the revolutionary convention of North Carolina specifically authorized its delegates in Congress to vote for independence. On May 15 the Virginia convention instructed its deputies to offer the motion, which was brought forward in the Congress by Richard Henry Lee on June 7.

By that time the Congress had already taken long steps toward severing ties with Britain. It had denied Parliamentary sovereignty over the colonies as early as December 6, 1775, and it had declared on May 10, 1776, that the authority of the king ought to be "totally suppressed," advising all the several colonies to establish governments of their own choice.

The passage of Lee's resolution was delayed for several reasons. Some of the delegates had not yet received authorization to vote for separation; a few were opposed to taking the final step; and several men, among them John Dickinson, believed that the formation of a central government, together with attempts to secure foreign aid, should precede it. However, a committee consisting of Thomas Jefferson, John Adams, Benjamin Franklin, Roger Sherman, and Robert R. Livingston was promptly chosen on June 11 to prepare a statement justifying the decision to assert independence, should it be taken. The document was prepared, and on July 1 nine delegations voted for separation, despite warm opposition on the part of Dickinson.

On the following day at the Pennsylvania State House (now Independence Hall) in Philadelphia, with the New York delegation abstaining only because it lacked permission to act, the Lee resolution was voted on and endorsed. (The convention of New York

A 19th-century engraving of the Declaration of Independence committee, showing (from left to right): Benjamin Franklin, Thomas Jefferson, Robert R. Livingston, John Adams, and Roger Sherman.

THE NATURE AND INFLUENCE OF THE DECLARATION OF INDEPENDENCE

The Declaration of Independence was written largely by Jefferson, who had displayed talent as a political philosopher and polemicist in his *A Summary View of the Rights of British America*, published in 1774. At the request of his fellow committee members he wrote the first draft. The members of the committee made a number of merely semantic changes, and they also expanded somewhat the list of charges against the king. The Congress made more substantial changes, deleting a condemnation of the British people, a reference to "Scotch & foreign mercenaries" (there were Scots in the Congress), and a denunciation of the African slave trade (this being offensive to some Southern and New England delegates).

gave its consent on July 9, and the New York delegates voted affirmatively on July 15.) On July 19 the Congress ordered the document to be engrossed as "The Unanimous Declaration of the Thirteen United States of America." It was accordingly put on parchment, probably by Timothy Matlack of Philadelphia. Members of the Congress present on August 2 affixed their signatures to this parchment copy on that day, and others later. The last signer was Thomas McKean of Delaware, whose name was not placed on the document before 1777.

It can be said, as John Adams did, that the declaration contained nothing really novel in its political philosophy, which was derived from John Locke, Algernon Sidney, and other English theorists. It may also be asserted that the argument offered was not without flaws in history and logic. Substantially abandoning contention on the basis of the rights of Englishmen, the declaration put forth the more fundamental doctrines of natural rights and of government under social contract.

Claiming that Parliament never truly possessed sovereignty over the colonies and that the crown of right exercised it only under contract, the declaration contended that George III, with the support of a "pretended" legislature, had persistently violated the agreement between himself as governor and the Americans as the governed. A long list of accusations was offered toward proving this contention. The right and duty of revolution were then invoked.

Few will now claim that government arose among men as Locke and Jefferson said it did, and the social-contract theory has lost vogue among political scientists. It is likewise true, from a British viewpoint, that Parliament and crown could not be separated and that the history of the colonies after 1607 was not entirely consistent with the assertion that Parliament had never as of right possessed sovereignty over them. Furthermore, the specific charges brought against the king were partisan and not uniformly defensible, and the general accusation that he intended to establish an "absolute Despotism" is hardly warranted. It should be added that several of the heaviest specific complaints condemned actions of the British government taken after the beginning of hostilities.

THE Declaration of Independence has also been a source of inspiration outside the United States. It encouraged Antonio de Nariño and Francisco de Miranda to strive toward overthrowing the Spanish empire in South America, and it was quoted with enthusiasm by the Marquis de Mirabeau during the French Revolution. It remains a great historical landmark in that it contained the first formal assertion by a whole people of their right to a government of their own choice. What Locke had contended for as an individual, the Americans proclaimed as a body politic; moreover, they made good the argument by force of arms.

The defects in the Declaration of Independence are not sufficient to force the conclusion that the document is unsound. On the contrary, it was in essence morally just and politically valid. If the right of revolution cannot be established on historical grounds, it nevertheless rests solidly upon ethical ones. The right of the colonists to government ultimately of their own choice is valid. Some of the phrases of the declaration have steadily exerted profound influence in the United States, especially the proclamation that, "We hold these truths to be self-evident, that all men are created equal, that they are endowed by their Creator with certain unalienable Rights, that among these are Life, Liberty and the pursuit of Happiness." Although the meanings of these phrases, together with conclusions drawn from them, have been endlessly debated, the declaration has served to justify the extension of American political and social democracy.

Since 1952 the original parchment document of the Declaration of Independence has resided in the National Archives exhibition hall in Washington, D.C.

Text of the Declaration of Independence

IN CONGRESS, JULY 4, 1776
The Unanimous Declaration of the Thirteen United States of America

When in the Course of human events, it becomes necessary for one people to dissolve the political bands which have connected them with another, and to assume among the powers of the earth, the separate and equal station to which the Laws of Nature and of Nature's God entitle them, a decent respect to the opinions of mankind requires that they should declare the causes which impel them to the separation.

We hold these truths to be self-evident, that all men are created equal, that they are endowed by their Creator with certain unalienable Rights, that among these are Life, Liberty and the pursuit of Happiness.—That to secure these rights, Governments are instituted among Men, deriving their just powers from the consent of the governed,—That whenever any Form of Government becomes destructive of these ends, it is the Right of the People to alter or to abolish it, and to institute new Government, laying its foundation on such principles and organizing its powers in such form, as to them shall seem most likely to effect their Safety and Happiness.

Prudence, indeed, will dictate that Governments long established should not be changed for light and transient causes; and accordingly all experience hath shown, that mankind are more disposed to suffer, while evils are sufferable, than to right themselves by abolishing the forms to which they are accustomed. But when a long train of abuses and usurpations, pursuing invariably the same Object evinces a design to reduce them under absolute Despotism, it is their right, it is their duty, to throw off such Government, and to provide new Guards for their future security.—Such has been the patient sufferance of these Colonies; and such is now the necessity which constrains them to alter their former Systems of Government. The history of the present King of Great Britain is a history of repeated injuries and usurpations, all having in direct object the establishment of an absolute Tyranny over these States.

To prove this, let Facts be submitted to a candid world.

He has refused his Assent to Laws, the most wholesome and necessary for the public good.—He has forbidden his Governors to pass Laws of immediate and pressing importance, unless suspended in their operation till his Assent should be obtained; and when so suspended, he has utterly neglected to attend to them.

He has refused to pass other Laws for the accommodation of large districts of people, unless those people would relinquish the right of Representation in the Legislature, a right inestimable to them and formidable to tyrants only.

He has called together legislative bodies at places unusual, uncomfortable, and distant from the depository of their public Records, for the sole purpose of fatiguing them into compliance with his measures.

He has dissolved Representative Houses repeatedly, for opposing with manly firmness his invasions on the rights of the people.

He has refused for a long time, after such dissolutions, to cause others to be elected; whereby the Legislative powers, incapable of Annihilation, have returned to the People at large for their exercise; the State remaining in the mean time exposed to all the dangers of invasion from without, and convulsions within.

He has endeavored to prevent the population of these States; for that purpose obstructing the Laws for Naturalization of Foreigners; refusing to pass others to encourage their migration hither,and raising the conditions of new Appropriations of Lands.

He has obstructed the Administration of Justice, by refusing his Assent to Laws for establishing Judiciary powers.

He has made judges dependent on his Will alone, for the tenure of their offices, and the amount and payment of their salaries.

He has erected a multitude of New Offices, and sent hither swarms of Officers to harrass our people, and eat out their substance.

He has kept among us, in times of peace, Standing Armies, without the Consent of our legislatures.

He has affected to render the Military independent of and superior to the Civil power.

He has combined with others to subject us to a jurisdiction foreign to our constitution, and unacknowledged by our laws; giving his Assent to their Acts of pretended Legislation:

For quartering large bodies of armed troops among us:

For protecting them, by a mock Trial, from punishment for any Murders which they should commit on the Inhabitants of these States:

For cutting off our Trade with all parts of the world:

For imposing Taxes on us without our Consent:—For depriving us in many cases, of the benefits of Trial by Jury:

For transporting us beyond Seas to be tried for pretended offences:

For abolishing the free System of English Laws in a neighbouring Province, establishing therein an Arbitrary government, and enlarging its Boundaries so as to render it at once an example and fit instrument for introducing the same absolute rule into these Colonies:

For taking away our Charters, abolishing our most valuable Laws, and altering fundamentally the Forms of our Governments:

For suspending our own Legislatures, and declaring themselves invested with power to legislate for us in all cases whatsoever.

He has abdicated Government here, by declaring us out of his Protection and waging War against us.

He has plundered our seas, ravaged our Coasts, burnt our towns, and destroyed the lives of our people.

He is at this time transporting large Armies of foreign Mercenaries to compleat the works of death, desolation and tyranny, already begun with circumstances of Cruelty & perfidy scarcely paralleled in the most barbarous ages, and totally unworthy the Head of a civilized nation.

He has constrained our fellow Citizens taken Captive on the high Seas to bear Arms against their Country, to become the executioners of their friends and Brethren, or to fall themselves by their Hands.

He has excited domestic insurrections amongst us, and has endeavoured to bring on the inhabitants of our frontiers, the merciless Indian Savages, whose known rule of warfare, is an undistinguished destruction of all ages, sexes and conditions.

In every stage of these Oppressions We have Petitioned for Redress in the most humble terms: Our repeated Petitions have been answered only by repeated injury. A Prince, whose character is thus marked by every act which may define a Tyrant, is unfit to be the ruler of a free people.

Nor have We been wanting in attentions to our Brittish brethren. We have warned them from time to time of attempts by their legislature to extend an unwarrantable jurisdiction over us. We have reminded them of the circumstances of our emigration and settlement here.We have appealed to their native justice and magnanimity, and we have conjured them by the ties of our common kindred to disavow these usurpations, which, would inevitably interrupt our connections and correspondence. They too have been deaf to the voice of justice and of consanguinity. We must, therefore, acquiesce in the necessity, which denounces our Separation, and hold them, as we hold the rest of mankind. Enemies in War, in Peace Friends.—

We, therefore, the Representatives of the United States of America, in General Congress, Assembled, appealing to the Supreme Judge of the world for the rectitude of our intentions, do, in the Name, and by Authority of the good People of these Colonies, solemnly publish and declare, That these United Colonies are, and of Right ought to be Free and Independent States; that they are Absolved from all Allegiance to the British Crown, and that all political connection between them and the State of Great Britain, is and ought to be totally dissolved; and that as Free and Independent States, they have full Power to levy War, conclude Peace, contract Alliances, establish Commerce, and to do all other Acts and Things which Independent States may of right do.—And for the support of this Declaration, with a firm reliance on the protection of Divine Providence, we mutually pledge to each other our Lives, our Fortunes and our sacred Honor.

GEORGIA
Button Gwinnett, Lyman Hall, Geo. Walton

NORTH CAROLINA
Wm. Hooper, Joseph Hewes, John Penn

SOUTH CAROLINA
Edward Rutledge, Thos. Heyward, Junr.,
Thomas Lynch, Junr., Arthur Middleton

MARYLAND
Samuel Chase, Wm. Paca, Thos. Stone,
Charles Carroll of Carrollton

VIRGINIA
George Wythe, Richard Henry Lee,
Th. Jefferson, Benja. Harrison, Ths. Nelson, Jr.,
Francis Lightfoot Lee, Carter Braxton

PENNSYLVANIA
Robt. Morris, Benjamin Rush,
Benja. Franklin, John Morton, Geo. Clymer,
Jas. Smith, Geo. Taylor, James Wilson, Geo. Ross

DELAWARE
Caesar Rodney, Geo. Read, Tho. M'Kean

NEW YORK
Wm. Floyd, Phil. Livingston, Frans. Lewis, Lewis Morris

NEW JERSEY
Richd. Stockton, Jno. Witherspoon, Fras. Hopkinson,
John Hart, Abra. Clark

NEW HAMPSHIRE
Josiah Bartlett, Wm. Whipple, Matthew Thornton

MASSACHUSETTS
Saml. Adams, John Adams, Robt. Treat Paine,
Elbridge Gerry

MASSACHUSETTS BAY
John Hancock

RHODE ISLAND
Step. Hopkins, William Ellery

CONNECTICUT
Roger Sherman, Sam'el Huntington, Wm. Williams,
Oliver Wolcott

ARTICLES OF CONFEDERATION

The Articles of Confederation functioned as the first U.S. constitution, in force from 1781 to 1789 and serving as a bridge between the initial government by the Continental Congress of the Revolutionary period and the federal government provided under the U.S. Constitution of 1787. Because the experience of overbearing British central authority was vivid in colonial minds, the drafters of the Articles deliberately established a confederation of sovereign states.

On June 7, 1776, Richard Henry Lee moved that Congress appoint a committee to draw up articles of confederation among the several states—as they would soon be if his resolution for independence was adopted. One member of each state was chosen for this committee, which on July 12 presented a plan of union drafted by John Dickinson of Pennsylvania. Dickinson's plan was much debated, and not until November 15, 1777, was it adopted in greatly revised form. It did not go into effect until March 1, 1781, since the ratification of all the states was required for its adoption.

On paper, the Congress had power to regulate foreign affairs, war, and the postal service and to appoint military officers, control Indian affairs, borrow money, determine the value of coin, and issue bills of credit.

In reality, however, the Articles gave the Congress no power to enforce its requests to the states for money or troops, and by the end of 1786 governmental effectiveness had broken down.

Nevertheless, some solid accomplishments had been achieved: certain state claims to western lands were settled, and the Northwest Ordinance of 1787 established the fundamental pattern of evolving government in the territories north of the Ohio River. Equally important, the Confederation provided the new nation with instructive experience in self-government under a written document. In revealing their own weaknesses, the Articles paved the way for the Constitutional Convention of 1787 and the present form of U.S. government.

Text of the Articles of Confederation

To all to whom these presents shall come, We, the undersigned, Delegates of the States affixed to our names, send greeting: Whereas the Delegates of the United States of America in Congress assembled, did on the fifteenth day of November, in the year of our Lord one thousand seven hundred and seventy-seven, and in the second year of the Independence of America, agree to certain Articles of Confederation and Perpetual Union between the states of New Hampshire, Massachusetts Bay, Rhode Island and Providence Plantations, Connecticut, New York, New Jersey, Pennsylvania, Delaware, Maryland, Virginia, North Carolina, South Carolina, and Georgia, in the words following, viz.

ARTICLES OF CONFEDERATION AND PERPETUAL UNION

between the States of New Hampshire, Massachusetts Bay, Rhode Island and Providence Plantations, Connecticut, New York, New Jersey, Pennsylvania, Delaware, Maryland, Virginia, North Carolina, South Carolina, and Georgia.

ARTICLE I.

The style of this confederacy shall be "The United States of America."

ARTICLE II.

Each state retains its sovereignty, freedom, and independence, and every power, jurisdiction, and right which is not by this confederation expressly delegated to the United States in Congress assembled.

ARTICLE III.

The said states hereby severally enter into a firm league of friendship with each other, for their common defense, the security of their liberties, and their mutual and general welfare, binding themselves to assist each other against all force offered to, or attacks made upon them, or any of them, on account of religion, sovereignty, trade, or any other pretense whatever.

ARTICLE IV.

The better to secure and perpetuate mutual friendship and intercourse among the people of the different states in this union, the free inhabitants of each of these states, paupers, vagabonds, and fugitives from justice excepted, shall be entitled to all privileges and immunities of free citizens in the several states; and the people of each state shall have free ingress and regress to and from any other state and shall enjoy therein all the privileges of trade and commerce, subject to the same duties, impositions, and restrictions as the inhabitants thereof respectively, provided that such restrictions shall not extend so far as to prevent the removal of property imported into any state, to any other state of which the owner is an inhabitant; provided also that no imposition, duties, or restriction shall be laid by any state on the property of the United States, or either of them.

If any person guilty of or charged with treason, felony, or other high misdemeanor in any state shall flee from justice, and be found in any of the United States, he shall, upon demand of the governor or executive power of the state from which he fled, be delivered up and removed to the state having jurisdiction of his offense.

Full faith and credit shall be given in each of these states to the records, acts, and judicial proceedings of the courts and magistrates of every other state.

ARTICLE V.

For the more convenient management of the general interests of the United States, delegates shall be annually appointed in such manner as the legislature of each state shall direct, to meet in Congress on the first Monday in November, in every year, with a power reserved to each state to recall its delegates, or any of them, at any time within the year and to send others in their stead for the remainder of the year.

No state shall be represented in Congress by less than two nor by more than seven members; and no person shall be capable of being a delegate for more than three years in any term of six years; nor shall any person, being a delegate, be capable of holding any office under the United States for which he, or another for his benefit, receives any salary, fees, or emolument of any kind.

Each state shall maintain its own delegates in a meeting of the states and while they act as members of the Committee of the States.

In determining questions in the United States in Congress assembled, each state shall have one vote.

Freedom of speech and debate in Congress shall not be impeached or questioned in any court or place out of Congress, and the members of Congress shall be protected in their persons from arrests and imprisonments during the time of their going to and from, and attendance on, Congress, except for treason, felony, or breach of the peace.

ARTICLE VI.

No state, without the consent of the United States in Congress assembled, shall send any embassy to, or receive any embassy from, or enter into any conference, agreement, alliance, or treaty with any king, prince, or state; nor shall any person holding any office of profit or trust under the United States, or any of them, accept of any present, emolument, office, or title of any kind whatever from any king, prince, or foreign state; nor shall the United States in Congress assembled, or any of them, grant any title of nobility.

No two or more states shall enter into any treaty, confederation, or alliance whatever between them without the consent of the United States in Congress assembled, specifying accurately the purposes for which the same is to be entered into and how long it shall continue.

No state shall lay any imposts or duties which may interfere with any stipulations in treaties entered into by the United States in Congress assembled with any king, prince, or state, in pursuance of any treaties already proposed by Congress, to the courts of France and Spain.

No vessels of war shall be kept up in time of peace by any state except such number only as shall be deemed necessary by the United States in Congress assembled for the defense of such state or its trade; nor shall any body of forces be kept up by any state in time of peace except such number only as in the judgment of the United States in Congress assembled shall be deemed requisite to garrison the forts necessary for the defense of such state; but every state shall always keep up a well-regulated and disciplined militia, sufficiently armed and accoutered, and shall provide and constantly have ready for use, in public stores, a due number of field pieces and tents and a proper quantity of arms, ammunition, and camp equipage.

No state shall engage in any war without the consent of the United States in Congress assembled unless such state be actually invaded by enemies, or shall have received certain advice of a resolution being formed by some nation of Indians to invade such state, and the danger is so imminent as not to admit of a delay till the United States in Congress assembled can be consulted; nor shall any state grant commissions to any ships or vessels of war, nor letters of marque or reprisal, except it be after a declaration of war by the United States in Congress assembled, and then only against the kingdom or state and the subjects thereof against which war has been so declared and under such regulations as shall be established by the United States in Congress assembled, unless such state be infested by pirates, in which case vessels of war may be fitted out for that occasion and kept so long as the danger shall continue or until the United States in Congress assembled shall determine otherwise.

ARTICLE VII.

When land forces are raised by any state for the common defense, all officers of or under the rank of colonel shall be appointed by the legislature of each state respectively, by whom such forces shall be raised, or in such manner as such state shall direct, and all vacancies shall be filled up by the state which first made the appointment.

ARTICLE VIII.

All charges of war and all other expenses that shall be incurred for the common defense or general welfare, and allowed by the United States in Congress assembled, shall be defrayed out of a common treasury, which shall be supplied by the several states in proportion to the value of all land within each state, granted to or surveyed for any person, as such land the buildings and improvements thereon shall be estimated according to such mode as the United States in Congress assembled shall from time to time direct and appoint. The taxes for paying that proportion shall be laid and levied by the authority and direction of the legislatures of the several states within the time agreed upon by the United States in Congress assembled.

ARTICLE IX.

The United States in Congress assembled shall have the sole and exclusive right and power of determining on peace and war, except in the cases mentioned in the sixth article—of sending and receiving ambassadors—entering into treaties and alliances, provided that no treaty of commerce shall be made whereby the legislative power of the respective states shall be restrained from imposing such imposts and duties on foreigners as their own people are subjected to or from prohibiting the exportation or importation of any species of goods or commodities whatsoever—of establishing rules for deciding in all cases what captures on land or water shall be legal, and in what manner prizes taken by land or naval forces in the service of the United States shall be divided or appropriated—of granting letters of marque and reprisal in times of peace—appointing courts for the trial of piracies and felonies committed on the high seas and establishing courts for receiving and determining finally appeals in all cases of captures, provided that no member of Congress shall be appointed a judge of any of the said courts.

The United States in Congress assembled shall also be the last resort on appeal in all disputes and difference now subsisting or that hereafter may arise between two or more states concerning boundary, jurisdiction, or any other cause whatever, which authority shall always be exercised in the manner following: Whenever the legislative or executive authority or lawful agent of any state in controversy with another shall present a petition to Congress stating the matter in question and praying for a hearing, notice thereof shall be given by order of Congress to the legislative or executive authority of the other state in controversy, and a day assigned for the appearance of the parties by their lawful agents, who shall then be directed to appoint, by joint consent, commissioners or judges to constitute a court for hearing and determining the matter in question. But if they cannot agree, Congress shall name three persons out of each of the United States, and from the list of such persons each party shall alternately strike out one, the petitioners beginning, until the number shall be reduced to thirteen. And from that number not less than seven nor more than nine names, as Congress shall direct, shall in the presence of Congress be drawn out by lot, and the persons whose names shall be so drawn, or any five of them, shall be commissioners or judges to hear and finally determine the controversy, so always as a major part of the judges who shall hear the cause shall agree in the determination: and if either party shall neglect to attend at the day appointed, without showing reasons, which Congress shall judge sufficient, or being present shall refuse to strike, the Congress shall proceed to nominate three persons out of each state, and the secretary of Congress shall strike in behalf of such party absent or refusing. ... The judgment and sentence of the court to be appointed, in the manner before prescribed, shall be final and conclusive. ... If any of the parties shall refuse to submit to the authority of such court, or to appear or defend their claim or cause, the court shall nevertheless proceed to pronounce sentence or judgment, which shall in like manner be final and decisive, the judgment or sentence and other proceedings being in either case transmitted to Congress and lodged among the acts of Congress for the security of the parties concerned. Provided that every commissioner, before he sits in judgment, shall take an oath to be administered by one of the judges of the supreme or superior court of the state where the cause shall be tried, "well and truly to hear and determine the matter in question, according to the best of his judgment, without favor, affection, or hope of reward": provided, also, that no state shall be deprived of territory for the benefit of the United States.

All controversies concerning the private right of soil claimed under different grants of two or more states, whose jurisdictions as they may respect such lands, and the states which passed such grants are adjusted, the said grants or either of them being at the same time claimed to have originated antecedent to such settlement of jurisdiction shall, on the petition of either party to the Congress of the United States, be finally determined as near as may be in the same manner as is before prescribed for deciding disputes respecting territorial jurisdiction between different states.

The United States in Congress assembled shall also have the sole and exclusive right and power of regulating the alloy and value of coin struck by their own authority or by that of the respective states—fixing the standard of weights and measures throughout the United States—regulating the trade and managing all affairs with the Indians not members of any of the states, provided that the legislative right of any state within its own limits be not infringed or violated—establishing or regulating post offices from one state to another, throughout all the United States, and exacting such postage on the papers passing through the same as may be requisite to defray the expenses of the said office—appointing all officers of the land forces in the service of the United States excepting regimental officers—appointing all the officers of the naval forces, and commissioning all officers whatever in the service of the United States—making rules for the government and regulation of the said land and naval forces, and directing their operations.

The United States in Congress assembled shall have authority to appoint a committee, to sit in the recess of Congress, to be denominated "A Committee of the States," and to consist of one delegate from each state; and to appoint such other committees and civil officers as may be necessary for managing the general affairs of the United States under their direction—to appoint one of their number to preside, provided that no person be allowed to serve in the office of President more than one year in any term of three years; to ascertain the necessary sums of money to be raised for the service of the United States, and to appropriate and apply the same for defraying the public expenses—to borrow money or emit bills on the credit of the United States, transmitting every half-year to the respective states an account of the sums of money so borrowed or emitted—to build and equip a navy—to agree upon the number of land forces, and to make requisitions from each state for its quota, in proportion to the number of white inhabitants in such state, which requisition shall be binding. ...

Thereupon the legislature of each state shall appoint the regimental officers, raise the men and clothe, arm, and equip them in a soldier-like manner, at the expense of the United States; and the officers and men so clothed, armed, and equipped shall march to the place appointed and within the time agreed on by the United States in Congress assembled. But if the United States in Congress assembled shall, on consideration of circumstances, judge proper that any state should not raise men or should raise a smaller number than its quota and that any other state should raise a greater number of men than the quota thereof, such extra number shall be raised, officered, clothed, armed, and equipped in the same manner as the quota of such state, unless the legislature of such state shall judge that such extra number cannot be safely spared out of the same, in which case they shall raise, officer, clothe, arm, and equip as many of such extra number as they judge can be safely spared. And the officers and men so clothed, armed, and equipped shall march to the place appointed and within the time agreed on by the United States in Congress assembled.

The United States in Congress assembled shall never engage in a war, nor grant letters of marque and reprisal in time of peace, nor enter into any treaties or alliances, nor coin money, nor regulate the value thereof, nor ascertain the sums and expenses necessary for the defense and welfare of the United States, or any of them, nor emit bills, nor borrow money on the credit of the United States, nor appropriate money, nor agree upon the number of vessels of war to be built or purchased or the number of land or sea forces to be raised, nor appoint a commander in chief of the Army or Navy , unless nine states assent to the same; nor shall a question on any other point, except for adjourning from day to day, be determined unless by the votes of a majority of the United States in Congress assembled.

The Congress of the United States shall have power to adjourn to any time within the year, and to any place within the United States, so that no period of adjournment be for a longer duration than the space of six months, and shall publish the journal of their proceedings monthly, except such parts thereof relating to treaties, alliances, or military operations as in their judgment require secrecy; and the yeas and nays of the delegates of each state on any question shall be entered on the journal when it is desired by any delegate; and the delegates of a state, or any of them, at his or their request, shall be furnished with a transcript of the said journal, except such parts as are above excepted, to lay before the legislatures of the several states.

ARTICLE X.

The Committee of the States, or any nine of them, shall be authorized to execute, in the recess of Congress, such of the powers of Congress as the United States in Congress assembled, by the consent of nine states, shall from time to time think expedient to vest them with; provided that no power be delegated to the said committee, for the exercise of which, by the Articles of Confederation, the voice of nine states in the Congress of the United States assembled is requisite.

ARTICLE XI.

Canada acceding to this Confederation, and joining in the measures of the United States, shall be admitted into and entitled to all the advantages of this union; but no other colony shall be admitted into the same unless such admission be agreed to by nine states.

ARTICLE XII.

All bills of credit emitted, moneys borrowed, and debts contracted by or under the authority of Congress, before the assembling of the United States, in pursuance of the present Confederation, shall be deemed and considered as a charge against the United States, for payment and satisfaction whereof the said United States and the public faith are hereby solemnly pledged.

ARTICLE XIII.

Every state shall abide by the determinations of the United States in Congress assembled on all questions which by this Confederation are submitted to them. And the Articles of this Confederation shall be inviolably observed by every state, and the union shall be perpetual; nor shall any alteration at any time hereafter be made in any of them; unless such alteration be agreed to in a Congress of the United States and be afterward confirmed by the legislatures of every state.

And whereas it has pleased the Great Governor of the world to incline the hearts of the legislatures we respectively represent in Congress to approve of, and to authorize us to ratify the said Articles of Confederation and Perpetual Union. Know ye that we the undersigned delegates, by virtue of the power and authority to us given for that purpose, do by these presents, in the name and in behalf of our respective constituents, fully and entirely ratify and confirm each and every of the said Articles of Confederation and Perpetual Union and all and singular the matters and things therein contained. And we do further solemnly plight and engage the faith of our respective constituents that they shall abide by the determinations of the United States in Congress assembled on all questions which by the said Confederation are submitted to them. And that the articles thereof shall be inviolably observed by the states we respectively represent and that the union shall be perpetual. In witness whereof we have hereunto set our hands in Congress.

CONSTITUTION OF THE UNITED STATES OF AMERICA

The U.S. Constitution is a landmark document of the Western world, the oldest written national constitution in use. It created a federal system of government and defines the principal organs of government and their jurisdictions and the basic rights of citizens. The document created in Philadelphia has been amended 27 times since its ratification, and the following essay discusses the Constitution both as it was written and how it has been amended since, as well as how it has been interpreted by the Supreme Court over more than two centuries.

CONSTITUTIONAL CONVENTION

The Constitution was written during the summer of 1787 in Philadelphia, by 55 delegates to a Constitutional Convention that was called ostensibly to amend the Articles of Confederation (1781–1789), the country's first written constitution. The Constitution was the product of political compromise after long and often rancorous debates over issues such as states' rights, representation, and slavery. Delegates from small and large states disagreed over whether the number of representatives in the new federal legislature should be the same for each state—as was the case under the Articles of Confederation—or different depending on a state's population. In addition, some delegates from Northern states sought to abolish slavery or, failing that, to make representation dependent on the size of a state's free population.

At the same time, some Southern delegates threatened to abandon the convention if their demands to keep slavery and the slave trade legal and to count slaves for representation purposes were not met. Eventually the framers resolved their disputes by adopting a proposal put forward by the Connecticut delegation. The Great Compromise, as it came to be known, created a bicameral legislature with a Senate, in which all states would be equally represented, and a House of Representatives, in which representation would be apportioned on the basis of a state's free population plus three-fifths of its slave population. (The inclusion of the slave population was known separately as the three-fifths compromise.) A further compromise on slavery prohibited Congress from banning the importation of slaves until 1808 (Article I, Section 9). After all the disagreements were bridged, the new Constitution was submitted for ratification to the 13 states on September 28, 1787. In 1787–1788, in an effort to persuade New York to ratify the Constitution, Alexander Hamilton, John Jay, and James Madison published a series of essays on the Constitution and republican government in New York newspapers. Their work, written under the pseudonym "Publius" and collected and published in book form as *The Federalist* (1788), became a classic exposition and defense of the Constitution. In June 1788, after the Constitution had been ratified by nine states (as required by Article VII), Congress set March 4, 1789, as the date for the new government to commence proceedings (the first elections under the Constitution were held late in 1788). Because ratification in many states was contingent on the promised addition of a Bill of Rights, Congress proposed 12 amendments in September 1789; 10 were ratified by the states, and their adoption was certified on December 15, 1791.

The authors of the Constitution were heavily influenced by the country's experience under the Articles of Confederation, which had attempted to retain as much independence and sovereignty for the states as possible and to assign to the central government only those nationally important functions that the states could not handle individually. But the events of the years 1781 to 1787, including the national government's inability to act during Shays's Rebellion (1786–1787) in Massachusetts, showed that the Articles were unworkable because they deprived the national government of many essential powers, including direct taxation and the ability to regulate interstate commerce. It was hoped that the new Constitution would remedy this problem.

The framers of the Constitution were especially concerned with limiting the power of government and securing the liberty of citizens. The doctrine of legislative, executive, and judicial separation of powers, the checks and balances of each branch against the others, and the explicit guarantees of individual liberty were all designed

ONE of the original 12 proposed amendments to the Constitution, which prohibited midterm changes in compensation for members of Congress, was ratified in 1992 as the Twenty-seventh Amendment. The last one, concerning the ratio of citizens per member of the House of Representatives, has never been adopted.

to strike a balance between authority and liberty—the central purpose of American constitutional law.

PROVISIONS

The Constitution concisely organizes the country's basic political institutions. The main text comprises seven articles. Article I vests all legislative powers in the Congress—the House of Representatives and the Senate. The Great Compromise stipulated that representation in the House would be based on population, and each state is entitled to two senators. Members of the House serve terms of two years, senators terms of six. Among the powers delegated to Congress are the right to levy taxes, borrow money, regulate interstate commerce, provide for military forces, declare war, and determine member seating and rules of procedure. The House initiates impeachment proceedings, and the Senate adjudicates them.

Article II vests executive power in the office of the presidency of the United States. The president, selected by an electoral college to serve a four-year term, is given responsibilities common to chief executives, including serving as commander in chief of the armed forces, negotiating treaties (two-thirds of the Senate must concur), and granting pardons. The president's vast appointment powers, which include members of the federal judiciary and the cabinet, are subject to the "advice and consent" (majority approval) of the Senate (Article II, Section 2). Originally presidents were eligible for continual reelection, but the Twenty-second Amendment (1951) later prohibited any person from being elected president more than twice. Although the formal powers of the president are constitutionally quite limited and vague in comparison with those of the Congress, a variety of historical and technological factors—such as the centralization of power in the executive branch during war and the advent of television—have increased the informal responsibilities of the office extensively to embrace other aspects of political leadership, including proposing legislation to Congress.

Article III places judicial power in the hands of the courts. The Constitution is interpreted by the courts, and the Supreme Court of the United States is the final court of appeal from the state and lower federal courts. The power of American courts to rule on the constitutionality of laws, known as judicial review, is held by few other courts in the world and is not explicitly granted in the Constitution. The principle of judicial review was first asserted by Supreme Court Chief Justice John Marshall in *Marbury v. Madison* (1803), when the court ruled that it had the authority to void national or state laws.

Beyond the body of judicial rulings interpreting it, the Constitution acquires meaning in a broader sense at the hands of all who use it. Congress on innumerable occasions has given new scope to the document through statutes, such as those creating executive departments, the federal courts, territories, and states; controlling succession to the presidency; and setting up the executive budget system. The chief executive also has contributed to constitutional interpretation, as in the development of the executive agreement as an instrument of foreign policy. Practices outside the letter of the Constitution based on custom and usage are often recognized as constitutional elements; they include the system of political parties, presidential nomination procedures, and the conduct of election campaigns. The presidential cabinet is largely a constitutional "convention" based on custom, and the actual operation of the electoral college system is also a convention.

Article IV deals, in part, with relations between the states and privileges of the citizens of the states. These provisions include the full faith and credit clause, which requires states to recognize the official acts and judicial proceedings of other states; the requirement that each state provide citizens from other states with all the privileges and immunities afforded the citizens of that state; and the guarantee of a republican form of government for each state.

Article V stipulates the procedures for amending the Constitution. Amendments may be proposed by a two-thirds vote of both houses of Congress or by a convention called by Congress on the application of the legislatures of two-thirds of the states. Proposed amendments must be ratified by three-fourths of the state legislatures or by conventions in as many states, depending on the decision of Congress. All subsequent amendments have been proposed by Congress, and all but one—the Twenty-first Amendment, which repealed prohibition—have been ratified by state legislatures.

Article VI, which prohibits religious tests for officeholders, also deals with public debts and the supremacy of the Constitution, citing the document as "the supreme Law of the Land;…any Thing in the Constitution or Laws of any State to the Contrary notwithstanding." Article VII stipulated that the Constitution would become operational after being ratified by nine states.

The national government has only those constitutional powers that are delegated to it either expressly or by implication; the states, unless otherwise restricted, possess all the remaining powers (Tenth Amendment).

Thus, national powers are enumerated (Article I, Section 8, paragraphs 1–17), and state powers are not. The state powers are often called residual, or reserved, powers. The elastic, or necessary and proper, clause (Article I, Section 8, paragraph 18) states that Congress shall have the authority "To make all Laws which shall be necessary and proper for carrying into Execution" the various powers vested in the national government. Thus, it follows that, in addition to the delegated powers, Congress possesses implied powers, a proposition established by Chief Justice Marshall in *McCulloch v. Maryland* (1819). The issue of national versus state power was not fully resolved by this decision, however, and many political battles in American history—including debates on nullification, slavery, racial segregation, and abortion—often have been disputes over constitutional interpretations of implied and residual powers.

Competing concepts of federal supremacy and states' rights were brought into sharp relief in questions about commercial regulation. The commerce clause simply authorized Congress "To regulate Commerce with foreign Nations, and among the several States, and with the Indian Tribes." Particularly since a series of decisions in 1937, the court has interpreted Congress's regulatory power broadly under the commerce clause as new methods of interstate transportation and communication have come into use. States may not regulate any aspect of interstate commerce that Congress has preempted.

CIVIL LIBERTIES AND THE BILL OF RIGHTS

The federal government is obliged by many constitutional provisions to respect the individual citizen's basic rights. Some civil liberties were specified in the original document, notably in the provisions guaranteeing the writ of habeas corpus and trial by jury in criminal cases (Article III, Section 2) and forbidding bills of attainder and ex post facto laws (Article I, Section 9). But the most significant limitations to government's power over the individual were added in 1791 in the Bill of Rights. The Bill of Rights derives from the Magna Carta (1215), the English Bill of Rights (1689), the colonial struggle against king and Parliament, and a gradually broadening concept of equality among the American people. Virginia's 1776 Declaration of Rights, drafted chiefly by George Mason, was a notable forerunner. Besides being axioms of government, the guarantees in the Bill of Rights have binding legal force. Acts of Congress in conflict with them may be voided by the U.S. Supreme Court when

THE Bill of Rights originally protected citizens only from the national government. For example, although the Constitution prohibited the establishment of an official religion at the national level, the official state-supported religion of Massachusetts was Congregationalism until 1833. Thus, individual citizens had to look to state constitutions for protection of their rights against state governments.

the question of the constitutionality of such acts arises in litigation.

The Constitution's First Amendment guarantees the rights of conscience, such as freedom of religion, speech, and the press, and the right of peaceful assembly and petition. Other guarantees in the Bill of Rights require fair procedures for persons accused of a crime—such as protection against unreasonable search and seizure, compulsory self-incrimination, double jeopardy, and excessive bail—and guarantees of a speedy and public trial by a local, impartial jury before an impartial judge and representation by counsel. Rights of private property are also guaranteed. Although the Bill of Rights is a broad expression of individual civil liberties, the ambiguous wording of many of its provisions—such as the Second Amendment's right "to keep and bear arms"

and the Eighth Amendment's prohibition of "cruel and unusual punishments"—has been a source of constitutional controversy and intense political debate. Further, the rights guaranteed are not absolute, and there has been considerable disagreement about the extent to which they limit governmental authority.

THE FOURTEENTH AMENDMENT

After the American Civil War, three new constitutional amendments were adopted: the Thirteenth, which abolished slavery; the Fourteenth, which granted citizenship to former slaves; and the Fifteenth, which guaranteed former male slaves the right to vote. The Fourteenth Amendment placed an important federal limitation on the states by forbidding them to deny to any person "life, liberty, or property, without due process of law" and guaranteeing every person within a state's jurisdiction "the equal protection of its laws." Later interpretations by the Supreme Court in the 20th century gave these two clauses added significance. In *Gitlow v. New York* (1925), the due process clause was interpreted by the Supreme Court to broaden the applicability of the Bill of Rights' protection of speech to the states, holding both levels of government to the same constitutional standard. During subsequent decades, the Supreme Court selectively applied the due process clause to protect other liberties guaranteed in the Bill of Rights, including freedom of religion and the press and guarantees of a fair trial, including the defendant's right to an impartial judge and the assistance of counsel. Most controversial was the Supreme Court's application of this due process clause to the *Roe v. Wade* case, which led to the legalization of abortion in 1973.

The Supreme Court applied the equal protection clause of the Fourteenth Amendment in its landmark decision in *Brown v. Board of Education of Topeka* (1954), in which it ruled that racial segregation in public schools was unconstitutional. In the 1960s and '70s the equal protection clause was used by the Supreme Court to extend protections to other areas, including zoning laws, voting rights, and gender discrimination. The broad interpretation of this clause has also caused considerable controversy.

THE CONSTITUTION AS A LIVING DOCUMENT

Twenty-seven amendments have been added to the Constitution since 1789. In addition to those mentioned above, other far-reaching amendments include the Sixteenth (1913), which allowed Congress to impose an income tax; the Seventeenth (1913), which provided for direct election of senators; the Nineteenth (1920), which mandated woman suffrage; and the Twenty-sixth (1971), which granted suffrage to citizens 18 years of age and older.

In more than two centuries of operation, the United States Constitution has proved itself a dynamic document. It has served as a model for other countries, its provisions being widely imitated in national constitutions throughout the world. Although the Constitution's brevity and ambiguity have sometimes led to serious disputes about its meaning, they also have made it adaptable to changing historical circumstances and ensured its relevance in ages far removed from the one in which it was written.

Text of the Constitution of the United States

We the People of the United States, in Order to form a more perfect Union, establish Justice, insure domestic Tranquility, provide for the common defence, promote the general Welfare, and secure the Blessings of Liberty to ourselves and our Posterity, do ordain and establish this Constitution for the United States of America.

ARTICLE I

Section 1

All legislative Powers herein granted shall be vested in a Congress of the United States, which shall consist of a Senate and House of Representatives.

Section 2

The House of Representatives shall be composed of Members chosen every second Year by the People of the several States, and the Electors in each State shall have the Qualifications requisite for Electors of the most numerous Branch of the State Legislature.

No person shall be a Representative who shall not have attained to the Age of twenty five Years, and been seven Years a Citizen of the United States, and who shall not, when elected, be an Inhabitant of that State in which he shall be chosen.

[Representatives and direct Taxes shall be apportioned among the several States which may be included within this Union, according to their respective Numbers, which shall be determined by adding to the whole Number of free Persons, including those bound to Service for a

Term of Years, and excluding Indians not taxed, three fifths of all other Persons.][1] The actual Enumeration shall be made within three Years after the first Meeting of the Congress of the United States, and within every subsequent Term of ten Years, in such Manner as they shall by Law direct. The Number of Representatives shall not exceed one for every thirty Thousand, but each State shall have at Least one Representative; and until such enumeration shall be made, the State of New Hampshire shall be entitled to chuse three, Massachusetts eight, Rhode-Island and Providence Plantations one, Connecticut five, New-York six, New Jersey four, Pennsylvania eight, Delaware one, Maryland six, Virginia ten, North Carolina five, South Carolina five, and Georgia three.

When vacancies happen in the Representation from any State, the Executive Authority thereof shall issue Writs of Election to fill such Vacancies.

The House of Representatives shall chuse their Speaker and other Officers; and shall have the sole Power of Impeachment.

Section 3

The Senate of the United States shall be composed of two Senators from each State, [chosen by the Legislature thereof,][2] for six Years; and each Senator shall have one Vote.

Immediately after they shall be assembled in Consequence of the first Election, they shall be divided as equally as may be into three Classes. The Seats of the Senators of the first Class shall be vacated at the Expiration of the second Year, of the second Class at the Expiration of the fourth Year, and of the third Class at the Expiration of the sixth Year, so that one third may be chosen every second Year; [and if Vacancies happen by Resignation, or otherwise, during the Recess of the Legislature of any State, the Executive thereof may make temporary Appointments until the next Meeting of the Legislature, which shall then fill such Vacancies].[3]

No Person shall be a Senator who shall not have attained to the Age of thirty Years, and been nine Years a Citizen of the United States, and who shall not, when elected, be an Inhabitant of that State for which he shall be chosen.

The Vice President of the United States shall be President of the Senate, but shall have no Vote, unless they be equally divided.

The Senate shall chuse their other Officers, and also a President pro tempore, in the Absence of the Vice President, or when he shall exercise the Office of President of the United States.

The Senate shall have the sole Power to try all Impeachments. When sitting for that Purpose, they shall be on Oath or Affirmation. When the President of the United States is tried, the Chief Justice shall preside: And no Person shall be convicted without the Concurrence of two thirds of the Members present.

Judgment in Cases of Impeachment shall not extend further than to removal from Office, and disqualification to hold and enjoy any Office of honor, Trust or Profit under the United States: but the Party convicted shall nevertheless be liable and subject to Indictment, Trial, Judgment and Punishment, according to Law.

Section 4

The Times, Places and Manner of holding Elections for Senators and Representatives, shall be prescribed in each State by the Legislature thereof; but the Congress may at any time by Law make or alter such Regulations, except as to the Places of chusing Senators.

The Congress shall assemble at least once in every Year, and such Meeting shall [be on the first Monday in December,]⁴ unless they shall by Law appoint a different Day.

Section 5

Each House shall be the Judge of the Elections, Returns and Qualifications of its own Members, and a Majority of each shall constitute a Quorum to do Business; but a smaller Number may adjourn from day to day, and may be authorized to compel the Attendance of absent Members, in such Manner, and under such Penalties as each House may provide.

Each House may determine the Rules of its Proceedings, punish its Members for disorderly Behaviour, and, with the Concurrence of two thirds, expel a Member.

Each House shall keep a Journal of its Proceedings, and from time to time publish the same, excepting such Parts as may in their Judgment require Secrecy; and the Yeas and Nays of the Members of either House on any question shall, at the Desire of one fifth of those Present, be entered on the Journal.

Neither House, during the Session of Congress, shall, without the Consent of the other, adjourn for more than three days, nor to any other Place than that in which the two Houses shall be sitting.

Section 6

The Senators and Representatives shall receive a Compensation for their Services, to be ascertained by Law, and paid out of the Treasury of the United States. They shall in all Cases, except Treason, Felony and Breach of the Peace, be privileged from Arrest during their Attendance at the Session of their respective Houses, and in going to and returning from the same; and for any Speech or Debate in either House, they shall not be questioned in any other Place.

No Senator or Representative shall, during the Time for which he was elected, be appointed to any civil Office under the Authority of the United States, which shall have been created, or the Emoluments whereof shall have been encreased during such time; and no Person holding any Office under the United States, shall be a Member of either House during his Continuance in Office.

Section 7

All Bills for raising Revenue shall originate in the House of Representatives; but the Senate may propose or concur with Amendments as on other Bills.

Every Bill which shall have passed the House of Representatives and the Senate, shall, before it become a Law, be presented to the President of the United States; If he approve he shall sign it, but if not he shall return it, with his Objections to that House in which it shall have originated, who shall enter the Objections at large on their Journal, and proceed to reconsider it. If after such Reconsideration two thirds of that House shall agree to pass the Bill, it shall be sent, together with the Objections, to the other House, by which it shall likewise be reconsidered, and if approved by two thirds of that House, it shall become a Law. But in all such Cases the Votes of both Houses shall be determined by yeas and Nays, and the Names of the Persons voting for and against the Bill shall be entered on the Journal of each House respectively. If any Bill shall not be returned by the President within ten Days (Sundays excepted) after it shall have been presented to him, the Same shall be a Law, in like Manner as if he had signed it, unless the Congress by their Adjournment prevent its Return, in which Case it shall not be a Law.

Every Order, Resolution, or Vote to which the Concurrence of the Senate and House of Representatives may be necessary (except on a question of Adjournment) shall be presented to the President of the United States; and before the Same shall take Effect, shall be approved by him, or being disapproved by him, shall be repassed by two thirds of the Senate and House of Representatives, according to the Rules and Limitations prescribed in the Case of a Bill.

Section 8

The Congress shall have Power To lay and collect Taxes, Duties, Imposts and Excises, to pay the Debts and provide for the common Defence and general Welfare of the United States; but all Duties, Imposts and Excises shall be uniform throughout the United States;

To borrow Money on the credit of the United States;

To regulate Commerce with foreign Nations, and among the several States, and with the Indian Tribes;

To establish an uniform Rule of Naturalization, and uniform Laws on the subject of Bankruptcies throughout the United States;

To coin Money, regulate the Value thereof, and of foreign Coin, and fix the Standard of Weights and Measures;

To provide for the Punishment of counterfeiting the Securities and current Coin of the United States;

To establish Post Offices and post Roads;

To promote the Progress of Science and useful Arts, by securing for limited Times to Authors and Inventors the exclusive Right to their respective Writings and Discoveries;

To constitute Tribunals inferior to the supreme Court;

To define and punish Piracies and Felonies committed on the high Seas, and Offences against the Law of Nations;

To declare War, grant Letters of Marque and Reprisal, and make Rules concerning Captures on Land and Water;

To raise and support Armies, but no Appropriation of Money to that Use shall be for a longer Term than two Years;

To provide and maintain a Navy;

To make Rules for the Government and Regulation of the land and naval Forces;

To provide for calling forth the Militia to execute the Laws of the Union, suppress Insurrections and repel Invasions;

To provide for organizing, arming, and disciplining, the Militia, and for governing such Part of them as may be employed in the Service of the United States, reserving to the States respectively, the Appointment of the Officers, and the Authority of training the Militia according to the discipline prescribed by Congress;

To exercise exclusive Legislation in all Cases whatsoever, over such District (not exceeding ten Miles square) as may, by Cession of particular States, and the Acceptance of Congress, become the Seat of the Government of the United States, and to exercise like Authority over all Places purchased by the Consent of the Legislature of the State in which the Same shall be, for the Erection of Forts, Magazines, Arsenals, dock-Yards, and other needful Buildings;—And

To make all Laws which shall be necessary and proper for carrying into Execution the foregoing Powers, and all other Powers vested by this Constitution in the Government of the United States, or in any Department or Officer thereof.

Section 9

The Migration or Importation of such Persons as any of the States now existing shall think proper to admit, shall not be prohibited by the Congress prior to the Year one thousand eight hundred and eight, but a Tax or duty may be imposed on such Importation, not exceeding ten dollars for each Person.

The Privilege of the Writ of Habeas Corpus shall not be suspended, unless when in Cases of Rebellion or Invasion the public Safety may require it.

No Bill of Attainder or ex post facto Law shall be passed.

No Capitation, or other direct, Tax shall be laid, unless in Proportion to the Census or Enumeration herein before directed to be taken.[5]

No Tax or Duty shall be laid on Articles exported from any State.

No Preference shall be given by any Regulation of Commerce or Revenue to the Ports of one State over those of another: nor shall Vessels bound to, or from, one State, be obliged to enter, clear, or pay Duties in another.

No Money shall be drawn from the Treasury, but in Consequence of Appropria-tions made by Law; and a regular Statement and Account of the Receipts and Expenditures of all public Money shall be published from time to time.

No Title of Nobility shall be granted by the United States: And no Person holding any Office of Profit or Trust under them, shall, without the Consent of the Congress, accept of any present, Emolument, Office, or Title, of any kind whatever, from any King, Prince, or foreign State.

Section 10

No State shall enter into any Treaty, Alliance, or Confederation; grant Letters of Marque and Reprisal; coin Money; emit Bills of Credit; make any Thing but gold and silver Coin a Tender in Payment of Debts; pass any Bill of Attainder, ex post facto Law, or Law impairing the Obligation of Contracts, or grant any Title of Nobility.

No State shall, without the Consent of the Congress, lay any Imposts or Duties on Imports or Exports, except what may be absolutely necessary for executing it's inspection Laws: and the net Produce of all Duties and Imposts, laid by any State on Imports or Exports, shall be for the Use of the Treasury of the United States; and all such Laws shall be subject to the Revision and Controul of the Congress.

No State shall, without the Consent of Congress, lay any Duty of Tonnage, keep Troops, or Ships of War in time of Peace, enter into any Agreement or Compact with another State, or with a foreign Power, or engage in War, unless actually invaded, or in such imminent Danger as will not admit of delay.

ARTICLE II

Section I

The executive Power shall be vested in a President of the United States of America. He shall hold his Office during the Term of four Years, and, together with the Vice President, chosen for the same Term, be elected, as follows

Each State shall appoint, in such Manner as the Legislature thereof may direct, a Number of Electors, equal to the whole Number of Senators and Representatives to which the State may be entitled in the Congress: but no Senator or Representative, or Person holding an Office of Trust or Profit under the United States, shall be appointed an Elector.

[The Electors shall meet in their respective States, and vote by Ballot for two Persons, of whom one at least shall not be an Inhabitant of the same State with themselves. And they shall make a List of all the Persons voted for, and of the Number of Votes for each; which List they shall sign and certify, and transmit sealed to the Seat of the Government of the United States, directed to the President of the Senate. The President of the Senate shall, in the Presence of the Senate and House of Representatives, open all the Certificates, and the Votes shall then be counted. The Person having the greatest Number of Votes shall be the President, if such Number be a Majority of the whole Number of Electors appointed; and if there be more than one who have such Majority, and have an equal Number of Votes, then the House of Representatives shall immediately chuse by Ballot one of them for President; and if no Person have a Majority, then from the five highest on the List the said House shall in like Manner chuse the President. But in chusing the President, the Votes shall be taken by States, the Representation from each State having one Vote; A quorum for this Purpose shall consist of a Member or Members from two thirds of the States, and a Majority of all the States shall be necessary to a Choice. In every Case, after the Choice of the President, the Person having the greatest Number of Votes of the Electors shall be the Vice PresidSent. But if there should remain two or more who have equal Votes, the Senate shall chuse from them by Ballot the Vice President.][6]

The Congress may determine the Time of chusing the Electors, and the Day on which they shall give their Votes; which Day shall be the same throughout the United States.

No Person except a natural born Citizen, or a Citizen of the United States, at the time of the Adoption of this Constitution, shall be eligible to the Office of President; neither shall any Person be eligible to that Office who shall not have attained to the Age of thirty five Years, and been fourteen Years a Resident within the United States.

In Case of the Removal of the President from Office, or of his Death, Resignation, or Inability to discharge the Powers and Duties of the said Office,[7] the Same shall devolve on the Vice President, and the Congress may by Law provide for the Case of Removal, Death, Resignation or Inability, both of the President and Vice President, declaring what Officer shall then act as President, and such Officer shall act accordingly, until the Disability be removed, or a President shall be elected.

The President shall, at stated Times, receive for his Services, a Compensation, which shall neither be encreased nor diminished during the Period for which he shall have been elected, and he shall not receive within that Period any other Emolument from the United States, or any of them.

Before he enter on the Execution of his Office, he shall take the following Oath or Affirmation:—"I do solemnly swear (or affirm) that I will faithfully execute the Office of President of the United States, and will to the best of my Ability, preserve, protect and defend the Constitution of the United States."

Section 2

The President shall be Commander in Chief of the Army and Navy of the United States, and of the Militia of the several States, when called into the actual Service of the United States; he may require the Opinion, in writing, of the principal Officer in each of the executive

Departments, upon any Subject relating to the Duties of their respective Offices, and he shall have Power to grant Reprieves and Pardons for Offences against the United States, except in Cases of Impeachment.

He shall have Power, by and with the Advice and Consent of the Senate, to make Treaties, provided two thirds of the Senators present concur; and he shall nominate, and by and with the Advice and Consent of the Senate, shall appoint Ambassadors, other public Ministers and Consuls, Judges of the supreme Court, and all other Officers of the United States, whose Appointments are not herein otherwise provided for, and which shall be established by Law: but the Congress may by Law vest the Appointment of such inferior Officers, as they think proper, in the President alone, in the Courts of Law, or in the Heads of Departments.

The President shall have Power to fill up all Vacancies that may happen during the Recess of the Senate, by granting Commissions which shall expire at the End of their next Session.

Section 3

He shall from time to time give to the Congress Information of the State of the Union, and recommend to their Consideration such Measures as he shall judge necessary and expedient; he may, on extraordinary Occasions, convene both Houses, or either of them, and in Case of Disagreement between them, with Respect to the Time of Adjournment, he may adjourn them to such Time as he shall think proper; he shall receive Ambassadors and other public Ministers; he shall take Care that the Laws be faithfully executed, and shall Commission all the Officers of the United States.

Section 4

The President, Vice President and all civil Officers of the United States, shall be removed from Office on Impeachment for, and Conviction of, Treason, Bribery, or other high Crimes and Misdemeanors.

ARTICLE III

Section 1

The judicial Power of the United States, shall be vested in one supreme Court, and in such inferior Courts as the Congress may from time to time ordain and establish. The Judges, both of the supreme and inferior Courts, shall hold their Offices during good Behaviour, and shall, at stated Times, receive for their Services, a Compensation, which shall not be diminished during their Continuance in Office.

Section 2

The judicial Power shall extend to all Cases, in Law and Equity, arising under this Constitution, the Laws of the United States, and Treaties made, or which shall be made, under their Authority;—to all Cases affecting Ambassadors, other public Ministers and Consuls;—to all Cases of admiralty and maritime Jurisdiction;—to Controversies to which the United States shall be a Party;—to Controversies between two or more States;—between a State and Citizens of another State;[8]—between Citizens of different States,—between Citizens of the same State claiming Lands under Grants of different States, and between a State, or the Citizens thereof, and foreign States, Citizens or Subjects.

In all Cases affecting Ambassadors, other public Ministers and Consuls, and those in which a State shall be Party, the supreme Court shall have original Jurisdiction. In all the other Cases before mentioned, the supreme Court shall have appellate Jurisdiction, both as to Law and Fact, with such Exceptions, and under such Regulations as the Congress shall make.

The Trial of all Crimes, except in Cases of Impeachment, shall be by Jury; and such Trial shall be held in the State where the said Crimes shall have been committed; but when not committed within any State, the Trial shall be at such Place or Places as the Congress may by Law have directed.

Section 3

Treason against the United States, shall consist only in levying War against them, or in adhering to their Enemies, giving them Aid and Comfort. No Person shall be convicted of Treason unless on the Testimony of two Witnesses to the same overt Act, or on Confession in open Court.

The Congress shall have Power to declare the Punishment of Treason, but no Attainder of Treason shall work Corruption of Blood, or Forfeiture except during the Life of the Person attainted.

ARTICLE IV

Section 1

Full Faith and Credit shall be given in each State to the public Acts, Records, and judicial Proceedings of every other State. And the Congress may by general Laws prescribe the Manner in which such Acts, Records and Proceedings shall be proved, and the Effect thereof.

Section 2

The Citizens of each State shall be entitled to all Privileges and Immunities of Citizens in the several States.

A Person charged in any State with Treason, Felony, or other Crime, who shall flee from Justice, and be found in another State, shall on Demand of the executive Authority of the State from which he fled, be delivered up, to be removed to the State having Jurisdiction of the Crime.

[No Person held to Service or Labour in one State, under the Laws thereof, escaping into another, shall, in Consequence of any Law or Regulation therein, be discharged from such Service or Labour, but shall be delivered up on Claim of the Party to whom such Service or Labour may be due.][9]

Section 3

New States may be admitted by the Congress into this Union; but no new State shall be formed or erected within the Jurisdiction of any other State; nor any State be formed by the Junction of two or more States, or Parts of States, without the Consent of the Legislatures of the States concerned as well as of the Congress.

The Congress shall have Power to dispose of and make all needful Rules and Regulations respecting the Territory or other Property belonging to the United States; and nothing in this Constitution shall be so construed as to Prejudice any Claims of the United States, or of any particular State.

Section 4

The United States shall guarantee to every State in this Union a Republican Form of Government, and shall protect each of them against Invasion; and on Application of the Legislature, or of the Executive (when the Legislature cannot be convened) against domestic Violence.

ARTICLE V

The Congress, whenever two thirds of both Houses shall deem it necessary, shall propose Amendments to this Constitution, or, on the Application of the Legislatures of two thirds of the several States, shall call a Convention for proposing Amendments, which, in either Case, shall be valid to all Intents and Purposes, as Part of this Constitution, when ratified by the Legislatures of three fourths of the several States, or by Conventions in three fourths thereof, as the one or the other Mode of Ratification may be proposed by the Congress; Provided [that no Amendment which may be made prior to the Year One thousand eight hundred and eight shall in any Manner affect the first and fourth Clauses in the Ninth Section of the first Article; and][10] that no State, without its Consent, shall be deprived of its equal Suffrage in the Senate.

ARTICLE VI

All Debts contracted and Engagements entered into, before the Adoption of this Constitution, shall be as valid against the United States under this Constitution, as under the Confederation.

This Constitution, and the Laws of the United States which shall be made in Pursuance thereof; and all Treaties made, or which shall be made, under the Authority of the United States, shall be the supreme Law of the Land; and the Judges in every State shall be bound thereby, any Thing in the Constitution or Laws of any State to the Contrary notwithstanding.

The Senators and Representatives before mentioned, and the Members of the several State Legislatures, and all executive and judicial Officers, both of the United States and of the several States, shall be bound by Oath or Affirmation, to support this Constitution; but no religious Test shall ever be required as a Qualification to any Office or public Trust under the United States.

ARTICLE VII

The Ratification of the Conventions of nine States, shall be sufficient for the Establishment of this Constitution between the States so ratifying the Same.

Done in Convention by the Unanimous Consent of the States present the Seventeenth Day of September in the Year of our Lord one thousand seven hundred and Eighty seven and of the Independence of the United States of America the Twelfth

IN WITNESS whereof We have hereunto subscribed our Names,

Go. Washington—Presidt. and deputy from Virginia

NEW HAMPSHIRE
John Langdon, Nicholas Gilman

MASSACHUSETTS
Nathaniel Gorham, Rufus King

CONNECTICUT
Wm. Saml. Johnson, Roger Sherman

NEW YORK
Alexander Hamilton

NEW JERSEY
Wil: Livingston, David Brearley, Wm. Paterson,
Jona: Dayton

PENNSYLVANIA
B Franklin, Thomas Mifflin, Robt Morris, Geo. Clymer,
Thos. FitzSimons, Jared Ingersoll, James Wilson, Gouv Morris

DELAWARE
Geo: Read, Gunning Bedford jun, John Dickinson,
Richard Bassett, Jaco: Broom

MARYLAND
James McHenry, Dan of St Thos. Jenifer, Danl Carroll

VIRGINIA
John Blair, James Madison Jr.

NORTH CAROLINA

Wm. Blount, Rich'd Dobbs Spaight, Hu Williamson

SOUTH CAROLINA

J. Rutledge, Charles Cotesworth Pinckney, Charles Pinckney, Pierce Butler

GEORGIA

William Few, Abr Baldwin

ATTEST:

William Jackson, Secretary

AMENDMENTS TO THE CONSTITUTION

Articles in addition to, and amendment of, The Constitution of the United States of America, proposed by Congress, and ratified by the legislatures of the several states pursuant to the fifth article of the original Constitution.

The first 10 amendments to the Constitution were proposed by the Congress on September 25, 1789. They were ratified by the following states, and the notifications of the ratification by the governors thereof were successively communicated by the President to the Congress: New Jersey, November 20, 1789; Maryland, December 19, 1789; North Carolina, December 22, 1789; South Carolina, January 19, 1790; New Hampshire, January 25, 1790; Delaware, January 28, 1790; New York, February 4, 1790; Pennsylvania, March 10, 1790; Rhode Island, June 7, 1790; Vermont, November 3, 1791; and Virginia, December 15, 1791. Ratification was completed on December 15, 1791.

The amendments were subsequently ratified by Massachusetts, March 2, 1939; Georgia, March 18, 1939; and Connecticut, April 19, 1939.

Two other amendments were concurrently proposed in 1789. One failed of ratification. The other (Amendment XXVII) was not ratified until May 7, 1992, when the Michigan legislature gave it the required number of state approvals.

AMENDMENT I

Congress shall make no law respecting an establishment of religion, or prohibiting the free exercise thereof; or abridging the freedom of speech, or of the press; or the right of the people peaceably to assemble, and to petition the Government for a redress of grievances.[11]

AMENDMENT II

A well regulated Militia, being necessary to the security of a free State, the right of the people to keep and bear Arms, shall not be infringed.

AMENDMENT III

No Soldier shall, in time of peace be quartered in any house, without the consent of the Owner, nor in time of war, but in a manner to be prescribed by law.

AMENDMENT IV

The right of the people to be secure in their persons, houses, papers, and effects, against unreasonable searches and seizures, shall not be violated, and no Warrants shall issue, but upon probable cause, supported by Oath or affirmation, and particularly describing the place to be searched, and the persons or things to be seized.

AMENDMENT V

No person shall be held to answer for a capital, or otherwise infamous crime, unless on a presentment or indictment of a Grand Jury, except in cases arising in the land or naval forces, or in the Militia, when in actual service in time of War or public danger; nor shall any person be subject for the same offence to be twice put in jeopardy of life or limb; nor shall be compelled in any criminal case to be a witness against himself, nor be deprived of life, liberty, or property, without due process of law; nor shall private property be taken for public use without just compensation.

AMENDMENT VI

In all criminal prosecutions, the accused shall enjoy the right to a speedy and public trial, by an impartial jury of the State and district wherein the crime shall have been committed, which district shall have been previously ascertained by law, and to be informed of the nature and cause of the accusation; to be confronted with the witnesses against him; to have compulsory process for obtaining Witnesses in his favor, and to have the assistance of counsel for his defence.

AMENDMENT VII

In Suits at common law, where the value in controversy shall exceed twenty dollars, the right of trial by jury shall be preserved, and no fact tried by a jury, shall be otherwise reexamined in any Court of the United States, than according to the rules of the common law.

AMENDMENT VIII

Excessive bail shall not be required, nor excessive fines imposed, nor cruel and unusual punishments inflicted.

AMENDMENT IX

The enumeration in the Constitution, of certain rights, shall not be construed to deny or disparage others retained by the people.

AMENDMENT X

The powers not delegated to the United States by the Constitution, nor prohibited by it to the States, are reserved to the States respectively, or to the people.

AMENDMENT XI [1795]

The Judicial power of the United States shall not be construed to extend to any suit in law or equity, commenced or prosecuted against one of the

United States by Citizens of another State, or by Citizens or Subjects of any Foreign State.

AMENDMENT XII [1804]

The electors shall meet in their respective states and vote by ballot for President and Vice President, one of whom, at least, shall not be an inhabitant of the same state with themselves; they shall name in their ballots the person voted for as President, and in distinct ballots the person voted for as Vice President, and they shall make distinct lists of all persons voted for as President, and of all persons voted for as Vice President, and of the number of votes for each, which lists they shall sign and certify, and transmit sealed to the seat of the government of the United States, directed to the President of the Senate;—The President of the Senate shall, in the presence of the Senate and House of Representatives, open all the certificates and the votes shall then be counted;—The person having the greatest number of votes for President, shall be the President, if such number be a majority of the whole number of Electors appointed; and if no person have such majority, then from the persons having the highest numbers not exceeding three on the list of those voted for as President, the House of Representatives shall choose immediately, by ballot, the President. But in choosing the President, the votes shall be taken by states, the representation from each state having one vote; a quorum for this purpose shall consist of a member or members from two-thirds of the states, and a majority of all the states shall be necessary to a choice. [And if the House of Representatives shall not choose a President whenever the right of choice shall devolve upon them, before the fourth day of March next following, then the Vice President shall act as President, as in the case of the death or other constitutional disability of the President.][12] The person having the greatest number of votes as Vice President, shall be the Vice President, if such number be a majority of the whole number of Electors appointed, and if no person have a majority, then from the two highest numbers on the list, the Senate shall choose the Vice President; a quorum for the purpose shall consist of two-thirds of the whole number of Senators, and a majority of the whole number shall be necessary to a choice. But no person constitutionally ineligible to the office of President shall be eligible to that of Vice President of the United States.

AMENDMENT XIII [1865]

Section 1

Neither slavery nor involuntary servitude, except as a punishment for crime whereof the party shall have been duly convicted, shall exist within the United States, or any place subject to their jurisdiction.

Section 2

Congress shall have power to enforce this article by appropriate legislation.

AMENDMENT XIV [1868]

Section 1

All persons born or naturalized in the United States, and subject to the jurisdiction thereof, are citizens of the United States and of the State wherein they reside. No State shall make or enforce any law which shall abridge the privileges or immunities of citizens of the United States; nor shall any State deprive any person of life, liberty, or property, without due process of law; nor deny to any person within its jurisdiction the equal protection of the laws.

Section 2

Representatives shall be apportioned among the several States according to their respective numbers, counting the whole number of persons in each State, excluding Indians not taxed. But when the right to vote at any election for the choice of electors for President and Vice President of the United States, Representatives in Congress, the Executive and Judicial officers of a State, or the members of the Legislature thereof, is denied to any of the male inhabitants of such State, being twenty-one years of age,[13] and citizens of the United States, or in any way abridged, except for participation in rebellion, or other crime, the basis of representation therein shall be reduced in the proportion which the number of such male citizens shall bear to the whole number of male citizens twenty-one years of age in such State.

Section 3

No person shall be a Senator or Representative in Congress, or elector of President and Vice President, or hold any office, civil or military, under the United States, or under any State, who, having previously taken an oath, as a member of Congress, or as an officer of the United States, or as a member of any State legislature, or as an executive or judicial officer of any State, to support the Constitution of the United States, shall have engaged in insurrection or rebellion against the same, or given aid or comfort to the enemies thereof. But Congress may by a vote of two-thirds of each House, remove such disability.

Section 4

The validity of the public debt of the United States, authorized by law, including debts incurred for payment of pensions and bounties for services in suppressing insurrection or rebellion, shall not be questioned. But neither the United States nor any State shall assume or pay any debt or obligation incurred in aid of insurrection or rebellion against the

United States, or any claim for the loss or emancipation of any slave; but all such debts, obligations and claims shall be held illegal and void.

Section 5

The Congress shall have power to enforce, by appropriate legislation, the provisions of this article.

AMENDMENT XV [1870]

Section 1

The right of citizens of the United States to vote shall not be denied or abridged by the United States or by any State on account of race, color, or previous condition of servitude.

Section 2

The Congress shall have power to enforce this article by appropriate legislation.

AMENDMENT XVI [1913]

The Congress shall have power to lay and collect taxes on incomes, from whatever source derived, without apportionment among the several States, and without regard to any census or enumeration.

AMENDMENT XVII [1913]

The Senate of the United States shall be composed of two Senators from each State, elected by the people thereof, for six years; and each Senator shall have one vote. The electors in each State shall have the qualifications requisite for electors of the most numerous branch of the State legislatures.

When vacancies happen in the representation of any State in the Senate, the executive authority of such State shall issue writs of election to fill such vacancies: *Provided,* That the legislature of any State may empower the executive thereof to make temporary appointments until the people fill the vacancies by election as the legislature may direct.

This amendment shall not be so construed as to affect the election or term of any Senator chosen before it becomes valid as part of the Constitution.

AMENDMENT XVIII [1919] [14]

Section 1

After one year from the ratification of this article the manufacture, sale, or transportation of intoxicating liquors within, the importation thereof into, or the exportation thereof from the United States and all territory subject to the jurisdiction thereof for beverage purposes is hereby prohibited.

Section 2

The Congress and the several States shall have concurrent power to enforce this article by appropriate legislation.

Section 3

This article shall be inoperative unless it shall have been ratified as an amendment to the Constitution by the legislatures of the several States, as provided in the Constitution, within seven years from the date of the submission hereof to the States by the Congress.

AMENDMENT XIX [1920]

The right of citizens of the United States to vote shall not be denied or abridged by the United States or by any State on account of sex.

Congress shall have power to enforce this article by appropriate legislation.

AMENDMENT XX [1933]

Section 1

The terms of the President and Vice President shall end at noon on the 20th day of January, and the terms of Senators and Representatives at noon on the 3d day of January, of the years in which such terms would have ended if this article had not been ratified; and the terms of their successors shall then begin.

Section 2

The Congress shall assemble at least once in every year, and such meeting shall begin at noon on the 3d day of January, unless they shall by law appoint a different day.

Section 3—XV

If, at the time fixed for the beginning of the term of the President, the President elect shall have died, the Vice President elect shall become President. If a President shall not have been chosen before the time fixed for the beginning of his term, or if the President elect shall have failed to qualify, then the Vice President elect shall act as President until a President shall have qualified; and the Congress may by law provide for the case wherein neither a President elect nor a Vice President elect shall have qualified, declaring who shall then act as President, or the manner in which one who is to act shall be selected, and such person shall act accordingly until a President or Vice President shall have qualified.

Section 4

The Congress may by law provide for the case of the death of any of the persons from whom the House of Representatives may choose a President whenever the right of choice shall have devolved upon them, and for the case of the death of any of the persons from whom the Senate may choose a Vice President whenever the right of choice shall have devolved upon them.

Section 5

Sections 1 and 2 shall take effect on the 15th day of October following the ratification of this article.

Section 6

This article shall be inoperative unless it shall have been ratified as an amendment to the Constitution by the legislatures of three-fourths of the several States within seven years from the date of its submission.

AMENDMENT XXI [1933]

Section 1

The eighteenth article of amendment to the Constitution of the United States is hereby repealed.

Section 2

The transportation or importation into any State, Territory, or possession of the United States for delivery or use therein of intoxicating liquors, in violation of the laws thereof, is hereby prohibited.

Section 3

This article shall be inoperative unless it shall have been ratified as an amendment to the Constitution by conventions in the several States, as provided in the Constitution, within seven years from the date of the submission hereof to the States by the Congress.

AMENDMENT XXII [1951]

Section 1

No person shall be elected to the office of the President more than twice, and no person who has held the office of President, or acted as President, for more than two years of a term to which some other person was elected President shall be elected to the office of the President more than once. But this Article shall not apply to any person holding the office of President when this Article was proposed by the Congress, and shall not prevent any person who may be holding the office of President, or acting as President, during the term within which this Article becomes operative from holding the office of President or acting as President during the remainder of such term.

Section 2

This article shall be inoperative unless it shall have been ratified as an amendment to the Constitution by the legislatures of three-fourths of the several States within seven years from the date of its submission to the States by the Congress.

AMENDMENT XXIII [1961]

Section 1

The District constituting the seat of Government of the United States shall appoint in such manner as the Congress may direct:

A number of electors of President and Vice President equal to the whole number of Senators and Representatives in Congress to which the District would be entitled if it were a State, but in no event more than the least populous State; they shall be in addition to those appointed by the States, but they shall be considered, for the purposes of the election of President and Vice President, to be electors appointed by a State; and they shall meet in the District and perform such duties as provided by the twelfth article of amendment.

Section 2

The Congress shall have power to enforce this article by appropriate legislation.

AMENDMENT XXIV [1964]

Section 1

The right of citizens of the United States to vote in any primary or other election for President or Vice President, for electors for President or Vice President, or for Senator or Representative in Congress, shall not be denied or abridged by the United States or any State by reason of failure to pay any poll tax or other tax.

Section 2

The Congress shall have power to enforce this article by appropriate legislation.

AMENDMENT XXV [1967]

Section 1

In case of the removal of the President from office or of his death or resignation, the Vice President shall become President.

Section 2

Whenever there is a vacancy in the office of the Vice President, the President shall nominate a Vice President who shall take office upon confirmation by a majority vote of both Houses of Congress.

Section 3

Whenever the President transmits to the President pro tempore of the Senate and the Speaker of the House of Representatives his written declaration that he is unable to discharge the powers and duties of his office, and until he transmits to them a written declaration to the contrary, such powers and duties shall be discharged by the Vice President as Acting President.

Section 4

Whenever the Vice President and a majority of either the principal officers of the executive departments or of such other body as Congress may by law provide, transmit to the President pro tempore of the Senate and the Speaker of the House of Representatives their written declaration that the President is unable to discharge the powers and duties of his office, the Vice President shall immediately assume the powers and duties of the office as Acting President.

Thereafter, when the President transmits to the President pro tempore of the Senate and the Speaker of the House of Representatives his written declaration that no inability exists, he shall resume the powers and duties of his office unless the Vice President and a majority of either the principal officers of the executive department or of such other body as Congress may by law provide, transmit within four days to the President pro tempore of the Senate and the Speaker of the House of Representatives their written declaration that the President is unable to discharge the powers and duties of his office. Thereupon Congress shall decide the issue, assembling within forty-eight hours for that purpose if not in session. If the Congress, within twenty-one days after receipt of the latter written declaration, or, if Congress is not in session, within twenty-one days after Congress is required to assemble, determines by two-thirds vote of both Houses that the President is unable to discharge the powers and duties of his office, the Vice President shall continue to discharge the same as Acting President; otherwise, the President shall resume the powers and duties of his office.

AMENDMENT XXVI [1971]

Section 1

The right of citizens of the United States, who are eighteen years of age or older, to vote shall not be denied or abridged by the United States or by any State on account of age.

Section 2

The Congress shall have power to enforce this article by appropriate legislation.

AMENDMENT XXVII [1992]

No law, varying the compensation for the services of the Senators and Representatives, shall take effect, until an election of Representatives shall have intervened.

NOTES

[1] The part included in brackets was changed by section 2 of the 14th amendment.

[2] The part included in brackets was changed by section 1 of the 17th amendment.

[3] The part included in brackets was changed by clause 2 of the 17th amendment.

[4] The part included in brackets was changed by section 2 of the 20th amendment.

[5] See also the 16th amendment.

[6] This paragraph has been superseded by the 12th amendment.

[7] This provision has been affected by the 25th amendment.

[8] This clause has been affected by the 11th amendment.

[9] This paragraph has been superseded by the 13th amendment.

[10] Obsolete.

[11] Only Amendments XIII, XIV, XV, and XVI had numbers assigned to them at the time of ratification.

[12] The part included in brackets has been superseded by section 3 of Amendment XX.

[13] See Amendment XXVI.

[14] Repealed by section 1 of Amendment XXI.

[15] See Amendment XXV.

FEDERALIST PAPERS

The Federalist papers, formally known as *The Federalist*, were a series of 85 essays on the proposed new Constitution of the United States and on the nature of republican government, published between 1787 and 1788 by Alexander Hamilton, James Madison, and John Jay in an effort to persuade New York state voters to support ratification. Seventy-seven of the essays first appeared serially in New York newspapers, were reprinted in most other states, and were published in book form as *The Federalist* on May 28, 1788; the remaining eight papers appeared in New York newspapers between June 14 and August 16.

The authors of the Federalist papers presented a masterly defense of the new federal system and of the major departments in the proposed central government. They also argued that the existing government under the Articles of Confederation, the country's first constitution, was defective and that the proposed Constitution would remedy its weaknesses without endangering the liberties of the people.

As a general treatise on republican government, the Federalist papers are distinguished for their comprehensive analysis of the means by which the ideals of justice, the general welfare, and the rights of individuals could be realized. The authors assumed that the primary political motive of man was self-interest and that men—whether acting individually or collectively—were selfish and only imperfectly rational. The establishment of a republican form of government would not of itself provide protection against such characteristics: the representatives of the people might betray their trust; one segment of the population might oppress another; and both the representatives and the public might give way to passion or caprice. The possibility of good government, they argued, lay in man's capacity to devise political institutions that would compensate for deficiencies in both reason and virtue in the ordinary conduct of politics. This theme was predominant in late 18th-century political thought in America and accounts in part for the elaborate system of checks and balances that was devised in the Constitution.

In one of the most notable essays, "Federalist 10," Madison rejected the then common belief that republican government was possible only for small states. He argued that stability, liberty, and justice were more likely to be achieved in a large area with a numerous and heterogeneous population. Although frequently interpreted as an attack on majority rule, the essay is in reality a defense of both social, economic, and cultural pluralism and of a composite majority formed by compromise and conciliation. Decision by such a majority, rather than by a monistic one, would be more likely to accord with the proper ends of government. This distinction between a proper and an improper majority typifies the fundamental philosophy of the Federalist papers; republican institutions, including the principle of majority rule, were not considered good in themselves but were good because they constituted the best means for the pursuit of justice and the preservation of liberty.

All the papers appeared over the signature "Publius," and the authorship of some of the papers was once a matter of scholarly dispute. However, computer analysis and historical evidence has led nearly all historians to assign authorship in the following manner: Hamilton wrote numbers 1, 6–9, 11–13, 15–17, 21–36, 59–61, and 65–85; Madison, numbers 10, 14, 18–20, 37–58, and 62–63; and Jay, numbers 2–5 and 64.

Text of Federalist No. 1
(ALEXANDER HAMILTON)

After an unequivocal experience of the inefficiency of the subsisting federal government, you are called upon to deliberate on a new Constitution for the United States of America. The subject speaks its own importance; comprehending in its consequences nothing less than the existence of the Union, the safety and welfare of the parts of which it is composed, the fate of an empire in many respects the most interesting in the world. It has been frequently remarked that it seems to have been reserved to the people of this country, by their conduct and example, to decide the important question, whether societies of men are really capable or not of establishing good government from reflection and choice, or whether they are forever destined to depend for their political constitutions on accident and force. If there be any truth in the remark, the crisis at which we are arrived may with propriety be regarded as the era in which that decision is to be made;

and a wrong election of the part we shall act may, in this view, deserve to be considered as the general misfortune of mankind.

This idea will add the inducements of philanthropy to those of patriotism, to heighten the solicitude which all considerate and good men must feel for the event. Happy will it be if our choice should be directed by a judicious estimate of our true interests, unperplexed and unbiased by considerations not connected with the public good. But this is a thing more ardently to be wished than seriously to be expected. The plan offered to our deliberations affects too many particular interests, innovates upon too many local institutions, not to involve in its discussion a variety of objects foreign to its merits, and of views, passions, and prejudices little favorable to the discovery of truth.

Among the most formidable of the obstacles which the new Constitution will have to encounter may readily be distinguished the obvious interest of a certain class of men in every state to resist all changes which may hazard a diminution of the power, emolument, and consequence of the offices they hold under the state establishments; and the perverted ambition of another class of men who will either hope to aggrandize themselves by the confusions of their country or will flatter themselves with fairer prospects of elevation from the subdivision of the empire into several partial confederacies than from its union under one government.

It is not, however, my design to dwell upon observations of this nature. I am well aware that it would be disingenuous to resolve indiscriminately the opposition of any set of men (merely because their situations might subject them to suspicion) into interested or ambitious views. Candor will oblige us to admit that even such men may be actuated by upright intentions; and it cannot be doubted that much of the opposition which has made its appearance, or may hereafter make its appearance, will spring from sources, blameless at least, if not respectable—the honest errors of minds led astray by preconceived jealousies and fears.

So numerous, indeed, and so powerful are the causes which serve to give a false bias to the judgment that we, upon many occasions, see wise and good men on the wrong as well as on the right side of questions of the first magnitude to society. This circumstance, if duly attended to, would furnish a lesson of moderation to those who are ever so much persuaded of their being in the right in any controversy. And a further reason for caution, in this respect, might be drawn from the reflection that we are not always sure that those who advocate the truth are influenced by purer principles than their antagonists. Ambition, avarice, personal animosity, party opposition, and many other motives not more laudable than these, are apt to operate as well upon those who support as those who oppose the right side of a question. Were there not even these inducements to moderation, nothing could be more ill judged than that intolerant spirit which has, at all times, characterized political parties. For in politics, as in religion, it is equally absurd to aim at making proselytes by fire and sword. Heresies in either can rarely be cured by persecution.

And yet, however just these sentiments will be allowed to be, we have already sufficient indications that it will happen in this as in all former cases of great national discussion. A torrent of angry and malignant passions will be let loose. To judge from the conduct of the opposite parties, we shall be led to conclude that they will mutually hope to evince the justness of their opinions, and to increase the number of their converts by the loudness of their declamations and the bitterness of their invectives. An enlightened zeal for the energy and efficiency of government will be stigmatized as the offspring of a temper fond of despotic power and hostile to the principles of liberty.

An overscrupulous jealousy of danger to the rights of the people, which is more commonly the fault of the head than of the heart, will be represented as mere pretense and artifice, the stale bait for popularity at the expense of public good. It will be forgotten, on the one hand, that jealousy is the usual concomitant of love, and that the noble enthusiasm of liberty is apt to be infected with a spirit of narrow and illiberal distrust. On the other hand, it will be equally forgotten that the vigor of government is essential to the security of liberty; that, in the contemplation of a sound and well-informed judgment, their interest can never be separated; and that a dangerous ambition more often lurks behind the specious mask of zeal for the rights of the people than under the forbidding appearance of zeal for the firmness and efficiency of government. History will teach us that the former has been found a much more certain road to the introduction of despotism than the latter, and that of those men who have over-turned the liberties of republics, the greatest number have begun their career by paying an obsequious court to the people, commencing demagogues and ending tyrants.

In the course of the preceding observations, I have had an eye, my fellow citizens, to putting you upon your guard against all attempts, from whatever quarter, to influence your decision in a matter of the utmost moment to your welfare, by any impressions other than those which may result from the evidence of truth. You will, no doubt, at the same time, have collected from the general scope of them that they proceed from a source not unfriendly to the new Constitution. Yes, my countrymen, I own to you that, after having given it an attentive consideration, I am clearly of opinion it is your interest to adopt it. I am convinced that this is the safest course for your liberty, your dignity, and your happiness. I affect not reserves which I do not feel. I will not amuse you with an appearance of deliberation when I have decided. I frankly acknowledge to you my convictions, and I will freely lay before you the reasons on which they are founded. The consciousness of good intentions disdains ambiguity. I shall not, however, multiply professions on this head. My motives must remain in the depository of my own breast. My arguments will be open to all, and may be judged of by all. They shall at least be offered in a spirit which will not disgrace the cause of truth.

I propose, in a series of papers, to discuss the following interesting particulars: *the utility of the Union to your political prosperity; the insufficiency of the present Confederation to preserve that Union; the necessity of a government at least equally energetic with the one proposed, to the attainment of this object; the conformity of the proposed Constitution to the true principles of republican government; its analogy to your own state constitution; and, lastly, the additional security which its adoption will afford to the preservation of that species of government, to liberty, and to property.*

In the progress of this discussion I shall endeavor to give a satisfactory answer to all the objections, which shall have made their appearance, that may seem to have any claim to your attention.

It may perhaps be thought superfluous to offer arguments to prove the utility of the Union, a point, no doubt, deeply engraved on the hearts of the great body of the people in every state, and one which, it may be imagined, has no adversaries. But the fact is that we already hear it whispered in the private circles of those who oppose the new Constitution that the thirteen states are of too great extent for any general system, and that we must of necessity resort to separate confederacies of distinct portions of the whole. This doctrine will, in all probability, be gradually propagated, till it has votaries enough to countenance an open avowal of it. For nothing can be more evident, to those who are able to take an enlarged view of the subject, than the alternative of an adoption of the new Constitution or a dismemberment of the Union.

Text of Federalist No. 10

(JAMES MADISON)

Among the numerous advantages promised by a well-constructed Union, none deserves to be more accurately developed than its tendency to break and control the violence of faction. The friend of popular governments never finds himself so much alarmed for their character and fate as when he contemplates their propensity to this dangerous vice. He will not fail, therefore, to set a due value on any plan which, without violating the principles to which he is attached, provides a proper cure for it. The instability, injustice, and confusion introduced into the public councils have, in truth, been the mortal diseases under which popular governments have everywhere perished; as they continue to be the favorite and fruitful topics from which the adversaries to liberty derive their most specious declamations.

The valuable improvements made by the American constitutions on the popular models, both ancient and modern, cannot certainly be too much admired; but it would be an unwarrantable partiality to contend that they have as effectually obviated the danger on this side, as was wished and expected. Complaints are everywhere heard from our most considerate and virtuous citizens, equally the friends of public and private faith, and of public and personal liberty, that our governments are too unstable, that the public good is disregarded in the conflicts of rival parties, and that measures are too often decided, not according to the rules of justice and the rights of the minor party, but by the superior force of an interested and overbearing majority. However anxiously we may wish that these complaints had no foundation, the evidence of known facts will not permit us to deny that they are in some degree true.

It will be found, indeed, on a candid review of our situation, that some of the distresses under which we labor have been erroneously charged on the operation of our governments; but it will be found, at the same time, that other causes will not alone account for many of our heaviest misfortunes; and, particularly, for that prevailing and increasing distrust of public engagements, and alarm for private rights, which are echoed from one end of the continent to the other. These must be chiefly, if not wholly, effects of the unsteadiness and injustice with which a factious spirit has tainted our public administrations.

By a faction, I understand a number of citizens, whether amounting to a majority or minority of the whole, who are united and actuated by some common impulse of passion, or of interest, adverse to the rights of other citizens, or to the permanent and aggregate interests of the community.

There are two methods of curing the mischiefs of faction: the one, by removing its causes; the other, by controlling its effects.

There are again two methods of removing the causes of faction: the one, by destroying the liberty which is essential to its existence; the other, by giving to every citizen the same opinions, the same passions, and the same interests.

It could never be more truly said than of the first remedy that it was worse than the disease. Liberty is to faction what air is to fire, an aliment without which it instantly expires. But it could not be less folly to abolish liberty, which is essential to political life, because it nourishes faction, than it would be to wish the annihilation of air, which is essential to animal life, because it imparts to fire its destructive agency.

The second expedient is as impracticable as the first would be unwise. As long as the reason of man continues fallible, and he is at liberty to exercise it, different opinions will be formed. As long as the connection subsists between his reason and his self-love, his opinions and his passions will have a reciprocal influence on each other; and the former will be objects to which the latter will attach themselves. The diversity in the faculties of men, from which the rights of property originate, is not less an insuperable obstacle to a uniformity of interests. The protection of these faculties is the first object of government. From the protection of different and unequal faculties of acquiring property, the possession of different degrees and kinds of property immediately results; and from the influence of these on the sentiments and views of the respective proprietors ensues a division of the society into different interests and parties.

The latent causes of faction are thus sown in the nature of man; and we see them everywhere brought into different degrees of activity, according to the different circumstances of civil society. A zeal for different opinions concerning religion, concerning government, and many other points, as well of speculation as of practice; an attachment of different leaders ambitiously contending for preeminence and power; or to persons of other descriptions whose fortunes have been interesting to the human passions, have, in turn, divided mankind into parties, inflamed them with mutual animosity, and rendered them much more disposed to vex and oppress each other than to cooperate for their common good. So strong is this propensity of mankind to fall into mutual animosities that, where no substantial occasion presents itself, the most frivolous and fanciful distinctions have been sufficient to kindle their unfriendly passions and excite their most violent conflicts. But the most common and durable source of factions has been the various and unequal distribution of property.

Those who hold and those who are without property have ever formed distinct interests in society. Those who are creditors and those who are debtors fall under a like discrimination. A landed interest, a manufacturing interest, a mercantile interest, a moneyed interest, with many lesser interests, grow up of necessity in civilized nations and divide them into different classes, actuated by different sentiments and views. The regulation of these various and interfering interests forms the principal task of modern legislation and involves the spirit of party and faction in the necessary and ordinary operations of the government.

No man is allowed to be a judge in his own cause, because his interest would certainly bias his judgment and, not improbably, corrupt his integrity. With equal, nay, with greater reason, a body of men are unfit to be both judges and parties at the same time; yet what are many of the most important acts of legislation but so many judicial determinations, not indeed concerning the rights of single persons, but concerning the rights of large bodies of citizens? And what are the different classes of legislators but advocates and parties to the causes which they determine? Is a law proposed concerning private debts? It is a question to which the creditors are parties on one side and the debtors on the other. Justice ought to hold the balance between them. Yet the parties are, and must be, themselves the judges; and the most numerous party or, in other words, the most powerful faction must be expected to prevail.

Shall domestic manufactures be encouraged, and in what degree, by restrictions on foreign manufactures? [These] are questions which would be differently decided by the landed and the manufacturing classes, and probably by neither with a sole regard to justice and the public good. The apportionment of taxes on the various descriptions of property is an act which seems to require the most exact impartiality; yet there is, perhaps, no legislative act in which greater opportunity and temptation are given to a predominant party to trample on the rules of justice. Every shilling with which they overburden the inferior number is a shilling saved to their own pockets.

It is in vain to say that enlightened statesmen will be able to adjust these clashing interests and render them all subservient to the public good. Enlightened statesmen will not always be at the helm. Nor, in many cases, can such an adjustment be made at all without taking into view indirect and remote considerations, which will rarely prevail over the immediate interest which one party may find in disregarding the rights of another or the good of the whole.

The inference to which we are brought is that the *causes* of faction cannot be removed and that relief is only to be sought in the means of controlling its *effects*.

If a faction consists of less than a majority, relief is supplied by the republican principle, which enables the majority to defeat its sinister views by regular vote. It may clog the administration, it may convulse the society; but it will be unable to execute and mask its violence under the forms of the Constitution. When a majority is included in a faction, the form of popular government, on the other hand, enables it to sacrifice to its ruling passion or interest both the public good and the rights of other citizens. To secure the public good and private rights against the danger of such a faction, and at the same time to preserve the spirit and the form of popular government, is then the great object to which our inquiries are directed. Let me add that it is the great desideratum by which this form of government can be rescued from the opprobrium under which it has so long labored and be recommended to the esteem and adoption of mankind.

By what means is this object attainable? Evidently by one of two only. Either the existence of the same passion or interest in a majority at the same time must be prevented, or the majority, having such coexistent passion or interest, must be rendered, by their number and local situation, unable to concert and carry into effect schemes of oppression. If the impulse and the opportunity be suffered to coincide, we well know that neither moral nor religious motives can be relied on as an adequate control. They are not found to be such on the injustice and violence of individuals and lose their efficacy in proportion to the number combined together, that is, in proportion as their efficacy becomes needful.

From this view of the subject it may be concluded that a pure democracy, by which I mean a society consisting of a small number of citizens who assemble and administer the government in person, can admit of no cure for the mischiefs of faction. A common passion or interest will, in almost every case, be felt by a majority of the whole; a communication and concert result from the form of government itself; and there is nothing to check the inducements to sacrifice the weaker party or an obnoxious individual. Hence it is that such democracies have ever been spectacles of turbulence and contention; have ever been found incompatible with personal security or the rights of property; and have in general been as short in their lives as they have been violent in their deaths. Theoretic politicians, who have patronized this species of government, have erroneously supposed that by reducing mankind to a perfect equality in their political rights, they would, at the same time, be perfectly equalized and assimilated in their possessions, their opinions, and their passions.

A republic, by which I mean a government in which the scheme of representation takes place, opens a different prospect and promises the cure for which we are seeking. Let us examine the points in which it varies from pure democracy, and we shall comprehend both the nature of the cure and the efficacy which it must derive from the Union.

The two great points of difference between a democracy and a republic are: first, the delegation of the government, in the latter, to a small number of citizens elected by the rest; secondly, the greater number of citizens, and greater sphere of country, over which the latter may be extended.

The effect of the first difference is, on the one hand, to refine and enlarge the public views by passing them through the medium of a chosen body of citizens, whose wisdom may best discern the true interest of their country, and whose patriotism and love of justice will be least likely to sacrifice it to temporary or partial considerations. Under such a regulation, it may well happen that the public voice, pronounced by the representatives of the people, will be more consonant to the public good than if pronounced by the people themselves, convened for the purpose. On the other hand, the effect may be inverted. Men of factious tempers, of local prejudices, or of sinister designs may, by intrigue, by corruption, or by other means, first obtain the suffrages, and then betray the interests of the people. The question resulting is, whether small or extensive republics are more favorable to the election of proper guardians of the public weal; and it is clearly decided in favor of the latter by two obvious considerations:

In the first place, it is to be remarked that, however small the republic may be, the representatives must be raised to a certain number, in order to guard against the cabals of a few; and that, however large it may be, they must be limited to a certain number, in order to guard against the confusion of a multitude. Hence, the number of representatives in the two cases not being in proportion to that of the two constituents, and being proportionally greater in the small republic, it follows that, if the proportion of fit characters be not less in the large than in the small republic, the former will present a greater option, and consequently a greater probability of a fit choice.

In the next place, as each representative will be chosen by a greater number of citizens in the large than in the small republic, it will be more difficult for unworthy candidates to practice with success the vicious arts by which elections are too often carried; and the suffrages of the people being more free, will be more likely to center in men who possess the most attractive merit and the most diffusive and established character.

It must be confessed that in this, as in most other cases, there is a mean, on both sides of which inconveniences will be found to lie. By enlarging too much the number of electors, you render the representative too little acquainted with all their local circumstances and lesser interests; as by reducing it too much, you render him unduly attached to these and too little fit to comprehend and pursue great and national objects. The federal Constitution forms a happy combination in this respect: the great and aggregate interests being referred to the national, the local and particular to the state legislatures.

The other point of difference is the greater number of citizens and extent of territory which may be brought within the compass of republican than of democratic government; and it is this circumstance principally which renders factious combinations less to be dreaded in the former than in the latter. The smaller the society, the fewer probably will be the distinct parties and interests composing it; the fewer the distinct parties and interests, the more frequently will a majority be found of the same party; and the smaller the number of individuals composing a majority, and the smaller the compass within which they are placed, the more easily will they concert and execute their plans of oppression. Extend the sphere and you take in a greater variety of parties and interests; you make it less probable that a majority of the whole will have a common motive to invade the rights of other citizens; or if such a common motive exists, it will be more difficult for all who feel it to discover their own strength and to act in unison with each other. Besides other impediments it may be remarked that, where there is a consciousness of unjust or dishonorable purposes, communication is always checked by distrust in proportion to the number whose concurrence is necessary.

Hence, it clearly appears that the same advantage which a republic has over a democracy, in controlling the effects of factions, is enjoyed by a large over a small republic—is enjoyed by the Union over the states composing it. Does the advantage consist in the substitution of representatives whose enlightened views and virtuous sentiments render them superior to local prejudices and to schemes of injustice? It will not be denied that the representation of the Union will be most likely to possess these requisite endowments. Does it consist in the greater security afforded by a greater variety of parties, against the event of any one party being able to outnumber and oppress the rest? In an equal degree does the increased variety of parties comprised within the Union increase this security? Does it, in fine, consist in the greater obstacles opposed to the concert and accomplishment of the secret wishes of an unjust and interested majority? Here, again, the extent of the Union gives it the most palpable advantage.

The influence of factious leaders may kindle a flame within their particular states but will be unable to spread a general conflagration through the other states. A religious sect may degenerate into a political faction in a part of the Confederacy; but the variety of sects dispersed over the entire face of it must secure the national councils against any danger from that source. A rage for paper money, for an abolition of debts, for an equal division of property, or for any other improper or wicked project will be less apt to pervade the whole body of the Union than a particular member of it; in the same proportion as such a malady is more likely to taint a particular county or district than an entire state.

In the extent, and proper structure of the Union, therefore, we behold a republican remedy for the diseases most incident to republican government. And according to the degree of pleasure and pride we feel in being republicans, ought to be our zeal in cherishing the spirit and supporting the character of Federalists.

GLOSSARY

Alien and Sedition Acts — Four internal security laws passed in 1798 by the U.S. Congress, restricting aliens and curtailing the excesses of an unrestrained press, in anticipation of an expected war with France.

Anti-Federalists — Loose political coalition of popular politicians such as Patrick Henry who unsuccessfully opposed the strong central government envisioned in the U.S. Constitution of 1787 and whose agitations led to the addition of a Bill of Rights.

Articles of Confederation — First U.S. constitution (1781–1789), which served as a bridge between the initial government by the Continental Congress of the Revolutionary period and the federal government provided under the U.S. Constitution of 1787.

Bill of Rights — First 10 amendments to the U.S. Constitution, which were adopted as a single unit on December 15, 1791, and which constitute a collection of mutually reinforcing guarantees of individual rights and of limitations on federal and state governments.

Boston Massacre — Skirmish on March 5, 1770, between British troops and a crowd in Boston that contributed to the unpopularity of the British regime in America in the years before the American Revolution.

Boston Tea Party — Incident on December 16, 1773, in which 342 chests of tea belonging to the British East India Company were thrown from ships into Boston Harbor by American patriots disguised as Mohawk Indians.

Checks and balances — Principle of government under which separate branches are empowered to prevent actions by other branches and are induced to share power.

"Common Sense" — Irreverent pamphlet by Thomas Paine advocating independence for the colonies.

Constitution of the United States — Fundamental law of the U.S. federal system of government and the oldest written national constitution in use, defining the principal organs of government and their jurisdictions and the basic rights of citizens.

Constitutional Convention — Meeting between May 25, 1787, and September 17, 1787, in which a new Constitution of the United States was approved.

Continental Congress — Body of delegates who met from 1774 to 1789 and who spoke and acted collectively for the people of the colony-states that later became the United States of America.

Declaration of Independence — Document approved by the Continental Congress on July 4, 1776, that announced the separation of 13 North American British colonies from Great Britain.

Declaratory Act — Declaration in 1766 by the British Parliament that accompanied the repeal of the Stamp Act, stating that the British Parliament's taxing authority was the same in America as in Great Britain.

Deism — Unorthodox Christian religious belief that human experience and ratio-nality—rather than religious dogma and mystery—determine the validity of human beliefs.

Electoral college — System by which the president and vice president of the United States are chosen, selected by the framers to provide a method of election that was feasible, desirable, and consistent with a republican form of government.

Federalist papers — Series of 85 essays (known formally as *The Federalist*) on the proposed new Constitution of the United States and on the nature of republican government, published between 1787 and 1788 under the name Publius by Alexander Hamilton, James Madison, and John Jay in a successful effort to persuade New York state voters to support ratification.

Federalist Party — Early U.S. national political party, which advocated a strong central government and held power from 1789 to 1801.

Great Compromise — Plan put forward by Roger Sherman of Connecticut that devised that representation would be based on population in the House of Representations and would be equal in the Senate, helping bridge differences between small and large states at the Constitutional Convention.

Intolerable Acts — Four punitive measures enacted in 1774 by the British Parliament in retaliation for acts of colonial defiance, together with the Quebec Act establishing a new administration for the territory ceded to Britain after the French and Indian War (1754–1763).

Necessary and proper clause — Section of the U.S. Constitution (Article I, Section 8, paragraph 18) that gives Congress implied powers, stating that Congress shall have the authority "To make all Laws which shall be necessary and proper for carrying into Execution" the various powers vested in the national government.

Separation of church and state — Concept that the religious and political powers in society are clearly distinct and should not overlap, an approach advocated strongly by Thomas Jefferson.

Separation of powers — Division of the legislative, executive, and judicial functions of government among separate and independent bodies.

Stamp Act — First British parliamentary attempt (1765) to raise revenue through direct taxation of all colonial commercial and legal papers, newspapers, pamphlets, cards, almanacs, and dice.

Sugar Act — British legislation (1764) aimed at ending the smuggling trade in sugar and molasses from the French and Dutch West Indies and at providing increased revenues to fund enlarged British Empire responsibilities following the French and Indian War.

Virginia and Virginia Resolutions — Measures passed by the legislatures of Virginia (1798) and Kentucky (1799) as a protest against the Federalist Alien and Sedition Acts.

IMAGE CREDITS

INDEX